Emotions, Senses, Spaces

This book is available as a free fully-searchable ebook from
www.adelaide.edu.au/press

Emotions, Senses, Spaces:

Ethnographic Engagements and Intersections

edited by

Susan R. Hemer and Alison Dundon

UNIVERSITY OF
ADELAIDE PRESS

Published in Adelaide by

University of Adelaide Press
Barr Smith Library
The University of Adelaide
South Australia 5005
press@adelaide.edu.au
www.adelaide.edu.au/press

The University of Adelaide Press publishes peer reviewed scholarly books. It aims to maximise access to the best research by publishing works through the internet as free downloads and for sale as high quality printed volumes.

© 2016 The Contributors

This work is licenced under the Creative Commons Attribution-NonCommercial-NoDerivatives 4.0 International (CC BY-NC-ND 4.0) License. To view a copy of this licence, visit http://creativecommons.org/licenses/by-nc-nd/4.0 or send a letter to Creative Commons, 444 Castro Street, Suite 900, Mountain View, California, 94041, USA. This licence allows for the copying, distribution, display and performance of this work for non-commercial purposes providing the work is clearly attributed to the copyright holders. Address all inquiries to the Director at the above address.

For the full Cataloguing-in-Publication data please contact the National Library of Australia: cip@nla.gov.au

ISBN (paperback) 978-1-925261-26-4
ISBN (ebook: pdf) 978-1-925261-27-1
ISBN (ebook: epub) 978-1-925261-28-8
ISBN (ebook: kindle) 978-1-925261-29-5
DOI: http://dx.doi.org/10.20851/emotions

Editor: Rebecca Burton
Editorial support: Julia Keller
Book design: Zoë Stokes
Cover design: Emma Spoehr
Cover images: © 2016 Dianne Rodger and Anthony Heathcote

Contents

	Biographies	vii
1	Ethnographic intersections: Emotions, senses and spaces *Alison Dundon and Susan R. Hemer*	1
2	'Dancing for joy': Gender and relational spaces in Papua New Guinea *Alison Dundon*	17
3	Creating the right 'vibe': Exploring the utilisation of space at Hip Hop concerts in Adelaide and Melbourne *Diane Rodger*	31
4	Pontic dance: Feeling the absence of homeland *Valerie Liddle*	49
5	Emotional actors/Affective agents: Interspecies edgework and sociotechnical networks in the Spanish bullfight from horseback (*rejoneo*) *Kirrilly Thompson*	67
6	Sensual feasting: Transforming spaces and emotions in Lihir *Susan R. Hemer*	91
7	Anxious spaces: The intersection of sexuality, the senses and emotion in fieldwork in Nepal *Sarah Homan*	107
8	Interrupted research: Emotions, senses and social space in (and out of) the field *Anthony Heathcote*	123
9	Voices in the park: The composition of sacred space and public place *Judith Haines*	137
10	Ngadha being-in-common: Emotional attachment to people and place in Flores, Indonesia *Jayne Curnow*	159
11	Trust your senses: Growing wine and making place in McLaren Vale *William Skinner*	175

Biographies

Jayne Curnow is the Research Program Manager for Agricultural Systems Management at the Australian Centre for International Agriculture Research. Jayne is a social scientist with expertise in international development, program management, anthropology and gender. Jayne's previous role was at the International Water Management Institute, Sri Lanka, where she has led, *inter alia*, a project mapping gender data and statistics related to water and agriculture with research teams in the Volta, Nile, Ganges and Mekong river basins. She was previously lecturer in anthropology and development studies at The University of Adelaide; qualitative evaluation co-ordinator with the World Bank in Indonesia; program manager with the Australian Department of Health and Ageing; and has worked for extended periods with several NGOs in East Timor on gender-based violence.

Alison Dundon is an anthropologist with extensive and long-term field research in rural Papua New Guinea and recent research online. Dundon has published on medical anthropology, particularly sexual and gendered health and HIV/AIDS; the anthropology of Christianity, and ancestral and environmental spirituality; community development; art and material culture; space, place and dance; and embodiment, sexuality and gender, including gendered and sexual violence. More recently, she has conducted research on the anthropology of online interactions, particularly online dating, love, intimacy and wellbeing in both Papua New Guinea and Australia. Dundon is also researching technological advancements in Papua New Guinea more broadly, and their impact on local communities, as well as the development of global networks between Papua New Guinea, Australia, and Israel.

Judith Haines is writing a PhD thesis in anthropology. The topic of her thesis is Spiritual Ecology. She is developing her chapter in this volume as a chapter in her thesis. Judith's research interests include the relationship between humans and their environment. Judith carried out her field research in eco-spiritual networks in and around the Adelaide environment movement.

Anthony Heathcote completed his PhD in anthropology at the University of Adelaide in 2015. Based on twelve months' fieldwork in Vietnam, Anthony situated online relationships with the dead within the wider continuum of ancestor worship. Drawing on the key themes of remembering, community and emotion, he demonstrated how online memorialisation reflected ancestral practices, while also adapting them to contemporary social realities and concerns. Anthony has taught and guest lectured at several universities in Adelaide and Melbourne, and his publications feature in Australian and international curricula. He is currently working on a monograph of his research.

Susan R. Hemer is a social anthropologist based at The University of Adelaide in Australia, whose work focuses on emotion and psychological wellbeing, on health, and also on the impact of development, particularly in Papua New Guinea. She regularly returns to Papua New Guinea for fieldwork. Her book *Tracing the Melanesian Person: Emotions and Relationships in Lihir* (2013) explores what it means to be Lihirian in a world that has rapidly changed in the last century through the work of Christian missions, government administration and the development of the Lihir gold mine.

Sarah Homan is a post-graduate candidate of anthropology and development studies at The University of Adelaide. Her honours thesis in anthropology explored the sociality of coffee culture and the ways in which consumers of fair-trade products construct 'relationships of care' with coffee producers. She has conducted fieldwork in Nepal, focusing on the gendered subjectivities of Nepali women. Her doctoral thesis argues that urban Nepali womanhood is practised and understood through local understandings of what it means to be 'honourable'. Her research interests encompass gender, honour, shame, violence, sexualities, surveillance, tradition and modernity. In Aotearoa/New Zealand, she worked with a team under the guidance of the Alexander Turnbull Library on the Pakaitore/Moutua Gardens Oral History Project, documenting the living memories of Maori participants of the 1995 Pakaitore/Moutua Gardens land-rights occupation in Whanganui.

Valerie Liddle completed her PhD at The University of Adelaide in 2013. Her research focused on how loss is experienced by members of the Greek Pontian community in Adelaide and in Greece. She is currently a Visiting Research Fellow in the anthropology department at The University of Adelaide.

Dianne Rodger is an anthropologist whose work focuses on media, popular culture and communication. Her research explores issues including the tensions between globalisation and localisation, processes of distinction and taste-making and the culturally specific and contested nature of 'authenticity'. She is particularly interested in the production and consumption of music and the use of new information and communication technologies in a number of domains, including health promotion. Dianne completed her PhD on Hip Hop culture in Australia in 2012. Her thesis is entitled 'Living Hip Hop: Defining authenticity in the Adelaide and Melbourne Hip Hop scenes'.

William Skinner is a PhD graduate in anthropology from The University of Adelaide. His thesis, entitled 'Fermenting place: Wine production and terroir in McLaren Vale, South Australia', explores the ways local producers experience, understand and represent place and landscape in the near-urban context of McLaren Vale. Based on extensive ethnographic fieldwork in the region, the thesis argues that the 'terroir perspective' taken by producers in the Vale is informed both by direct phenomenological engagement with the land and by broader, globalised wine discourse. William's present research interests relate to conceptualisations of vineyard heritage and relationships between city and country in South Australia. He enjoys playing soccer, surfing, and playing guitar. For the past couple of years he has also tried making his own wine, with questionable success.

Kirrilly Thompson is an Associate Professor at CQUni's Appleton Institute. She uses ethnographic methods to research the cultural dimensions of human-animal relations, with a specialisation in equestrian cultures. Her research into interspecies risk and safety has particular applications in behaviour change and risk management. Her work on the public understanding of science saw her receive one of the inaugural Top 5 Under 40 awards for science communication in Australia in 2015. Kirrilly is the President Elect of the Society for Risk Analysis Australia and New Zealand, as well as the Vice Chair of the Board of the Horse Federation of South Australia.

1

Ethnographic intersections:
Emotions, senses and spaces

Alison Dundon and Susan R. Hemer

In his book *Paths toward a Clearing* Jackson (1989) describes the Kuranko girls' initiation rites that he witnessed in 1970:

> Each night from the veranda of the house where I was staying I would watch the girls performing the graceful and energetic yatuiye and yamayili dances ... With their hair specially braided and adorned with snail-shell toggles and wearing brightly coloured beaded headbands, groups of girls passed from house to house around the village, dancing, clapping, and singing that their girlhood days were almost over. The daylight hours too were crowded with activities. Visitors poured into the village ... all while the neophytes continued to circulate around the village in the company of indefatigable drummers ... Then women performers danced before us too. One was dressed in men's clothes with a wild fruit hung from a chord across her forehead. She imitated the maladroit dance movements of men, her face expressionless, while other women surrounded her, clapping, singing, and laughing. (Jackson 1989:124-5)

At the time Jackson puzzled over the meanings of the rites and, with great fervour, sought answers to the questions he posed about the rites, 'decoding the ritual activities as if they were symbolic representations of unconscious concerns' (125). Looking back, Jackson acknowledged that he assumed that there was a distinction to be made between pragmatic work and ritual activity, and that ritual could be analysed and interpreted outside of its action and experience. He wrote that the

> quest for semantic truths also explained my inability to participate in the spirit of the performances and why I spent time asking people to tell me what was going on, what it all meant, as if the painted bodies and mimetic dances were only the insipid remnants of what had perhaps once been a symbolically coherent structure of myths and masks. (127)

In this later analysis, Jackson argued the need for a primary focus on experiential, sensory and bodily aspects of ritual and other forms of social action, and pointed to how 'the body is the ground for what is thought and said' (131). Yet even in his second analysis of the initiations, Jackson is still largely absent. What might we have gained had Jackson used his senses and emotions to render the event *sensible*? There are hints in the description above that point to the flurry of excitement, the crowding of the village, confusion or embarrassment as women turned gendered performances upside down. We get some understanding of the transformation not only of girls and women, but also of the emotional tenor and spaces of the village.

In this volume we aim to explore this nexus of emotions, senses and spaces — where the ethnographer is engaged in understanding the relations between them. The chapters illustrate the ways in which people in various contexts and regions articulate and mediate the intersection of emotions, spaces and senses. Like Bondi, Davidson and Smith (2005), we seek to explore the negotiation and expression of emotional landscapes, but also the ways in which these engage, or are engaged by, the senses and the sensual. In many ways, anthropologists are only beginning 'to understand how sensory and affective bodies articulate at the interface of cultural difference' (Wise & Chapman 2005:1) as well as how these are expressed and experienced in the spatial dynamics and dimensions of their lives (see also Chapman 2005).

This collection of chapters engages Ross's call (2004:41) to take seriously 'the ways that we engage in and with space/place, filling it with activity, relations, sensual engagements, interpretive activity, [and] emotions'. As such, it seeks to contribute to 'sensuous scholarship' (Stoller 1997) through situating conceptual insights about emotions, the senses, and space in ethnographically generated experiences and understandings. This book draws together three contemporary core concerns for the social sciences, and anthropology in particular: the senses and embodiment, emotions, and space and place. Over the last few decades these three topics have gained prominence in social science analysis, yet tend to be explored individually or in pairs, and very rarely together. In drawing these themes together, this work is able to consider the ways that they are mutually constitutive. We question how spaces evoke or constrain senses and emotions, and how space is composed through the senses and emotion.

In the late 1980s and early 1990s, anthropologists of emotion worked to 'pry emotion loose from psychobiology' (Abu-Lughod & Lutz 1990:12), with a focus on emotion as discourse and social judgement. This yielded fruitful insights into the process of the social, cultural and political constitution of emotion, its cultural interpretation and expression, and the constitution of emotion in language (for example, Abu-Lughod 1986; Lutz 1988; Rosaldo 1980; Scheper-Hughes 1992; Wikan 1990). During the same period, anthropologists were turning their attention to the senses, 'emphasizing the lived and emergent nature of the senses' and 'the cultural embeddedness of sensory experience' (Porcello, Meintjes, Ochoa & Samuels 2010:53). Analyses that foregrounded the senses emphasised communication and phenomenological experience grounded in the body. Early writings tended to explore specific sensory domains, such as sound, taste, smell or touch (for example, Corbin 1986; Feld 1991; Seremetakis 1994; Stoller 1989), and critiqued the visual focus of much anthropology (Jackson 1989). However, in more recent work the emphasis has been on the integration of different senses — moving beyond the five senses, and incorporating them ethnographically into analyses of everyday practices, experiences and communications (Howes 2003; Jackson 1996; Taussig 1993).

The shift toward embodiment and the senses suggested new ways of understanding emotion and the need to return to the body to reconceptualise the sensual experience of emotion (Lyon & Barbalet 1994; Schilling 1997; Sobo 1996). Feld, for example, explored how sound can be an embodiment of sentiment (1990), while Schieffelin analysed how song evokes sorrow that provokes the burning of dancers (1977). Stoller and Oakes aimed to show how the sense of taste can convey emotions such as anger (1986). More recently, Beatty has implored once again for the centrality of emotion to human experience, arguing the need for anthropological analyses that address emotion in its temporal dimension and through engaging narratives of ethnographic experience (2014).

Two key concepts in the social sciences have linked emotion to place or space: topophilia from Tuan (1977), which has been taken up in anthropology by Hastrup (2011) as emotional topographies, and emotional geographies (Davidson & Milligan 2004; Bondi et al. 2005). These concepts have aimed to aid our understanding of the ways in which spaces and emotions are interlinked — how spaces come to hold particular emotional nuances, or evoke feelings (Smith 2005). Work in this field has addressed how people feel at home in certain spaces or how they feel when they are away from them or return: feelings of emplacement or displacement, and how we may feel in unfamiliar places (McKay 2005; Urry 2005; Wise 2010).

In concert with these approaches, there has been attention to the links between the senses and space, particularly through the work of Rodaway (1994) and Paterson (2007; 2009). These authors have sought to broaden an analysis of the senses beyond the classic 'five senses model' to look at somatic senses such as balance, felt muscular position or movement, and pressure, often termed the 'haptic system'; they emphasise more than simply the visual experience of space and place (Paterson 2009:771). Rodaway, for example, notes that

> the haptic system gives us the ability to discriminate key characteristics of the environment and our place as a separate entity in the environment or world, but it is not just a physical relationship, it is also an emotional bond between ourself and our world. (1994:44)

This approach to the senses foregrounds not only the embodied experience of sensing the world, but also the emotional experience. While relatively rare, there are a number of contributions that encompass these three core themes of senses, emotions and space. These direct attention to this area as worthy of study, such as the editorial by Davidson and Milligan (2004), Ross's call for more work in this area (2004), and Nichter's account of sensorial anthropology as addressing 'the study of how the spaces and places in which bodies are situated predispose perceptions of sensation that are associated with feelings of fear and vulnerability, well-being and protection' (2008:164). Also needed, however, in conjunction with these seminal texts, are ethnographic analyses that tease out the interrelationships of emotion, senses and space — the key work of this collection.

Each contributor to this collection develops a critical ethnographic analysis of the sensual/emotional/spatial dynamic, privileging local experiences and understandings of the intersection of space, emotion and the senses in a variety of contexts including Vietnam, Nepal, Papua New Guinea, Australia, Indonesia and Spain. The chapters explore the experiential and conceptual imbrications of space, sensuality and emotion in music, dance, feasting, bullfighting, meeting, healing and speaking. In the chapters, noise, voice and speech, proximity and sweat, sight and hearing, taste and movement are evoked and explored in ways that articulate the engagement of emotions and the senses with the spaces in which they take place or from which they are generated — from Spanish bullrings, Hip Hop venues or public parks in central Adelaide, to village centres and spaces in rural Papua New Guinea and Indonesia. Joy, anxiety, distress, love, loss, aspiration, harmony, triumph and anger arise in these spaces and are felt, embodied and articulated through sensual engagement and perception. All chapters engage the 'bodily, sensory and affective dimensions' (Wise and Chapman 2004:1) of interacting with, living in and through, or generating spaces in the process and practice of life through dance, music and performance; food, feasting and gendered bodies; and through voice, speech and agency.

The chapters in this book highlight four central processes of ethnographic engagement with spaces, senses and emotions. First, the engagement of emotions and senses in ethnographic research is critical to the processes of constructing anthropological knowledge. Second, attending to senses, emotions and space in performances deepens our understanding of what makes a good performance, and how performances may evoke or reflect emotions. Third, emotions and senses are crucial in the relationships between people and space, and in the composition of space. Finally, in the intersection of senses, spaces and emotions, emotions can be evoked, constrained or transformed. These key themes of the nexus of senses, spaces and emotions revolve around processes, practices and experiences of engagement, performance, composition and transformation.

The chapters cannot be simply aligned with, or divided between, the four processes, as these are interwoven in many ethnographic contexts, and such a division would undermine the nuance and complexity of the nexus of emotions, senses and spaces. All chapters in the book are based in long-term fieldwork where the ethnographers utilised their senses and emotions to engage with particular people and places. Two chapters, by Sarah Homan and Anthony Heathcote, focus more closely on these processes of engaging emotionally and sensorially in fieldwork in Nepal and Vietnam, and the implications for renewed insight and understanding of the lives and experiences of research participants. Many of the chapters in the book explore performative contexts of dances performed in Greece, Adelaide and Papua New Guinea, bullfighting on horseback in Spain, feasting in Papua New Guinea or Indonesia, or Reiki healing in Adelaide. A number of chapters also highlight how emotions may be evoked, constrained or transformed, particularly through ethnographic examples in Vietnam and Papua New Guinea. The final three chapters place emphasis on the composition of spaces through the senses and emotions through participation in Reiki healing practices in public parks in Adelaide, clan land and spaces of commonality in Central Flores, Indonesia, and the sensual and emotional constitution of wine places in McLaren Vale, South Australia.

Engaging emotions, senses and ethnographic spaces

A sensual and emotional engagement with the spaces of research is pivotal to the ethnographic experience and hence processes of the production of anthropological knowledge, particularly given that ethnographic research is often conducted in 'another place'. For all contributors to this volume, an emotional and sensorial engagement with the space of fieldwork was crucial. The contributors aim to 'retrieve' emotion and the interplay of the senses 'from the methodological margins of fieldwork' (Davies 2010:1) and to explore how the evocation and experience of the emotional and sensual informs the production and embodiment of anthropological knowledge. This resonates with Stoller's call for scholarship that engages with the sensorial experience of the fieldwork encounter (1997). Beatty has recently argued that to 'give emotion its due, to restore the heartbeat to ethnography, we have to think harder about what goes on in the field *and* how best to put experience into words' (2014:546, italics in the original text). Emotions mediate methodological distinctions drawn between the 'research subject' and the 'researched object', and allow for the prioritisation of the intersubjective and experiential aspects of anthropological fieldwork (Davies 2010:12). Chapters here, particularly those by Homan and Heathcote, demonstrate that awkwardness, disorientation and discomfort, not to mention ambivalence and anxiety (Jackson 2010), can be instrumental in gaining a more nuanced and embodied understanding of the people and places amongst whom anthropologists conduct their research (Davies 2010:12).

In the sensual and emotional engagement of ethnographic spaces, distinctions between anthropology and autobiography blur (Hastrup & Hervick 1994:1). Kahn (1996) has argued persuasively that it is difficult and even problematic to talk about the intersections of places and people without encompassing the biographies of the anthropologist as well as the subjects of their research. In Chapter 8 of this volume, Heathcote writes that he found that shared emotional and sensual scapes led to heightened ethnographic and interpersonal understandings in research conducted on online memorialisation in Vietnam. Initially feeling emotionally distanced from his research participants, who talked about the impact of deaths from abortion, accidents, murder or old age, Heathcote felt as if he were a 'pseudo-anthropologist'. Coming home to be with his critically ill mother only four months into the fieldwork, senses dulled by the hospital spaces and what he refers to as 'the monotony of illness', Heathcote found a new social space opened up to him in his research. This space was one he shared with his informants; it was underscored by common human experiences of illness, death, grief and anxiety, which had arisen out of a personal understanding of the depth of emotions experienced by his informants.

A reflexive analysis of emotional and sensory experiences in the field engages the anthropologist in the spatial, sensual and emotional landscapes of those they seek to study and elucidate (see Pink 2003:48; 2007).

> Whether serendipitously or as part of an intentional research method, researchers who have 'shared' the sensory embodied experiences of their informants in these ways have variously claimed that this approach has led to heightened understandings of the identities, moralities, values, beliefs and concerns of the people they do their research with. (2007:244)

Emotional and sensual engagement of the ethnographer is central to the negotiation of the blurred boundaries between academic practice and embodied experience, and to the acknowledgement that all anthropological knowledge is emotional, spatial and sensual (see also Basso 1988; Stoller 1989; 1997). Homan, in Chapter 7, explores the impact of emotional and sensorial experiences on the production of anthropological knowledge during her fieldwork on violence against women in remote Western Nepal. Homan writes that being a 'woman' in Nepal made her acutely aware of her gendered body and of the impact of its presence in terms of sexual harassment and maintenance of honour and reputation. It made her aware of her emotional state, and the ways in which she 'dulled' her senses in order to allay some of the anxiety she experienced.

This intersection of a heightened emotional state and sensual disengagement in Nepali spaces, in turn, led to a greater understanding of the contradictions and constraints Nepali women face on an everyday basis and how it 'felt' to be a woman in Nepal.

Performative spaces, senses and emotions

A number of chapters in this volume explore performative aspects of the nexus of senses, spaces and emotions: that the space of performance is critical to its constitution; that the spaces and sensory aspects of performance combine to create the right 'vibe' for performance success; and finally that the enactment of emotion in this context is not simulated, but is structured and evoked by the spaces and sensorial aspects of performance. Performances consist of routines and regulations about the production and reproduction of subjectivities and identities — the 'doings' of actions and performances (Wood & Smith 2004:534). Of course, as Wood and Smith (535) argue, performances come into being in terms of relationships which are 'simultaneously and indivisibly emotional, political and economic, and indeed which are inflected in all kinds of other ways'. Whether highly structured like the Pontic dances described by Valerie Liddle in Chapter 4, or largely informal or spontaneous like both the joyful dancing in Papua New Guinea analysed by Alison Dundon in Chapter 2 and the Reiki healing discussed by Judith Haines in Chapter 9, performances are shaped by the spaces in which they take place or are constituted. In this sense, they are time-spaces associated with high levels of affective and sensual interaction, which can play a 'critical role in provoking and encouraging people to engage with embodied emotional ways of being and knowing' (Wood & Smith 2004:535).

Performances are emotional relationships between performers and audiences. 'Neither party necessarily understands *why* they are engaging in such emotionally powerful ways, but the power of the experience is palpable to both performers and to those with whom they are bound within a particular performative space' (538, italics in the original text). In this emotional bond or relationship established between performer and audience, a dynamic of intimacy can be established, which may be experienced sensually and/or emotionally as something 'beyond words'. Performances thus create spaces that allow, and are maintained through, the establishment of an intimacy that is usually experienced in less public settings or contexts (539). At times it may appear that this intimacy is contrived, yet it is the sensorial and spatial structuring of performance that allows the evocation of emotion.

Performers themselves may experience these emotions, as discussed by Dundon in this volume, or act as a conduit for the audience (see also Liddle). In Chapter 2, Dundon analyses a dance performance referred to as 'dancing for joy' among Gogodala speakers in the Western province of Papua New Guinea. Performed only by women, dancing for joy, Dundon argues, is generated by emotions like pride, joy and happiness, and a sensual engagement with sporting events, 'traditional' dancing, or canoe races. At such events, women rise out of the audience in seemingly spontaneous outbursts of bodily movements, either thrusting themselves into the middle of these performances or dancing on the sidelines. In this context, dancing for joy, argues Dundon, creates a transient but highly visible and public space in which women's relationships with family members are foregrounded, as well as the pivotal role that women play in the constitution of relationality and kinship.

The focus of a performance may be more on evoking emotion in an audience, and this evocation may be a critical indicator of the success of the performance. In some cases the performance is structured to allow the enactment of sentiments that may normally be submerged or even subversive, such as is the case for the Bedouin poetry described by Abu-Lughod (1986), or the powerfully emotive dances of the Gisaro dances of the Kaluli (Schieffelin 1977). In Chapter 4, Liddle explores the role of emotion in an analysis of Pontic dancing, arguing that part of the 'feeling' and authenticity of Pontic dance is based on a shared sense of loss of the homeland. This 'feeling' of the dance, expressed by participants as an 'inward feeling' expressed in and through the dance, comes into being in two ways: through an engagement with the historical materiality of the dance itself through the instruments and costumes, and through the passionate embodied movements of the dance. The 'feel of the dance inside' is what makes both the dance and the dancer quintessentially Pontian, and it is also what makes the performers and those in the audience feel the 'presence of absence' of Pontos, a homeland that remains in the passion and materiality of the dance but no longer in reality.

A good or authentic performance, one that 'works', as the chapters demonstrate, has much to do with the ways in which its 'emotional geography' (see Wood & Smith 2004:536) is generated and mediated through sensual engagement and spatial structure. Emotional geographies of performances, however, are also about improvisation and interaction and, as such, are truly a 'way of life in the making' or a 'conversation of practices' that never is entirely complete or finished (537). Given this, performances can fall flat or fail. Schieffelin explores this in terms of the performer-audience relationship and the careful structuring of sensorial aspects of performance through timing and tone of voice (1996). In this volume, both Dianne Rodger and Kirrilly Thompson explore the success of performances in terms of the right level of emotional engagement and tension created by the sensorial engagement in spaces. In Chapter 3, Rodger explores the intersection of emotion, space and senses in Hip Hop performances in Adelaide and Melbourne, Australia. She argues that senses are employed through techniques and technologies associated with creating the right 'vibe' in Hip Hop concerts. Organisers aim to control the performance space in order to evoke an emotional response from the audience through the careful manipulation of lights, sounds and the layout of the venue. Rodger argues that particular spaces, and the ways in which they are arranged and utilised, can both constrain and/or evoke emotional responses and experiences in and from the audience.

In Chapter 5, Thompson examines a different kind of performance: the dynamic between interspecies edgework and sociotechnical networks at work in the Spanish bullfight on horseback. Thompson focuses on how space, emotion and the senses interact with technological mediation to draw together a more useful framework for understanding the dynamics of the bullfight on horseback, and how it is experienced by the bodies of the horses and riders in the performative space. Thompson argues that the Spanish mounted bullfight is an ideal performance to explore the interrelationships between space, emotions and the senses, as emotional intensity is achieved with the increasingly close merging of bull, fighter, horse and technology during the bullfight, providing the tension for a 'good' fight and performance.

Transforming emotions through space and the senses

A third theme of the book focuses on how emotions are evoked or constrained in particular contexts. Emotions, Davidson and Milligan write, are only understandable in the context of certain or specific places, and places must be 'felt' to make sense — so that 'meaningful senses of space emerge only via movements *between* people and places' (2004:524, italics in the original text). Beginning with the insight that emotions are understood as appropriate given particular contexts — otherwise called 'feeling rules' (Hochschild 1979) — this theme questions how we know what it is appropriate to feel, and what spatial and sensorial cues evoke and constrain emotions. A number of chapters relate to this theme — Heathcote's work demonstrates how his emotions were shaped and experienced through the different spatial and sensorial aspects of fieldwork in Vietnam in comparison to the hospital environments in Australia. Homan also demonstrates how the fieldwork conditions in Nepal led her to try to transform her own emotions through sensorially closing off her exposure to people in her field site.

Following Nussbaum (2001), Beatty (2014:557) notes that emotions have three interrelated aspects: they have features that are universal, culturally constructed, and individual or idiosyncratic to the person. Hochschild's work (1979) particularly focused on the ways that individuals shaped their emotions in order to fit with sociocultural norms of appropriate feeling. In this view, sociocultural norms were largely assumed as given, and the agency of individuals was understood in terms of altering feelings to fit with such norms. What is not clear here is how certain feeling rules come to be, particularly given different cultural understandings of emotions, their causes and the appropriate responses to them; how individuals may react differently given their own history and biography; and the extent to which feeling rules may be challenged or changed.

Beatty argues for the need for narrative and historical approaches to writing about emotion and social life (2014). Here we would agree, but argue that emotions cannot adequately be addressed without exploring their intersection with the senses and space. In Chapter 6 of the collection, Susan R. Hemer explores the transformation of emotions through the mediation of the senses and space, in a women's development project on Lihir in Papua New Guinea. She contends that the process of organising and building certain office spaces for this project created a context in which there was a great deal of resentment and anger between the parties involved. Drawing on Hochschild's concepts of feeling rules, Hemer argues that it became apparent in this context that it was not considered appropriate for women to openly express this anger. However, through the sensorial and spatial experiences of feasting — a form of collective emotion work — a transformation of feeling rules was achieved, and the women were henceforth able to express anger collectively.

Composing spaces, senses and emotions

Howes (1991:8) argued early that anthropologists should conceptualise cultures as 'ways of sensing the world' rather than as texts or symbols to be deciphered. Similarly, Classen (1991:254) wrote that cultures or cosmologies are not detached 'views' or structures of the world but are 'wet and warm, fragrant and foul, full of sound, colour, and feeling'. The senses not only provide people with a means to experience the world, but also link people to place, most notably through the emotions. Topophilia is the affective bond between people and place (Tuan 1990:4), and it has been argued that this affects the perception of place through the senses (Hastrup 2010:195). Bhatti, Church, Claremont and Stenner (2009) explore the ways that people are 'enchanted', or encounter particular places in the world in ways that are transformative, through mundane tasks such as gardening, activities that include sensory and emotional engagement. They note that 'enchantment in the garden involves a certain kind of sensibility: a "doing" through haptic perception; a caring through cultivating; and emotionality through memory' (73). In this way, emotions clearly and emphatically shape the ways in which we inhabit the spaces of our everyday worlds and have the potential to transform or shape how the world is for us, affecting our sense of space and time (Davidson & Milligan 2004:524). These sensorial and emotional links between people and place are discussed in Chapter 10, where Jayne Curnow explores the emotional significance of residential clan land for the Ngadhu of Central Flores, Indonesia, understood as the locus of key clan symbols, ceremony and Ancestors. The Ngadhu post and Bhaga miniature house are key grounding symbols of this emotional connection between clanspeople and their Ancestors. Curnow argues that clan land is the centre of the spatial, material and emotional expression of clan unity and being with others or 'being singular plural'.

Spaces are also shaped or composed by senses and emotions. This is powerfully argued by Ross (2004), who describes the experience of being lost in a previously familiar place, and notes that '[o]ur understandings of the landscape reflect our emplacement within it as social and phenomenal beings' (41-2). Sensory aspects to space and people's emotional responses to them shape the physical and emotional landscape, so that moving beyond the experience of, and links between, people and place, the constitution of spaces is central to human experience. 'Bodily ways of knowing' (Howes 1991:3), through the senses and emotions, are primary in this experience and interaction. After all, as Davidson and Milligan suggest (2004:523, italics in the original text), the 'most immediate and intimately *felt* geography is the body', which is the space of emotional and sensual articulation and experience.

This shaping or composition of space is explored through chapters by Judith Haines and William Skinner. In Chapter 9, Haines explores the 'voices in the park' in the parklands of the city of Adelaide, South Australia. Haines traces the experiences of one group of young environmental activists involved in Reiki spiritual healing, which they practise in Rymill Park. She argues that by drawing on spiritual healing and emotion in this way and in these public parklands, these activists begin a process whereby public spaces are recomposed as cosmic and spiritual spaces. This is achieved, partly at least, through the ambient vocalisation utilised by those participating in the healing session, whereby spiritual practices and the group itself are integrated into the public setting of the parklands. In the process, modernist constructions of binaries based on private, public, rational, irrational, and the atomised or individualised self are overturned.

In the final chapter of the book, Skinner explores the constitution and habitation of space in the context of winemaking amongst small producers in McLaren Vale in South Australia. He argues that the processes and activities associated with winemaking undertaken by small-scale wine producers, who privilege a 'hands on' approach to wine production, not only create a sense of place, but also create place itself in the process of making wine. In this process, senses predicate the relationship between winegrowers and the world through smells, touch and taste.

Integrating senses, spaces, emotions

In his later work, Jackson built on some of his early insights about the importance of sensory and emotional aspects of social life. In a recent contribution, he made clear the value of his own participation in the field and the emotional engagement of research (2010). Even as early as 1989, he discussed returning to the field after the loss of his wife and a key field interlocutor.

> I remember him now as he appears in the one photograph I managed to take of him
> … He and Pauline died in the same year, 1983. In 1985 I returned to Firawa to

find his house a charred ruin — the house he had given me and my family to use six years before ... I sat on the fire-blackened porch where we had spent so many hours together ... I stood awhile in the darkness. Insects shrilled in the grass. I thought if I was patient enough, if I had enough faith, he would appear out of the shadows, leaning on his stave, a conspiratorial grin on his face ... In the difficult weeks that followed, I often pondered the way the old medicine master had met and dealt with tribulation in his life. (1989:19)

This sensual and emotive writing conveys the engagement of ethnographers with those whom we work and argues for more than the elucidation of cultural patterns in analysis — for the significance of 'the lived world of contingent experience' (34). The chapters in this volume aim to do just this: to interrogate and explore the cultural patterns and lived experiences, particularly in terms of the points of intersection of emotions, senses and spaces. Providing integrated analyses of emotions, senses and spaces is not necessarily easy, however, and what becomes clear in this process is that writing is always positioned and partial. Jackson's quote illustrates his own connections to his research subjects, and his ponderings demonstrate a sensory and intellectual engagement with the 'field'. In this book, we seek to acknowledge our own partiality, perspective and research engagement through senses, emotions and spaces, offering an insight into the complexities of the intersections and mutual interrelationships with those with whom we work.

In bringing together these three elements, we resist moves to privilege one aspect over others as more important or illuminating of the ways humans engage with the world. In this, we mirror the move away from analyses focused on a single sense to those that integrate all senses in the process of engagement with the world. As can be seen in Jackson's writing above, being engaged ethnographically through our emotions and senses in the places we work can bring our own experience and those of others into view, and help us connect with other people's experiences and understandings of the world.

References

Abu-Lughod, L. 1986. *Veiled Sentiments: Honor and Poetry in a Bedouin Society*. Berkeley: University of California Press.

Abu-Lughod, L. and C.A. Lutz. 1990. 'Introduction: Emotion, discourse and the politics of everyday life'. In C.A. Lutz and L. Abu-Lughod (Eds.), *Language and the Politics of Emotion* (pp. 1-23). Cambridge: Cambridge University Press.

Basso, K. 1988. '"Speaking with names": Language and landscape among the Western Appache', *Cultural Anthropology* 3(2): 99-130.

Beatty, A. 2014. 'Anthropology and emotion', *Journal of the Royal Anthropological Institute* 20(3): 545-563.

Bhatti, M., A. Church, A. Claremont and P. Stenner. 2009. '"I love being in the garden": Enchanting encounters in everyday life', *Social and Cultural Geography* 10(1): 61-76.

Bondi, L., J. Davidson and M. Smith. 2005. 'Introduction: Geography's "Emotional Turn"'. In L. Bondi, J. Davidson and M. Smith (Eds.), *Emotional Geographies* (pp. 1-16). Surrey, UK and Burlington, VT: Ashgate.

Chapman, A. 2005. 'Breath and bamboo: Diasporic Lao identity and the Lao mouth organ', *Journal of Intercultural Studies* 26(1-2): 5-20.

Classen, C. 1991. 'Creation by sound/creation by light: A sensory analysis of two South American cosmologies'. In D. Howes (Ed.), *The Varieties of Sensory Experience: A Sourcebook in the Anthropology of the Senses* (pp. 239-256). Toronto: University of Toronto Press.

Corbin, A. 1986. *The Foul and the Fragrant: Odor and the French Social Imagination*. Cambridge, MA: Harvard University Press.

Davidson, J. and C. Milligan. 2004. 'Embodying emotion, sensing space: Introducing emotional geographies', *Social and Cultural Geography* 5(4): 523-532.

Davies, J. 2010. 'Introduction: Emotions in the field'. In J. Davies and D. Spencer (Eds.), *Emotions in the Field: The Psychology and Anthropology of Fieldwork Experience* (pp. 1-31). Stanford: Stanford University Press.

Dundon, A. 2005. 'The sense of sago: Motherhood and migration in Papua New Guinea and Australia', *Journal of Intercultural Studies* 26(1-2): 21-38.

Eves, R. 1996. 'Remembrance of things passed: Memory, body and the politics of feasting in New Ireland, Papua New Guinea', *Oceania* 66: 266-277.

Feld, S. 1990 [1982]. *Sound and Sentiment: Birds, Weeping, Poetics and Song in Kaluli Expression*. Philadelphia: University of Pennsylvania Press.

Feld, S. 1991. 'Sound as a symbolic system: The Kaluli drum'. In D. Howes (Ed.), *Varieties of Sensory Experience: A Sourcebook in the Anthropology of the Senses* (pp. 79-99). Toronto: University of Toronto Press.

Hastrup, K. 2011. 'Emotional topographies: The sense of place in the Far North'. In J. Davies and D. Spencer (Eds.), *Emotions in the Field: The Psychology and Anthropology of Fieldwork Experience* (pp. 191-211). Stanford: Stanford University Press.

Hastrup, K. and P. Hervick. 1994. *Social Experience and Anthropological Knowledge*. London: Routledge.

Hochschild, A.R. 1979. 'Emotion work, feeling rules and social structure', *The American Journal of Sociology* 85(3): 551-575.

Howes, D. 1991. *Varieties of Sensory Experience: A Sourcebook in the Anthropology of the Senses*. Toronto: University of Toronto Press.

Howes, D. 2003. *Sensual Relations: Engaging the Senses in Culture and Social Theory*. Ann Arbor, MI: University of Michigan Press.

Jackson, M. 1977. *The Kuranko: Dimensions of Social Reality in a West African Society*. London: C. Hurst.

Jackson, M. 1989. *Paths toward a Clearing: Radical Empiricism and Ethnographic Enquiry*. Bloomington, IN: Indiana University Press.

Jackson, M. 1996. *Things as They Are: New Directions in Phenomenological Anthropology*. Bloomington, IN: Indiana University Press.

Jackson, M. 2010. 'From anxiety to method in anthropological fieldwork: An appraisal of George Devereux's enduring ideas'. In J. Davies and D. Spencer (Eds.), *Emotions in the Field: The Psychology and Anthropology of Fieldwork Experience* (pp. 35-54). Stanford: Stanford University Press.

Kahn, M. 1996. 'Your place and mine: Sharing emotional landscapes in Wamira, Papua New Guinea'. In S. Feld and K.H. Basso (Eds.), *Senses of Place* (pp. 167-96). Santa Fe, NM: School of American Research Press.

Lutz, C.A. 1988. *Unnatural Emotions: Everyday Sentiments on a Micronesian Atoll and their Challenge to Western Theory*. Chicago: University of Chicago Press.

Lyon, M.L. and J.M. Barbalet. 1994 .'Society's body: Emotion and the "somatization" of social theory'. In T. Csordas (Ed.), *Embodiment and Experience: The Existential Ground of Culture and Self* (pp. 48-66). Cambridge: Cambridge University Press.

McKay, D. 2005. 'Migration and the sensuous geographies of re-emplacement in the Philippines', *Journal of Intercultural Studies* 26(1-2): 75-91.

Nichter, M. 2008. 'Coming to our senses: Appreciating the sensorial in Medical Anthropology', *Transcultural Psychiatry* 45(2): 163-197.

Nussbaum, M.C. 2001. *Upheavals of Thought: The Intelligence of Emotions*. Cambridge: Cambridge University Press.

Paterson, M. 2007. *The Senses of Touch: Haptics, Affects and Technologies*. Oxford: Berg.

Paterson, M. 2009. 'Haptic geographies: Ethnography, haptic knowledges and sensuous dispositions', *Progress in Human Geography* 33(6): 766-788.

Pink, S. 2003. 'Representing the sensory home: Ethnographic experience and anthropological hypermedia', *Social Analysis* 47(3): 46-63.

Pink, S. 2007. 'Walking with video', *Visual Studies* 22(3): 240-252.

Porcello, T., L. Meintjes, A.M. Ochoa and D.W. Samuels. 2010. 'The reorganisation of the sensory world', *Annual Review of Anthropology* 39: 51-66.

Rodaway, P. 1994. *Sensuous Geographies: Body, Sense, Place*. London: Routledge.

Rosaldo, M.Z. 1980. *Knowledge and Passion: Ilongot Notions of Self and Social Life*. Cambridge: Cambridge University Press.

Ross, F.C. 2004. 'Sense-scapes: Senses and emotions in the making of place', *Anthropology Southern Africa* 27(1-2): 35-42.

Scheper-Hughes, N. 1992. *Death without Weeping: The Violence of Everyday Life in Brazil*. Berkeley: University of California Press.

Schieffelin, E.L. 1977. *The Sorrow of the Lonely and the Burning of the Dancers*. St Lucia: University of Queensland Press.

Schieffelin, E.L. 1996. 'On failure and performance: Throwing the medium out of the séance'. In C. Laderman and M. Roseman (Eds.), *The Performance of Healing* (pp. 59-89). London: Routledge.

Schilling, C. 1997. 'Emotions, embodiment and the sensation of society', *The Sociological Review* 45(2): 195-219.

Seremetakis, N.C. 1994. *Perception and Memory as Material Culture in Modernity*. Boulder, CO: Westview Press.

Smith, M. 2005. 'On "being" moved by nature: Geography, emotion and environmental ethics'. In L. Bondi, J. Davidson and M. Smith (Eds.), *Emotional Geographies* (pp. 219-230). Surrey, UK and Burlington, VT: Ashgate.

Sobo, E.J. 1996. 'The Jamaican body's role in emotional experience and sense perception: Feelings, hearts, minds, and nerves', *Culture, Medicine and Psychiatry* 20: 313-342.

Stoller, P. 1989. *Taste of Ethnographic Things: The Senses in Anthropology*. Philadelphia: University of Pennsylvania Press.

Stoller, P. 1997. *Sensuous Scholarship*. Philadelphia: University of Pennsylvania Press.

Stoller, P. and C. Oakes. 1989. *The Taste of Ethnographic Things: The Senses in Anthropology*. Philadelphia: University of Pennsylvania Press.

Taussig, M. 1993. *Mimesis and Alterity: A Particular History of the Senses*. New York: Routledge.

Tuan, Y-F. 1977. *Space and Place: The Perspective of Experience*. Minneapolis: University of Minnesota Press.

Tuan, Y-F. 1990. *Topophilia: A Study of Environmental Perceptions, Attitudes, and Values*. New York: Columbia University Press.

Urry, J. 2005. 'The place of emotions within place'. In L. Bondi, J. Davidson and M. Smith (Eds.), *Emotional Geographies* (pp. 77-83). Surrey, UK and Burlington, VT: Ashgate.

Wikan, U. 1990. *Managing Turbulent Hearts: A Balinese Formula for Living*. Chicago: University of Chicago Press.

Wise, A. 2010. 'Sensuous multiculturalism: Emotional landscapes of inter-ethnic living in Australian suburbia', *Journal of Ethnic and Migration Studies* 36(6): 917-937.

Wise, A. and A. Chapman. 2005. 'Introduction: Migration, affect and the senses', *Journal of Intercultural Studies* 26(1-2): 1-3.

Wood, N. and S.J. Smith. 2004. 'Instrumental routes to emotional geographies', *Social and Cultural Geography* 5(4): 533-548.

2

'Dancing for joy':
Gender and relational spaces in Papua New Guinea

Alison Dundon

Abstract

Among the Gogodala of Papua New Guinea, a predominantly rural population in the Western Province, dance is a site of considerable emotion. Owama gi — 'dancing for joy' — is particularly so, a seemingly spontaneous series of sensuous movements through which women express both pleasure and pride in the beauty and ability of their male kin as well as the efficacy of their own webs of relatedness. Women express their compulsion to dance at these occasions in terms of expressions like 'you cannot help yourself'. In this chapter, I examine the performance of owama gi *as the sensual and embodied generation of what I refer to as relational space, in which happiness, pride and pleasure in relationships between women and their children, fathers, uncles and brothers are elicited and appreciated. At the same time, dancing for joy is an overtly public performance of the central role that women play in the lives and achievements of their kin. I analyse the ways in which, although understood as spontaneous expressions of pleasure and joy, such dances and the behaviour of those who perform them are highly proscribed. The chapter seeks to contribute to an analysis of the substantive connection between space, sensory experience and human emotions through an exploration of the ways in which the senses and emotions both generate, and are generated by, certain kinds of gendered relationships and performative spaces.*

Introduction

> The articulation of emotion is spatially mediated ... [W]hen we speak of the 'heights of joy' and the 'depths of despair', significant others are comfortingly close or distressingly distant. (Davidson & Milligan 2004:523)

It is September 1995. I am sitting behind a recently erected bamboo fence that runs the length and breadth of the football field in Balimo with over one thousand people who, like me, are there to watch the dances, canoe races, sports and other performances that make up the Balimo Show. Although I had been in the Gogodala-speaking area of the Western Province of Papua New Guinea for more than eight months by this stage, conducting research for my doctoral thesis, this was the first formal event that I had attended which brought together these performances. After one particularly arresting 'traditional' Gogodala dance, or *maiyata*, by a dance troupe consisting of both men and women clad in stately long grass skirts and colourful *ikewa*, or dance plaques, on their heads, two women hastily stood up in the crowd and, with loud cries, ran to join the dancers on the field.

As the dance made its way around the inside of the fence to the beat of the hand-held *kundu* (Tok Pisin) or *waluwa* drums played by the men and the cane rattles held by the women, the two interlopers weaved their way in amongst the performance, insinuating themselves into the careful movements and beat of the music. One of the women, the younger of the two, removed her shirt and danced in her bra and skirt. As she followed the troupe around the ground, she raised her hands above her head and exaggerated the roll of her buttocks, hips and legs. The older woman also began to dance in a similar fashion, making various facial contortions, including sticking out her tongue and emitting a startling yell. Both women seemed quite oblivious to the crowd who, by this time, had begun to respond to these new participants with whistles, shouted comments and a great deal of laughter at their antics. The dancers continued unperturbed in the performance, seemingly unaware of the noise, proximity and movements of the women in their path. But although there were many groups performing at the same time on the field, this particular troupe now seemed to have the attention of the majority of the audience, united by the movements of the two women and the response of the crowd.

In this chapter, I explore the dynamics of this seemingly spontaneous and informal dance-like performance of women, referred to in Gogodala as *owama gi* or in English as 'dancing for joy'. I argue that *owama gi* opens up a space in which Gogodala women can embody, experience and express the emotions elicited by certain kin-based relationships. Dancing for joy, which is generated by a sensual engagement with the performance and by intense emotions like pride and happiness, appears to be largely unrehearsed if not completely spontaneous: a celebration of motherhood, sisterhood or being a loved and valued daughter. Indeed, women, from single girls to grandmothers, express their compulsion to dance at these occasions in terms of phrases like 'you cannot help yourself'. It is in reality, however, proscribed not only in its movements and context but also in terms of who performs it and for whom it is performed — so that, understood as spontaneous expressions of pleasure, such dances involve certain types of bodily comportment and stylised movements. In addition, dancing for joy is always danced for someone, not only to draw attention to the quality of performer and performance, success or achievement, but also to chart public connections between the women who perform *owama gi* and those who are the source of the celebration. In this sense, dancing for joy is a performance in which 'the emotional content of human relations is deliberately laid bare' (Wood & Smith 2004:535); and an 'ephemeral' and 'intangible' dance performance (see Henry 2011) that is simultaneously 'a geographical act' (Wood & Smith 2004:535). It involves the sensual and embodied generation of space, in which emotions associated with relationships between women and their children, uncles, fathers, and brothers are elicited, and is a highly visible demonstration of the central role that women play in the lives and achievements of their close kin.

This account seeks to foreground the analysis of the substantive connection between space, sensory experience and human emotions through an exploration of the ways in which sensual immersion and emotion both generate, and are generated by, certain kinds of gendered relationships and spaces. Bader and Martin-Iverson (2014:154) note that while performances (like, I would argue, dancing for joy) negotiate and establish 'intersubjective relations and social values' at the time, they also 'extend beyond the performance experience as such, contributing to the construction, re-negotiation, maintenance and transformation of social groups and identities'. Like Bader and Martin-Iverson (156), I believe that it is analytically useful to see 'performance as a form of social action' and to focus on the ways in which 'performance both produces and is produced by social relationships'.

Marilyn Strathern (1988) has argued that, in Melanesia, performance is a form of social action that is a process of not just the production, but also the revelation of social and intimate relationships. In this chapter, I argue that the performance of dancing for joy is simultaneously constitutive and revelatory, and this is mediated by the ways in which both senses and emotions inform and structure these performances. In the process, performances of dancing for joy become 'powerful emotional ways of making the world, and they tap directly into the power of emotions to shape social life' (Bader & Martin-Iverson 2014:544). As Bondi, Davidson and Smith (2005:3) suggest, emotions are 'relational flows, fluxes or currents, in-between people and places rather than "things" or "objects" to be studied or measured'. In this context, bodies and persons are buffeted, created and moved by these 'flows, fluxes, or currents' (5). Here, I look at the extent to which the flow and flux of emotion is an inherent aspect of dancing for joy, and is both a source and expression of intimate, kin-based relationships. During the performance of *owama gi*, women utilise their moving bodies and those of their male kin to create spaces that embody as well as generate the emotional intimacy of gendered relationality.

In the following section, I explore the contexts of dancing for joy and the role of senses and emotions in the generation of a 'compulsion' or overwhelming desire to dance. I then discuss who performs *owama gi* and how this forms part of a wider set of work-based practices referred to as *ato ela gi*, which is the everyday basis of being a 'good' or 'true' woman. I then analyse this in terms of the gendered and relational constitution of people through blood and clan canoes, to which all Gogodala claim affiliation, and the ways in which dancing for joy is both generated by these relational and affective ties and constitutive of them. In this sense, I argue that the performance of *owama gi* is 'by its very nature a way of life "in the making"' (Wood & Smith 2004:535).

'Can't help myself': Sensual and emotive spaces

> Performance does not merely express, but rather constitutes and is constituted by social values and intersubjective relationships. (Bader & Martin-Iverson 2014:154)

Owama gi is performed exclusively by women, who, immersed in a sensual engagement with a performance, game or event, are moved by an overpowering emotion most closely translated as joy or intense happiness to take to their feet and dance. These women say that they find it impossible to resist 'the call' to move, dance and thus express the strong emotions that they experience at these times. Women note that their sensual interaction with significant others in engagement with their dance, game or race often makes it impossible to sit quietly. Some refer to the powerful beat of the drums in traditional dances or the haunting rattle of the bamboo cane repeatedly hitting the ground during the stately movements of the dance as the initial prompt or impulse to move. This is a common response to the sound of a beating drum or rattle used now most often during dancing held at cultural events (see Dundon 2002). In the past, when ceremonies or *maiyata* were still performed between two or three Gogodala villages, people were drawn to the village and ceremony by the sound of this music. Others say that the painted and stately beauty of the dancers or the full-faced youth of the children collecting prizes, or the sweaty, muscular and shiny-skinned evidence of the exertions and efforts of the players, paddlers or children playing sports bring about the feeling or compulsion to dance for joy. A certain kind of sensual engagement in the original performance or activity by women in the audience lies, then, at the base of the compulsion to dance *owama gi*.

Dancing for joy takes various forms but is generally recognisable — indeed, it is important that it is. Most women dance with extended arms, rolling hip or leg movements and rapid facial contortions that often include movement of the tongue and eyes. These are usually accompanied by loud whoops or calls, whether by the women themselves or women on the sidelines or in the audience. The removal of clothing, usually shirts or blouses (*meri*), often is seen as representative of the intensity of the emotion that gives rise to the compulsion to dance; it accentuates the loss of control over feelings and usual patterns of behaviour. While public nudity (particularly in mixed company and performed by women) in this predominantly evangelical Christian community is greatly discouraged, naked breasts are not perceived to be sexually provocative. In fact, breasts are in many ways indicative, more than any other part of a woman's body, of her ability and capacity to nurture her clan and her children. The revelation of a dancing woman's thighs is never part of *owama gi*, however, and would generate a great deal of immediate displeasure and censure from the crowd, and shame on the intended recipient of the dance.

Owama gi is performed in various contexts: from canoe races, traditional dancing performances like that described above, to school award nights or assemblies, and various sporting games and events. The context and space of dancing for joy is, like its movements and those who perform it, proscribed and focuses particularly on events that are understood to either be or have 'traditional' or 'customary' components, or, increasingly, on those events associated with performance and skills in educational arenas. The performance of 'dancing for joy' often accompanies the end of a canoe race, for example. Canoe races, *gawa maiyata* in the Gogodala language, have a long history in the area, noted first by A.P. Lyons, Resident Magistrate of Western Division in 1916 (1926:351-2); they were originally part of a series of *maiyata* or ceremonies held during cycles of male initiations (see Dundon 2013). They are usually now held as the penultimate 'customary' activity at the end of events like the one described above or at community school openings, national independence celebrations and, increasingly, as the basis of a 'cultural festival' (Dundon 2013). Canoe races are based on serious competitions between giant dugout canoes raced by men on the waterways of the area. Each canoe represents a clan and a village, and each of the paddlers is identified as a crew member through his affiliation with the village and/or clan. Towards the conclusion of the race, as the leading canoes make their way towards the finishing point, women closely related to the contestants and the canoes in the race begin to dance on the banks of the river. Some may jump into the water, initiating *owama gi*, celebrating the return of the men and the victory of their canoes. Others may even wade into the water and jump onto the front of the canoes, toppling the men into the shallow water. All of this generates a great deal of amusement from the watchers on the banks and substantially heightens enjoyment of the race (Dundon 2013:11). This was described to me by several people before I attended any canoe races as a source of some ribald humour and a great deal of both pride and amusement.

Dancing *owama gi* at sporting events is not as common an occurrence as it is at canoe races. Nonetheless, at venues like weekly football games (Australian Rugby League) held in Balimo town every Saturday on the main oval, women may feel moved enough to get up and dance. These games regularly draw crowds of hundreds of spectators, primarily from neighbouring or comparatively close villages and small towns. Spectators may spend hours travelling to the games and back to their own villages, while others stay in town or neighbouring villages with relatives. The enthusiasm of spectators and players alike is high during the football season, and emotions are evident in the physical and verbal violence that sometimes marks such sporting events. *Owama gi* in this context is most likely to take place after a goal has been scored or at the end of a match, during which a clan has been honoured by the valour and skill of the victorious team or certain 'star' players. Women may also dance for joy during and after school sporting events, particularly sports carnivals or games of basketball, football or soccer held on the weekends. These dances celebrate the skill and beauty of their children, grandchildren or those of close kin but are often muted. Many women dancing for joy at school events, for example, will not remove clothing but simply sway and dance on the sidelines to demonstrate and embody their emotion and inability to 'help themselves'.

Dancing for joy has correlates with performances by 'audience' members in various parts of the Torres Straits. Henry (2011:182), drawing on her own work as well as ethnography by Maureen Fuary and Jeremy Beckett, notes the presence of performances that resonate with dancing for joy among the Gogodala. During more formal or 'traditional' dance performances, audience members may spontaneously 'jump up' and dance close to their kin, thereby taking the opportunity to 'mark publicly particular kin relationships' (182). In this context, women jump up and dance briefly close to male kin or simply next to a kinsman with a kerosene lantern — thereby drawing attention to 'his performance, of which she as a kinswoman is immensely proud' (182). Dancers are also often sprayed with perfume or dusted with talcum powder, an expression of 'audience appreciation and delight' with extra perfume reserved for special kin (182). Henry (2011:183) also quotes Beckett recalling such an event in which 'women, mainly older women, and occasionally older men do a funny dance, while serious dancing is going'. To which, he noted, 'dancers are not supposed to respond'. While Beckett told Henry this was often just to 'make people happy', it was also often used to 'celebrate the dance of a favourite son or brother, or nephew' (as cited in Henry 2011:183). In the Western Torres Straits, during a performance referred to as *kaythian*, a woman 'will spontaneously join the dance team of men and perform in a comic or exaggerated way in front of one or more of them'. At the event Henry attended, 'exaggerated cavorting by women' occurred during several of the performances 'to the delight of the participant audience' (183).

Like *owama gi*, this kind of dance-like performance is based on emotional flows between performers and participant audience members, the latter of whom are 'active participants in the collective endeavour of dance performances or music-making' (Bader & Martin-Iverson 2014:154). Increasingly among the Gogodala, women have begun to perform *owama gi* during school assemblies or school prize-giving celebrations. In this context, women will only perform as their child or grandchild is collecting a prize or performing a drama during the assembly or prize-giving event and again may do so from their place in the audience and without the removal of any clothing. The actions of these women draw attention to the attributes and skill of the children and are much appreciated by audience members as long as they are more muted than *owama gi* performed on the oval during sports and 'traditional' cultural events.

Good and joyful women

So who performs dancing for joy among Gogodala speakers? Unlike among communities in the Torres Strait, dancing for joy is only ever performed by women and is part of a wider set of practices that characterise what is referred to in Gogodala as *ato ela gi*, or the 'women's way of life'. *Ato ela gi* is practised primarily by women living in villages in the Western Province, but also by Gogodala women living further afield, who continue to build their lives around certain central practices and principles that revolve around active participation in subsistence activities, and behaviour that ranges from regular attendance at church to birthing and raising children (see Dundon 2005). It is often rationalised by commonly held preconceptions about the role of women in families, clans and villages. What *ato ela gi* signifies in the contemporary context is somewhat ambivalent as well as differently experienced and articulated. Yet it emerges in this commentary as the appropriate moral and behavioural model for village women, one that women themselves generally embrace, and attribute their own actions to, however differently they understand it. It is also the basis for designating women as 'good or true women' — *susaegi bapi*.

Ato ela gi has changed considerably over the generations. According to the memories of elderly women who were brought up in the time either directly before the arrival of the first missionaries, or in the early period of their co-residence with the Gogodala, women's practices have been transformed. Along with this transformation, or perhaps coterminous with it, the moral and caring community of the past has also changed. A woman in her sixties, Sibalato, commented quite vehemently one day:

> When we were young, it was different: it was not the same. Nowadays ladies, everybody, want to get things from everybody, steal things. In those days, we never wanted to do those things. After making sago in the bush, we all came home. At the same time, we would help other people in need, help other women who didn't have sago, strings [for wrapping sago] or sago leaves [to cook the sago in]. At the same time, women nowadays are very greedy and selfish — they want to eat those things by themselves; they don't want to share things. Before, it was good when our parents taught us. Now the lifestyle [*ela gi*] is not that good. In the past it was good, people loved each other and shared. It was good. After catching fish, I bring them and put them in a balago [bark sheet] and share them among people in the village. (Sibalato, 7 October 2004)

This dialogue, which is the basis of a fairly common lament amongst women of the older generation, is hotly disputed by women in their late teens and early twenties — young women yet to marry, who provide diligently for their sister's husbands and children, or their elderly parents and grandparents, or newly married women with small children. These women maintain that they do, know and understand *ato ela gi* and that their lives are as distinctly patterned as their bodies by the cadence of women's work.

Ato ela gi is based largely on the kinds of *oko* 'work' or activities that bring together food, water and shelter and that strive to produce and maintain families, clans and villages. Of necessity, it revolves around the rhythms of village life and the seasonal transformations of the local landscape. Work is central to the Gogodala lifestyle — even paid employment, although this is understood as somewhat different from village 'work'. Although much work is shared between women and men, like gardening or the collection of water or firewood, and often carried out in unison, other activities are explicitly gendered. Certain jobs are predominantly performed by women, while others are performed by men and are the basis of *dala ela gi* — the male way of life — with a focus on hunting, game fishing, gardening and building houses.

But *ato ela gi* is more than a set of subsistence activities, constitutive of bodies and persons as they are, and *oko* or work is understood within a wide framework of practices. For women in particular, work encompasses the conception, pregnancy and birthing of children as well as their care and wellbeing. Marriage brings about a situation in which women and their husbands seek to establish their own family within the wider framework of extended family, clan and canoe as well as village. They are expected to do so through forming a partnership in which they undertake work that benefits not only themselves but this wider network of kin and clan relationships. In this sense, practising *ato ela gi* is also the basis of being *susaegi bapi* — a 'true' or 'good' woman. Gogodala women who practise *ato ela gi* aim to be perceived as a 'good woman', a phrase which encompasses the wider range of practices and commitments of *ato ela gi*. In this context, this is often a very significant source or site of conflict and contestation. A good woman is

> hardworking and rich; [good at] making sago *baya gi*; good at gathering things *lopala mowadae gi*; [fishing, firewood, water etc — bringing things back to the house]; *ila sala gi* — chopping firewood; *saba salamina gi* — sweeping [the] floor [and] organising the room; *aei lapela gi* — sweeping under the house, weeding. (Awato, 15 September 2004)

Owama gi can also be a part of being a good or true woman, but not all women perform *owama gi*. In fact, the majority of Gogodala women do not ever stand up in public and dance for their children, brothers, cousins or fathers. They represent themselves as 'shy' or quiet women who feel such emotions and happiness but resist the desire to stand up and dance. Others may dance at some moments or events but not at others. Yet these women are proud and empassioned by the emotions that they experience at these events. Those women who do dance, then, are referred to as *owama ato* — women who dance for joy. *Owama ato* are those women who often stand up in church or fellowship meetings to sing or lead the discussions or who are moved by the Holy Spirit during Christian revivals. They are women who are more easily or readily called into public displays of affection and emotion. Both types of women — whether they dance or not — can claim to be good or true women, but sometimes those who dance come under the imputation from others that their emotional readiness has the potential to lead to problems. In that sense, although *owama gi* is both a central part of *ato ela gi* and an emotional expression and experience of it, there is a limit to which women can authentically practise it and still be good women. Much of this relates specifically to the extent to which dancing for joy is understood to be legitimate in the instance it is performed — that is, whether the woman dancing is truly engaged in *ato ela gi* is a good woman.

Performing relationships: Blood and canoes

Relatedness and clan membership are central to *ato ela gi* and being *susaegi bapi*, and form the basis of 'authentic' or *gi bapi* ('real' or 'true') performances of dancing for joy. In Papua New Guinea, the importance of relatedness is foregrounded in analytic models that propose the Melanesian person as 'dividual' or 'partible' rather than as the Western 'individual'. That is, the Melanesian person is relationally conceived, nurtured and constituted (see Strathern 1988), a 'composite formed of relations with a plurality of other persons' (Mosko 2010:218). In this context, it is argued that these 'relational persons' are defined more by relationships than any kind of 'personality' or unique individual characteristics (Hemer 2013:17). Consequently, people situate themselves in a network of relationships that generate a variety of opportunities for, as well as constraints on, action and agency. This has been debated and disputed in various contexts (see for example Hemer 2013; Hess 2006; Mosko 2010; Robbins 2002; Smith 2012; Strathern 1988), and arose largely out of Marilyn Strathern's *Gender of the Gift* (1988), in which she proffered a primary metaphor for Melanesian sociality: that of the Melanesian person as multiple and relationally conceived. In this conception of the Melanesian person, people stood as 'a microcosm of social relations' (176). Strathern proposed that when a person acted and engaged in activities, social relations were objectified and thereby revealed. She wrote that in the process '[r]elations and persons become in effect homologous, the capabilities of persons revealing the social relations of which they are composed, and social relations revealing the persons they produce' (173). In this sense, people are the product or objectification of 'the gifts, contributions and detachments of others' — gifts generally expected to be reciprocated (Mosko 2010:218).

Various ethnographers have pointed to the problematic nature of positing (even metaphorically) an incommensurability between the 'Melanesian' and 'Western' person, which LiPuma (1998:75) notes is actually a comparison of ethnographically informed patterns of personhood in Melanesia with Western ideologies of personhood rather than its lived reality (see also Hess 2006; Mosko 2010). Several have pointed to the ethnographic reality of both the 'dividual' or partible and the 'individual' in both Melanesian and Western personhood (see for example Hemer 2013; Hess 2006; LiPuma 1998; Mosko 2010). Nonetheless, Melanesian societies do exhibit a primary focus on what Robbins (2002:190, 203) refers to as 'relationalism', which has at its base a paramount value for relationships and is based on 'relationalist assumptions'. Gogodala, too, speak in 'relationalist terms' and privilege a relational model of conception, nurture and maturation. This is particularly evident in contexts like performances of dancing for joy, where women dance at events and/or celebrations which demonstrate their connections of kinship and clanship — through 'blood' (*dede*) and 'clan canoes' (*udaga gawa*). Clan canoes are the smallest and most intimate Gogodala social grouping and clan canoes, as a social unit, are the source of people's names, access to land as well as potential marriage partners, and a variety of affiliations. Clan canoes are arranged into clans (*udaga*), of which there are eight, four in one moiety and four in the other. The two moieties are the most basic organisational unit, and divide Gogodala into either the red (Segela) moiety or the white (Paiya) one. As Gogodala clan groups are based on patrilineal ties, women and men derive their clan canoe affiliation from their father and are said to literally and metaphorically 'stand or sit' in that canoe — *naepe udaga gawala lelelowa*. In this way, clan canoes are a metaphorical space for membership, personhood and relatedness in the most basic sense.

Clan canoes, as much as people, objectify and thereby reveal the social relations of people who sit or ride in these spaces. During the time of the primary Gogodala ancestors, the original or 'real' canoes were given to the first ancestors by their father, one canoe for each of the eight clans or *udaga*: these eight canoes became the *kabigina gawa* or 'big clan canoes' for each of these clans. Big clan canoes hold the greatest number of people, which locate them within certain ancestral and contemporary social and political relationships. People in these clan canoes trace their genealogies from the first ancestral owner of the canoe to their own, collapsing the generations between this originary ancestor and the person's great-grandfather. Personal genealogies of this nature are utilised in the allocation of names, marriage alliances and for claims to land and resources.

But while a person's own clan canoe is the basis of claims to being a certain kind of person, people also ride or 'sit' in the canoe of their mother's clan — *agipe gawala dila waminaeno* — which also confers certain privileges and identification with that clan canoe. A person's relationship to their mother's clan canoe is very important and is often regarded with great affection: a man called Kelaki, for example, said in late 2004 that 'mothers [are] like a gateway to this world. Without mothers, we wouldn't be staying like this — it was her hard work that we are alive' (23 October). Women in particular are also marked, quite literally, by their work as *aeibaiga* — as the 'ground' out of which people and canoes are produced and constituted. Women are *aeibaiga*, providing the site and potential for development and growth — in terms of conception, pregnancy and birth, as well as through the reproduction of the clan canoe of their husbands. Women allow children and clan canoes to grow within their wombs (*sege ana*) — literally, the resting place of children: '[T]he child stays in there and is nourished through the food that the mother feeds it. The mother provides that *ana*, that mother provides that ground now' (Kelaki, 23 October 2004). Another man, Sagalu, pointed out that 'mothers are like a canoe to us because we came out of her body and we are connected through the umbilical cord, *dinipala*. [The] father is just [providing] the blood' (23 October 2004). Referring to the enduring connection between people and their mother's clan canoe, he pointed out that a 'mother's body is like a canoe and people are attached to their mother's canoe through something like an umbilical cord'. If people are always attached to the canoe and body of their mother through the enduring embodied relationship of pregnancy and birthing, they owe the continuing existence and significance of their own clan canoe to women as *aeibaiga* — the 'ground' that makes life possible.

It is not surprising, then, that Gogodala in general express not only an ongoing debt to the clan canoe of their mother and her brothers and male kin, but also a great emotion that often spills out in displays of *owama gi* at sporting events, canoe races and traditional dances held during the opening of new schools or trade-stores or events of national significance like Independence Day. In sporting events or canoe races, men, women and children play in the teams of their mother's clan canoe rather than in their own, or men paddle the village racing canoe that their mother or grandmother was born into. In this way, competitors demonstrate their ongoing connection to the canoe out of which they were born, into the clan canoe or social group of their father. Even in the case of children receiving commendations or prizes during school assemblies or speech days, mothers and maternal aunts are seen to be especially important in their children's achievements.

Yet despite the significance of mothers and their clan canoes on such occasions, they are not usually part of the official celebrations on such days and there is little space for the articulation of such ties or their impact on the success of these events. Women will not often stand in public to make speeches about their role in the success of their children, grandchildren or male kin, and they are offered few opportunities to make public declarations in general, even in a context of increased levels of education and employment for girls and women. Dancing for joy enables women to create a space in which they can 'perform' the significance of the emotive and substantial ties that connect people through their maternal clan canoes and blood — particularly through the bodies of their mothers and maternal kin. But while the performance of *owama gi* prefaces these relationalist values, it is a performance that also draws attention to the 'individual' aspects of the people involved — the agency and embodied power of the woman dancing for joy, the beauty, skill and capabilities of the dancer, child or sports player. In this way, dancing for joy is never simply a 'dividual' event or performance: the performance also foregrounds emotions and actions which emphasise individual aspects of those to whom it is directed and those who dance it.

Conclusions

Among the Gogodala, a spatial logic of intimacy is apparent in performances of *owama gi*, in which people not only take on 'particular rules and roles' (see Thein 2005:192), but also generate a visible space that foregrounds collective and personal foundational relationships. Wood and Smith note that

> performance spaces create settings in which relations of intimacy — those close, risky, emotionally charged relationships which are more usually reserved for 'private' encounters with familiar people — might be engaged in by comparative strangers in a 'public setting'. (2004:539)

In performances like dancing for joy, this can create or initiate bonds that give rise to intimacy or even 'nurture a sense of intimacy' (Wood & Smith 2004:539). In dancing for joy, the spaces between the dancers become, temporarily at least, spaces that prefigure intimate relationships in which women are primary social and physiological mediators. In this context, women enact and reveal not only pleasure and pride in the beauty and ability of their male kin or (grand)children, but also the efficacy of their own webs of relatedness, processes of nurture, enabling bodies and capabilities as good or true women. It is a very public but also intimate way in which Gogodala women underscore the importance of the role they play in their primary relationships.

Dancing for joy is generated by, and generates, a great deal of emotion, ranging from happiness and joy to pride. Wood and Smith (2004:537-8) argue that this kind of generation of shared emotions is essential for the 'making of performances that work' and that are thereby perceived as authentic. In many ways, while neither performers nor audience 'necessarily [understand] why they are engaging with each other in such emotionally powerful ways', the 'power of the experience is palpable to both performers and to those with whom they are bound within a particular performance space' (537-8). I have argued that the meaning of the performance of *owama gi* is clearly understood and people engage within the performance space in certain ways, whether that space is a canoe race, a dance contest or a school hall. As Henry (2011:180) writes about the mutually constitutive relationship between emotion and meaning in dance:

'[D]ance is about feeling, but it is also about meaning. We understand the meaning of dance through feeling and we feel dance through understanding what it might mean'.

Nonetheless, the performance of *owama gi* differs according to the women involved, the relatives for whom they dance, and the context in which it takes place. And the generation of emotional engagement is one that binds people within the performance space of *owama gi*. In this sense, then, what happens is not simply about 'what is heard or what is felt' — in this case, the importance of women in social and personal relationships — but is also about the relationship that is formed through the performance itself (Wood & Smith 2004:537). That dancing for joy occurs during performances that already celebrate and constitute shared identification through blood, clans and canoes is not surprising, given that women are perceived to be at the centre of such relationships, as the 'ground' out of which such collectives are possible.[1] Dancing for joy is both generated by relational and affective ties and constitutive of them, and in this sense, the performance is 'by its very nature a way of life "in the making"' (535) through the generation of emotions in others — the audience, dancers, sports players and children. Such emotions, whether expressed through happiness, laughter, pride, quiet or even ribald amusement, temporarily connect and unite the participating audience, the official performers and the women dancing for joy.

References

Bader, S. and S. Martin-Iverson. 2014. 'Creative intersubjectivity in performance: Perspectives from the Asia-Pacific', *Ethnomusicology Forum* 23(2): 149-162.

Bondi, L., J. Davidson and M. Smith. 2005. 'Introduction: Geography's "emotional turn"'. In L. Bondi, J. Davidson and M. Smith (Eds.), *Emotional Geographies* (pp. 1-16). Surrey, UK and Burlington, VT: Ashgate.

Davidson, J. and C. Milligan. 2004. 'Embodying emotion, sensing space: Introducing emotional geographies', *Social and Cultural Geography* 5(4): 523-532.

Dundon, A. 2002. 'Dancing around development: Crisis in Christian country in Western Province, Papua New Guinea', *Oceania* 72(3): 215-229.

Dundon, A. 2005. 'The Sense of sago: Motherhood and migration in Papua New Guinea and Australia', *Journal of Intercultural Studies* 26(1-2): 21-38.

Dundon, A. 2013. 'Gogodala canoe festivals, customary ways and cultural tourism in Papua New Guinea', *Oceania* 83(2): 88-101.

---

1 Henry (2011:183) notes this for similar performances in the Torres Straits, in which the 'particular intercorporeal aesthetic experience of the performance is flavoured by [the community's] ability to understand what the comic, sexually charged frolicking of the women, and other ribald interventions from the participant audience, symbolically represent in terms of the specific nature of the relationships being "spotlighted"'.

Hemer, S. R. 2013. *Tracing the Melanesian Person: Emotions and Relationships in Lihir*. Adelaide: University of Adelaide Press.

Henry, R. 2011. 'Dancing diplomacy: Performance and the politics of protocol in Australia'. In E. Hviding and K.M. Rio (Eds.), *Made in Oceania: Social Movements, Cultural Heritage and the State in the Pacific* (pp. 179-194). Wantage, UK: Sean Kingston Publishing.

Hess, S. 2006. 'Strathern's Melanesian "dividual" and the Christian "individual": A perspective from Vanua Lava, Vanuatu', *Oceania* 76(3): 285-296.

LiPuma, E. 1998. 'Modernity and forms of personhood in Melanesia'. In M. Lambek and A. Strathern (Eds.), *Bodies and Persons: Comparative Perspectives from Africa and Melanesia* (pp. 53-79). Cambridge: Cambridge University Press.

Lyons, A.P. 1926. 'Notes on the Gogodara tribes of Western Papua', *The Journal of the Royal Anthropological Institute of Great Britain and Ireland* 26: 329-359.

Mosko, M. 2010. 'Partible penitents: Dividual personhood and Christian practice in Melanesia and the West', *Journal of the Royal Anthropological Institute* 16: 215-240.

Robbins, J. 2002. 'My wife can't break off part of her belief and give it to me: Apocalyptic interrogations of Christian individualism among the Urapmin of Papua New Guinea', *Paideuma* 48: 189-206.

Smith, K. 2012. 'From dividual and individual selves to porous subjects', *The Australian Journal of Anthropology* 23: 50-64.

Strathern, M. 1988. *The Gender of the Gift: Problems with Women and Problems with Society in Melanesia*. Berkeley and Los Angeles, CA: California University Press.

Thein, D. 2005. 'Intimate distances: Considering questions of "us"'. In L. Bondi, J. Davidson and M. Smith (Eds.), *Emotional Geographies* (pp. 191-204). Surrey, UK and Burlington, VT: Ashgate.

Wood, N. and S.J. Smith. 2004. 'Instrumental routes to emotional geographies', *Social & Cultural Geography* 5(4): 533-548.

3

Creating the right 'vibe':
Exploring the utilisation of space at Hip Hop concerts in Adelaide and Melbourne

Dianne Rodger

Abstract

This chapter examines how space is utilised at Hip Hop concerts to promote certain sensual experiences. It is based on ethnographic fieldwork conducted in the Adelaide and Melbourne Hip Hop scenes. I explore how light, sound, venue layout and spacing are harnessed to foster specific reactions from the crowd and to create what Hip Hop fans colloquially referred to as the 'vibe'. I conclude that the practical realities of particular venue spaces (size, configuration, stage equipment and so on) can significantly influence the experiences of individuals attending Hip Hop concerts and the presence or absence of the 'vibe'.

Introduction

A successful Hip Hop concert is a dynamic event that overwhelms the senses. The music is loud enough to damage your hearing, the bass can be felt as well as heard and the whirling lights create a dramatic atmosphere. Hands are thrown in the air, heads are nodded to the beat, and people yell, clap and cheer their appreciation. Yet not all Hip Hop concerts evoke these kinds of reactions and emotions. Hip Hop concerts can be exciting and inspiring, but they can also be tedious and tiring. In this chapter, I draw on data compiled from participation observation at various Hip Hop shows in Adelaide and Melbourne, Australia, to explore the mutually constitutive relationship between space, emotion and cultural context. I demonstrate that the senses are engaged in specific ways at Hip Hop concerts to foster certain audience reactions and to create what Hip Hoppers colloquially refer to as the 'vibe'. Creating the right vibe is an important factor that contributes to the perceived 'success' or 'failure' of Hip Hop events. Concert organisers, promoters, performers and venue staff try to control the concert space and, therefore, the emotional and sensorial experiences of the audience. In particular, they harness light, sound and venue layout to try to promote particular emotional states and bodily movements. I argue that our understanding of the relationship between musical performance and emotion can be enhanced by research that accounts for spatial and cultural context in order to consider how the nature of particular spaces can both constrain and evoke emotion.

Music, emotion and methodology

The study of music and emotion is a multidisciplinary field that is characterised by diverse approaches. Theorists from psychology, anthropology, philosophy, musicology and biology have all explored how, when and why music evokes emotion. The variety of methodologies employed to study music and emotion is reflected in the content of the edited volume *Music and Emotion* (Juslin & Slobada 2001a). This collection features a broad range of perspectives from authors in disciplines such as neuropsychology (Peretz 2001), philosophy (Davies 2001) and music therapy (Bunt & Pavlicevic 2001). In the introduction to this book, Juslin and Sloboda (2001b:4) note that the field of music and emotion has been neglected in comparison to other domains of musical science because 'emotional reactions to music ... are difficult to observe under laboratory conditions'. Whether or not emotional responses to music can adequately be examined in a laboratory setting is an issue which is addressed in several of the chapters in their volume. Becker (2001:135-6) is critical of laboratory studies that involve people listening to a piece of music and communicating their emotions to a researcher. She demonstrates that this approach is grounded in 'Western' assumptions about how people listen to music that are not universal.

Becker argues that anthropology and ethnomusicology have contributed to the study of music and emotion by illustrating the 'degree to which emotional responses to musical events [are] culturally inflected' (136). Similarly, Sloboda and O'Neil state that

> music is always heard in a social context, in a particular place and time, with or without other individuals being present, and with other activities taking place which have their own complex sources of meaning and emotion. (2001:415)

As such, they note that the methodologies commonly utilised by laboratory researchers to study emotional responses to music do not account for 'everyday experience' (416) because they are not carried out in 'everyday contexts' (417). In order to address this weakness, Sloboda and O'Neil designed a study that used a pager system to prompt participants to fill out a response booklet about their most recent musical experience. This method allowed them to gather information about a broad range of everyday music-listening practices and their emotional effects.

Unlike Sloboda and O'Neil's work, my research was not designed to monitor how a cohort of individuals engaged with different music in diverse spaces.[1] Thus, while I support their argument that music may have different emotional functions in different contexts (cf. Becker 2001), my findings are based on an in-depth investigation of one cultural group, Hip Hoppers living in Adelaide and Melbourne, in one type of setting, Hip Hop concerts. This focus allows me to discuss in detail how the emotions and senses are engaged at a specific kind of musical event. This is important because when people listen to music they are always situated in a particular cultural context: 'every hearer occupies a position in a cultural field' (Becker 2001:136). Throughout my time in the field, I did observe people consuming and producing Hip Hop music outside of concerts, including in their own homes and cars; however, these practices are beyond the scope of this chapter.

Other theorists have examined the relationship between space, music and emotion by analysing a specific musical event or festival such as the Top Half Folk Festival (Duffy 2000), the West Coast Blues and Roots Festival (Jennings 2010), the Wangaratta Jazz Festival (Curtis 2010), the Swiss-Italian Festa Parade (Duffy, Waitt, Gorman-Murray & Gibson 2011), or the ChillOut Parade (Duffy et al. 2011). However, my research is not based on the analysis of a single event.[2] I conducted participant observation at several Hip Hop events over a sixteen-month period from September 2006 to January 2008.[3] Attending multiple Hip Hop events means that I am able to compare and contrast different concerts in order to evaluate how and why some events and not others were viewed as successful or as having the right vibe. In this chapter, I use the terms *Hip Hop concert*, *Hip Hop show* and *Hip Hop event* interchangeably to refer to live performances that featured Hip Hop music. I recognise that classifying musical genres and defining Hip Hop music can be a complex and divisive process. For this reason, I attended events that were advertised in media channels that targeted Hip Hop enthusiasts, such as the *Upcoming Oz Hip Hop Shows and Events* thread on the

---

1   For example, their participants reported listening to music in diverse settings and during activities such as having a bath, exercising, doing housework and doing deskwork (Sloboda & O'Neil 2001:420).
2   Jennings (2010) attended the same festival over a three-year period.
3   For further information about my (unpublished) fieldwork, see Rodger (2012).

Australian Hip Hop forum, Oz Hip Hop forum (n.d.), or events that people whom I interviewed were performing at or told me about.

The size, scale and set-up of the events that I attended varied; however, they were usually held in licensed premises, on a Friday or Saturday night.[4] Events commonly began at 9 pm or later and generally finished after 12 am. Timing was dependent on several factors including legal restrictions, the venue, the event organisers and the enthusiasm of the crowd. The vast majority of events that I attended throughout my fieldwork were held at in-door venues. This is significant because it enabled the event promoters, artists and venue owners to control aspects of the event space (such as temperature and lighting) with much greater predictability than they could at outdoor events, which must contend with the weather and natural light. These brief summative details demonstrate that Hip Hop concerts are primarily spaces of leisure that are organised around the model of the five-day working week. As I will argue later in this chapter, the assumption that Hip Hop concerts are spaces of leisure plays an important role in determining how people behave at these events and the kinds of emotional experiences that are privileged. All of the events that I refer to in this chapter had an entry fee (from under A$10 to over A$80) and all were advertised, although the format and the scale of these advertisements varied. My research has an urban bias: nearly all of the events that I attended were held in the central business district [CBD] of Adelaide or the inner suburbs of Melbourne.

The field notes that I wrote from 'scratch' notes after these events were a valuable resource that provided 'thick' descriptions (Geertz 2000 [1973]) of my own visceral, emotional responses to these concerts. These notes also described the layout of venues and the activities of concert attendees (that is, ebbs and flows in patron numbers, reactions and movement of the crowd, and so on). That said, it should be noted that at the time of my fieldwork, the relationship between space and emotion was not a central focus of my research. Although my field notes included detailed descriptions of Hip Hop events with a strong emphasis on emotional experiences and spatial geography, I did not employ methodologies which could have further elucidated the interrelationship between space and emotion such as Duffy et al.'s (2011) extension of Lefebvre's (2004) 'rhythmanalysis'. In their research, they utilised their bodies as 'research tools' to gather data about their own bodily rhythms (heart beat, breathing, pulse, movement and so on). They used this information in order to explore how these rhythms were triggered by sound in two different festival spaces. This approach is influenced by Probyn (2005) and by Wood, Duffy and Smith's auto-ethnography (2007).

---

4   Exceptions included events held on public holidays or when an international artist was touring. It is quite common for international acts to tour Adelaide mid-week as they perform to larger audiences on Friday or Saturday night interstate. This fact is resented by Adelaide fans.

Although I documented my own emotions and bodily responses in my field notes, I did not consistently record micro-details such as my pulse or breathing rate. While I support Duffy et al.'s (2011) argument that the body has been marginalised from geographical research (see also Driver 2011 for an account of how the body has been neglected in subcultural research), my analysis of Hip Hop concerts is not a 'rhythmanalysis' and does not centre on my own bodily responses to Hip Hop events. Rather, I use this information in conjunction with my observations of Hip Hop audiences and their own descriptions and analyses of their actions and emotions. Duffy et al. (2011:20) argue that interviews with participants at events or after events offer limited insight because they can only elucidate what 'festival goers think, and not how meaning is produced moment-by-moment'. Unlike Duffy et al., who used interviews as 'background' (20), I suggest that it is important to engage with festival and concert-goers in order to build holistic accounts of how different people respond to the same musical performance. For this reason, in addition to conducting participant observation at these events, I also carried out informal interviews with concert attendees during events and more formal, semi-structured interviews with Hip Hop fans and artists outside the concert setting. While I recognise that people may not always be able to articulate their emotions or reflect on how meaning is produced 'moment-by moment', relegating the thoughts of participants to the 'background' may result in an over-emphasis on the emotional and bodily experiences of the researcher, which may not be universal.

Defining the 'vibe'

Earlier, I noted that Hip Hop events are spaces of leisure for the majority of people who occupy them. Exceptions include performing artists, promoters and venue staff, such as lighting and sound technicians and bar staff. Because Hip Hop concerts are viewed as leisure spaces, people expect that they will experience particular emotions or a vibe when they inhabit them. They enter these spaces with the expectation that they will be entertained and that the concert will be an enjoyable experience. In his account of electronic dance music culture and religion, St John (2006:10) states that 'vibe' is insider slang that 'most commonly denotes a successful or optimum social dance experience'. Australian Hip Hoppers typically used the term 'vibe' to describe the atmosphere or the energy that they felt at Hip Hop shows. A show with a good vibe was 'electric', 'thrilling' and 'inspiring'. Conversely, a show with a bad vibe or, indeed with no vibe at all, was 'flat', 'dull' and 'tedious'.

It was much more common for people to use the term 'vibe' to refer to a positive Hip Hop show. When the term 'vibe' was used to describe a Hip Hop concert that was viewed as a failure or disappointment, an adjective was added to 'vibe' to qualify it, as in the above 'bad vibe' or, as another example, 'aggressive vibe'. Likewise, the absence of a vibe was typically understood as a negative quality. An event that did not have a vibe was defined as lacking certain elements; it did not evoke the positive emotions that audience members were anticipating. Hip Hoppers spoke about the vibe as an intangible but distinct feeling: as an almost magical aura. As such, it would be easy to assume that a vibe is invisible, unquantifiable and mysterious. However, as I will discuss, such an understanding overlooks both the cultural work that is required to create a particular vibe and the contextually specific nature of the vibe.

This chapter is informed by the work of authors who have examined the culturally constructed nature of taste distinctions like 'good' and 'bad' (Bourdieu 1984; Thornton 1996; Washburne & Derno 2004; Hibbett 2005). From this perspective, it is clear that the good vibe of a successful Hip Hop concert may have very different characteristics than those of a successful heavy metal show or other musical performance. This point is clearly articulated by Becker (2001; 2004) in her discussion of cross-cultural 'modes of listening' (2004:70):

> What is appropriate to say about musical affect, what is *not* appropriate to say, what one feels and what one does *not* feel may reveal underlying assumptions surrounding musical listening. What is *not* assumed in one mode (such as bodily movement in Western classical listening) may become central in another mode … [T]o sit quietly focused on musical structure at a salsa concert is as inappropriate as break dancing to a Schubert quintet. (Becker 2004:70, italics in the original text)

Becker argues that these 'modes of listening' are naturalised or taken for granted, and it is these taken-for-granted norms that I examine in this chapter. In the following section, I define the characteristics of what I call the 'Hip Hop mode of listening' — that is, the culturally appropriate and desired mode of listening at Hip Hop concerts in Adelaide and Melbourne. I then expand this discussion to explore how the practical realities of different Hip Hop venues constrained or enhanced this 'mode of listening' and, therefore, the vibe.

Creating the vibe: A Hip Hop mode of listening

> The date is the 12th of May 2007 and 7200 people are gathered in the Adelaide Entertainment Centre to see Adelaide Hip Hop group the Hilltop Hoods perform with the Adelaide Symphony Orchestra. The show is the album launch for 'The Hard Road: Restrung' a re-working of the Hilltop Hoods 2006 album 'The Hard Road' with orchestral backing. After the support acts have played[5] the lights are lowered, leaving the crowd murmuring in the darkness as the expectant atmosphere builds. Finally, a red curtain swings back to reveal the three members of the Hilltop

---

5   Support acts and guest artists who performed at this show were Adelaide locals *DJ Shep* and *DJ Reflux*, Melbourne group *Muph and Plutonic* with *DJ Slap 618*, British MC *Mystro* and American MC *Okwerdz*.

Hoods; DJ Debris, MC Suffa and MC Pressure. Debris is at the decks[6] on a raised platform and the 31 piece Adelaide Symphony Orchestra are seated behind him.

What follows is a whirlwind of sound and light. The orchestra adds a new dimension to the usual high energy of a Hip Hop show. Lyrics are yelled in unison as the crowd sings along to the unique combination of live strings, brass, woodwind, percussion, scratching, samples and rapping. After several tracks are performed the show comes to an end when the Hoods and the orchestra perform the album title track 'The Hard Road'. The crowd continues to applaud and stamp their feet after the Hilltop Hoods have left the stage. Eventually all the lights come back on and we re-adjust to our surroundings. Slowly we make our way out of the venue and into the cold night air, eagerly discussing the night's proceedings. (Field notes, 13 May 2007)

The Hilltop Hoods and Adelaide Symphony Orchestra Show [HTH/ASO Show] is an interesting case study because it featured the unusual combination of Hip Hop and a symphony orchestra. The majority of people that I spoke to about this show viewed it as an extremely positive event; it could be said that the show was the epitome of a concert with a good vibe. Below, I use the case study of the HTH/ASO Show and examples from other Hip Hop gigs to unpack the features of the Hip Hop mode of listening. I identify several factors (lighting, sight and venue layout, spacing, and sound) which play central roles in the evocation of the vibe. I argue that by exploring commonalities in the way that light, venue layout, spacing and sound are employed at Hip Hop concerts we can better understand the particularities of the Hip Hop mode of listening, a mode that privileges particular orientations and sensibilities. For ease of reading and analytical clarity, I have chosen to separate the key factors that contribute to the positive vibe of successful Hip Hop events. In practice, however, these factors are interrelated and intertwined.

Lighting

The transformative and affective capacities of light have been highlighted by scholars examining the relationship between 'light, material culture and social experience' (Bille & Sorensen 2007:263) and the role that both light and darkness play in the production of atmospheric effects (Edensor 2015). In his study of festival installations and musical performances which utilise both light and the absence of light, Edensor concludes that light and darkness are 'essential components in the formation and emergence of atmospheres of varying intensity' (332). The event organisers and/or artists at the HTH/ASO Show cleverly utilised stage lighting to create a range of sensory experiences and to encourage particular emotional responses. A blackout was used before the headlining act appeared on stage, in order to promote a sense of anticipation and heighten the sense of shock and awe facilitated by the pyrotechnics that followed.

---

6   Slang for turntables.

Throughout the entire performance, multicoloured lights created drama as they twirled around the Adelaide Entertainment Centre. While this show had a much larger budget than many events that I attended and utilised light in some novel ways that were not used at other venues, it also shared many commonalities with other Hip Hop performances. Most notably, the stage was always more heavily lit than the audience, a lighting set-up that was standard at every Hip Hop show that I attended and which meant that the audience was typically in semi-darkness.[7] This created opportunities for lights to cut through the darkness, temporarily highlighting the throng of the audience members, with arms outstretched and heads nodding to the beat.

I argue that this use of light is designed both to focus the audience's attention on the performance and to direct attention away from the everyday minutia of the venue. Edensor (2015) discusses how parks and everyday spaces can be transformed by light installations that are designed to foster a sense of unreality, unfamiliarity and amazement. Unlike art installations deployed in public spaces like parks, Hip Hop events are normally held in generalised venues designed for musical performances. While these spaces are often nondescript and fairly uninspiring when a performance is not occurring, during a performance Hip Hoppers can perceive them as places of enchantment. They are usually entered with the expectation of entertainment, excitement and good vibes. Lighting plays a key role in meeting these expectations by creating a sense of drama and shifting people's focus away from potential distractions. The effect of this is powerful enough to cause a sense of disorientation and a 'return to reality' when the performance is finished and the venue becomes fully lit by a bright, harsh light.

Being shrouded in semi-darkness also helps people to forget any bodily discomfort they may be experiencing. This is important because attending a Hip Hop concert can be a physically demanding and uncomfortable experience that typically requires standing for a long period of time in a confined space. As such, Hip Hop promoters and artists attempt to maximise the venue layout in order to draw people's attention away from these discomforts and onto the performance. Thus, at a Hip Hop event with a vibe, people are not looking at the empty drink cups lying crushed all over the floor or thinking about what that mysterious stain on the well-worn carpet is. Rather, lighting is used to focus on particular elements — most notably, the performers on stage. This focusing away from the individual self and onto one's position as a member of an audience has been argued to result in feelings of communal belonging or equality (Jennings 2010). In his account of a performance by Don McLean at the 2008 West Coast Blues and Roots Festival, Jennings (2010:80) describes how he entered a 'trance-like state' where some of his senses were heightened while others were bypassed.

---

7   One exception were events held outdoors during daylight hours. However, these events were rare, with most events being held after dark in venues with no natural light.

In this state he did not care about other sensations that he was also experiencing, like how much his feet hurt or what he looked like (80-1). What he experienced was a feeling of 'community' or 'togetherness' described by Turner (1969) as *communitas*, a concept Jennings applies to the study of musical concerts. However, Jennings also notes that people have critiqued Turner's account of *communitas*, arguing that it is utopian. He goes on to question whether or not the feeling of *communitas* that he experienced had any lasting ramifications beyond the event itself: 'What happens when the music dies?' (Jennings 2010:81).

Gerard (2004) is also critical of scholars who draw on Turner's theories or a more generalised account of 'ritual' to describe musical events like raves without adequately describing their structure. My own research suggests that we must be careful not to overstate the sense of unity that can be experienced by crowd members at musical performances. Indeed, the HTH/ASO Show was an event that divided many Hip Hoppers, some of whom felt that the Hilltop Hoods had 'sold out' by performing the show, or were alarmed by the number of newer fans who attended it who were not, in the eyes of the longer-term fans, 'authentic'. This was information that I was not aware of in 'the moment' (Duffy et al. 2011) at the HTH/ASO show itself because it did not manifest in any behaviours that I observed. However, at other events, the diverse motivations of audience members were clearly visible and at one event these differences erupted into physical violence. Thus while my research illustrates that lighting is used at Hip Hop concerts in specific ways to engender emotional reactions and to enhance the sensations felt by Hip Hoppers, further research is needed to explore whether *communitas* is produced at Hip Hop concerts and, if so, what the ramifications of this might be. My findings suggest that light is primarily deployed to focus attention on the stage, highlighting the significant interplay between hearing and sight in the Hip Hop mode of listening.

Sight and venue layout

Visual elements play a central role in the evocation of emotion at Hip Hop shows. Unlike other musical fans, who sometimes close their eyes in order to achieve a different sensorial appreciation of the music, Hip Hoppers' complaints about concerts frequently centred on the inability of audience members to adequately see the performance. While watching the performing artist is not always important in other musical genres such as electronic dance music (Haslam 1997; Fraser 2012), being able to see the performer was highly valued by Hip Hop fans. The significance placed on visually engaging with the performing artist/s was exemplified by the frequent use of projectors that displayed live stream shots of the performance to the crowd. Although these technologies were not typically used at smaller-scale shows where local acts were performing, they were a defining feature of larger events, in particular international

DJ acts. It was very common for a DJ set to include numerous shots of the DJ on different screens, including a close-up camera angle of the performer's hands. When these technologies were not used and/or the venue did not include a raised stage, it was difficult for the audience to view performers, and this caused frustration.

For example, I recorded in my field notes that I was extremely disappointed when I attended a Hip Hop concert that also featured a breakdancing or B-Boy/Girl battle. This battle was held in the middle of a large hall and a circle of audience members quickly formed around the breakers. This meant that only the audience members who made up the first and innermost circle of the crowd could properly view the event.[8] This problem was avoided at the HTH/ASO show because the stage was high and very large, and because the performance was being filmed and broadcast on large screens. This contributed to the vibe of the event because people were not craning to see the performance, or pushing and prodding other people to try to get a better view. This suggests that both the location and visibility of the stage, venue size and layout play a key role in the creation of the vibe. It is also important to note that the visibility of the performers facilitates communication between the audience and the Hip Hop act (facial gestures, smiling, laughing, instructions to the crowd, reaching out to audience members, and so on), and this also contributes to the production of emotion.

In his analysis of a musical concert conducted in total darkness as part of the Manchester International Festival, Edensor (2015:344-7) indicates that while the darkness did intensify the experience of the music, it also made audience members uncomfortable and stifled typical performer/audience interactions, which led to an absence of bonding. A musical concert conducted in total darkness is a fruitful event to analyse because it defies cultural expectations regarding appropriate modes of listening, and, in doing so, helps to reveal taken-for-granted listening behaviours. While it might seem self-evident that Hip Hop audience members place importance on having a clear view of the stage, it is worth remembering that attitudes towards the consumption and production of music are not universal and that culturally appropriate listening behaviours need to be investigated, not assumed.

For example, Overell's (2010:91) detailed ethnographic account of 'brutal belonging' in the Melbourne Grindcore scene found that participants preferred venues with low or no stages which allowed close bodily proximity between audience members and performers. In this scene, the facilitation of intermingling between the crowd and performers is highly valued (91). Like the participants in Overell's study, the Hip Hop fans and artists whom I engaged with had preferences for particular venues, and the Hip Hop mode of listening led Hip Hop promoters and artists to seek

---

8 Several other attendees and I tried to overcome this problem by standing on some tables that lined the outer edge of the hall and were probably used for other kinds of functions held in the space. However, we were promptly asked by Security to get down. This highlights how appropriate and inappropriate modes of listening can be dictated by authority figures.

out venue spaces that would best facilitate the emotional engagement of Hip Hop fans. As I discuss below, Hip Hop promoters, artists and venue owners clearly have a vested interest in ensuring that everyone who attends one of their events is feeling the vibe. Although they are often constrained by economic and other limitations, they do not leave these matters to chance, and they actively pursue venues that best suit Hip Hop events. As I discuss in the following section, spacing is a key concern that promoters consider when booking venues for Hip Hop performances.

Spacing

Venue size and layout are important considerations for Hip Hop promoters because these factors structure how people move through the venue space and therefore how their senses are engaged. The relationship between venue layout and the production, performance and experience of music has been explored by scholars like Nowotny, Fackler, Muschi, Vargas, Wilson and Kotarba (2010), who examined four Latino music scenes (conjunto, mariachi, salsa and Latin jazz) in Houston, Texas. Their account of these scenes demonstrates that different listening modes are facilitated by different venue layouts. For example, salsa venues take two forms in Houston: dance clubs and Latin restaurants (41). While both of these venue types feature salsa music, their layouts are designed to enable different forms of social interaction and to emphasise particular forms of movement (that is, dancing or dining).

The relationship between the physical space of a music venue and the movements of individuals has also been considered by scholars researching club culture in the United Kingdom (Malbon 1999; Wall 2006). Malbon (1999) examines the importance of spacing on the dance floor, arguing that the density of the crowd and the proximity of individual dancers contribute to the evocation of particular sensations. Wall (2006) draws on Malbon's work to explore how members of the British Northern Soul scene, a 'dance-based music culture' (Wall 2006:431), move within the space of a Northern Soul event. Both of these authors demonstrate that dancers make judgements about how dance venues should be organised and how people should move within those spaces. Hip Hoppers did not often dance but they did privilege other forms of bodily movement that centred on their relationship to the stage.

At every Hip Hop show that I attended, the performance took place on a stage, or in a demarcated area that the audience members orientated themselves toward. I say that the audience members orientated themselves, because there is generally no seating or very little seating at Hip Hop events. Unlike a typical classical music concert where everyone sits in ordered rows, the majority of audience members at a Hip Hop show stand. Because they are standing, they can choose to face in any direction, but the vast majority of audience members will face the stage for most of the event. Indeed, the assumption that crowd members will stand and not sit means that if you choose to sit down at a Hip Hop concert it can be almost impossible to find a seat. On one occasion when I was tired and decided to sit down at a Hip Hop show held at Earth nightclub in Adelaide, I managed to find one of three or four seats provided near the bar. Shortly after I sat down, I was approached by a man who was shocked that I was sitting down and asked me why I was not 'having fun'. Even though I was still enjoying the performance from my seat, my actions were contrary to the Hip Hop mode of listening which involves standing, usually as close to the stage as possible. Because I was not standing, I was perceived to be bored with the performance.

The association between sitting down and boredom or disengagement is illustrative of a mode of listening that privileges being able to stand and to perform movements like nodding your head, cheering and waving your arms. Many Hip Hoppers viewed sitting down as a constraint that limited their ability to express and to experience the vibe. For example, at the HTH/ASO Show there were two types of tickets: general admittance [GA], which gained people entrance to the central open space where the bulk of the audience stood, and reserved seating, which gained people entrance to an allocated seat in the tiers of seating that circled the stage. While it could be assumed that people would prefer allocated seating, GA tickets sold out first, and many Hip Hoppers who missed out on GA tickets and had to purchase allocated seating in order to attend the show were disappointed. People I spoke to who sat in an allocated seat reported feeling that they were somewhat disconnected from the performance and unable to fully express their emotional state through their bodily movements. Standing up was understood to be conducive to the sensation of particular emotions. Conversely, sitting down was often experienced as curtailing those senses and restricting bodily movements that contributed to emotions like joy and freedom.

This sense of frustration and restriction was not limited to Hip Hoppers who were unable to stand, however. Indeed, it was most frequently expressed by people who attended events that they thought were overcrowded. My research demonstrates that when people feel cramped and uncomfortable they are much less likely to enjoy themselves. I attended one show that was held in an oddly shaped and very small venue. The event had sold out and the space was packed with bodies. The people I interviewed thought that the promoter should have sold fewer tickets to the event, thus limiting the number of people in the space. Alternatively, they suggested that the promoter should have found a larger venue that could accommodate the audience without cramping them.

However, it should be noted that a tightly packed crowd is not always viewed negatively. It is only when the spacing of the crowd begins both to influence the ability of people to move and to limit their field of vision that they become frustrated. A dense crowd is also preferable to a very loosely spaced crowd or a largely empty space. This poses a significant dilemma for Hip Hop promoters who need to find the optimum-sized venue for their event. This decision is commonly made with an estimate for ticket sales that will not always be accurate. If the promoters hire a large venue and do not sell a high number of tickets, then the emptiness of the space can negatively affect the vibe. Similarly, if they hold a popular event in a small venue the audience can feel confined.

These concerns are illustrated in the following excerpt from an interview I conducted with a Hip Hop promoter who had organised several local Adelaide Hip Hop shows. In this interview, the promoter discussed how he planned events, noting that the size of the Adelaide Hip Hop scene was a factor that influenced which venues he booked. He had hosted several recent shows at the same venue, which he described as being a 'big venue to fill'. He explained that he purposely spaced these events out to ensure that people would not become 'sick' of the venue and the event would be close to capacity:

> With the size of [venue name] it just wouldn't work [holding events more regularly], because it can mean a lot, like you might have a big venue but if there's only a hundred people there it'll just … the vibe is just crap. But if you've got a room that just fits a hundred people, it'll be an awesome night. (Interview with Adelaide promoter, 17 July 2007)

Here the promoter notes that venue size plays a key role in the creation of the vibe — so much so, that the same hundred people could go from a experiencing a 'crap' vibe to an 'awesome' night, dependent on whether they were completely filling a small venue or were somewhat lost in a larger space. Choosing the best space for a Hip Hop event is a difficult task that involves making decisions about the best venue layout and size for the event. This choice is usually restricted by economic factors because the ideal venue for an event may be beyond the promoter's budget. While some spaces are viewed as being better suited to Hip Hop events than others, a broad range of factors influence venue choice, including venue availability and competition with other Hip Hop events.

Sound

Thus far I have demonstrated that concert organisers and performers utilise lighting and venue layout to try and create a particular vibe or emotional experience. Yet given that Hip Hop concerts are musical events, one of the most important factors in the evocation of a vibe is sound. When Hip Hoppers discuss the success or failure of a Hip Hop event, they commonly talk about the sound quality. Many Hip Hoppers believe that some venues are well configured neither for the loud bass that typically characterises Hip Hop music nor for the unique way that Hip Hoppers use microphones. Because Hip Hoppers rap rather than sing, the way that their music is mixed by a sound engineer or technician can be very different than at a rock show or other musical event, and it requires different skills. These differences were not always accounted for, and Hip

Hoppers told me that some sound desk operators were less able to successfully mix the sound at a Hip Hop show. Even when the sound engineers/technicians were proficient, unexpected problems or faulty equipment could result in inconsistent sound levels, failing microphones and other technical sound problems such as feedback, all of which were detrimental to the vibe.

At the HTH/ASO show, and indeed at every show that I attended, many people rapped along to the lyrics of the performing artist. Shouting lyrics in unison or yelling out a 'punch line' was a very enjoyable experience for Hip Hoppers. When the sound levels were unbalanced, people struggled to hear the performer's lyrics and to connect with the performance. The stop-and-start nature of events with sound problems was also discussed by Hip Hoppers as a disruption that stopped the vibe from developing. Throughout my time in the field, I observed that Hip Hop shows were much more likely to be viewed as successful if there were no delays or interruptions that distracted attendees from becoming immersed and engaged in the performance.

When Hip Hop fans are disgruntled and, indeed, when they are enjoying a performance, they also produce sounds that contribute to the vibe. Edensor (2015:333) notes that the atmosphere created at events should not be understood as 'conditions into which people are simply plunged and to which they passively respond'. Concert-goers are keen to ensure that they experience the right vibe, utilising measures such as cheering or clapping loudly both to show their appreciation for a performing artist and to contribute to an event's ambience. Thus, while audiences at musical performances are often depicted as merely receiving sound, it is important to note that they also create it. These sounds can play a critical role in the success or failure of a Hip Hop show. An audience that is loudly booing or is deathly quiet is a clear indicator of a bad vibe. Thus, as Edensor (2015:333) discusses, atmospheres (or, in this chapter, vibes) are shaped by numerous factors, including the current mood of audience members and their prior experiences, which can then 'feed back' into the vibe. For this reason, I want to be careful not to overstate my argument.

In this chapter, I have illustrated that the physical geography of Hip Hop venues plays a role in determining whether or not a Hip Hop event will be experienced as a success with the right vibe or as a failure with a bad vibe or no vibe. Details including the venue size, shape and layout, the number of attendees, and the spacing of the attendees in the venue, all influence how, and indeed if, the right vibe is felt. In particular, light and sound are harnessed to foster specific reactions from the crowd. The practical constraints of certain spaces influence the sensory and emotional experiences of the individuals at Hip Hop events and can inhibit the sensation of positive emotions. Nonetheless, a skilled performer can overcome all of these factors and can create an environment where aching feet, craned necks or that beer someone spilt down your back no longer matter. Artists often use humour to make light of any venue limitations or their own technical errors, and the way that they react to these situations has a definitive impact on the crowd's emotional engagement.

For example, well before I began my fieldwork, I went to a Hip Hop event that was held in a small venue and was not well attended. One of the performing rappers was clearly disappointed and actually said to the crowd, 'You are making me tired'. This did nothing to enhance the vibe of the event and it had an extremely negative impact on my own attitude towards this artist and the event itself. It is difficult to feel a vibe when the performing artist is so clearly disgruntled.

Conversely, during my fieldwork there were times when the vibe of an event appeared to be in jeopardy but the artist managed to prevent themselves from losing the engagement of the crowd — such as when technical difficulties threatened to derail the performance of MC Mystro, who was supported on the decks by DJ Reflux from the Adelaide group the Funkoars. During their set, Reflux appeared to cue and repeat the wrong track or to be having trouble with a skipping record that led to the repetition of a section of music and then sudden silence.[9] In order to fill the subsequent lull that occurred while DJ Reflux figured out the problem, MC Pressure from the Hilltop Hoods got on the microphone and said that while he didn't usually perform Funkoars material, he was going to make an exception. He then led the crowd in a chant by prompting them to yell 'Fuck Reflex'. This chant referenced the fact that the Funkoars often use the audience call and response 'Say, fuck the Funkoars/Fuck the Funkoars' during their performances. The chant occupied and amused the crowd, who may have otherwise begun to lose interest. In this case, the enthusiasm and skill of the performers kept the vibe 'alive'. Therefore, it is important to note that while concert organisers and performing artists try to control the concert space and thus the senses and emotions of attendees, many factors are often outside of their control or extremely unpredictable. Although some spaces are more conducive to the creation of a vibe than others, this does not mean that the vibe is never felt at an event that is not ideally suited to the Hip Hop 'mode of listening'. It may be more difficult to create a vibe in these circumstances, but it is certainly not impossible and indeed this is the joy of a great performance.

In this chapter, I have attempted to bring together a vast range of literature to examine the relationship between space, emotion and the production and consumption of music in specific cultural settings. The study of music and emotion is a multidisciplinary field that is characterised by diversity, both in terms of methodological approaches and the types of case studies examined. This contributes to a lack of consensus regarding key terms, which poses challenges when searching for relevant sources and can lead to missed opportunities for productive dialogue. Furthermore, each of the components of the vibe that I have investigated in this chapter, in particular

---

9   I was not close enough to the stage to see the precise cause.

light and sound, could be the focus of a stand-alone chapter drawing on a rich pool of studies from anthropology, geography and other disciplines that I have been unable to engage with here. I have chosen to examine these components together because I believe it is important to consider how these elements work in tandem to foster or constrain particular emotional experiences. I contend that future studies of emotion and music must attend to the particularities of space. By examining culturally inflected 'modes of listening' (Becker 2001; 2004), we are better able to understand the cultural norms and values that inform listening practices. In particular, I suggest that ethnographic accounts of musical performances enable us to move beyond abstractions and generalisations to consider how, when and why music stirs emotion in specific cultural contexts.

References

Becker, J. 2001. 'Anthropological perspectives on music and emotion'. In P.A. Juslin and J.A. Slobada (Eds.), *Music and Emotion: Theory and Research* (pp. 135-160). Oxford: Oxford University Press.

Becker, J. 2004. *Deep Listeners: Music, Emotion and Trancing*. Indianapolis: Indiana University Press.

Bille, M. and T.F. Sorensen. 2007. 'An anthropology of luminosity: The agency of light', *Journal of Material Culture* 12(3): 263-284.

Bourdieu, P. 1984. *Distinction: A Social Critique of the Judgement of Taste*. Trans. R. Nice. New York: Routledge.

Bunt, L. and M. Pavlicevic. 2001. 'Music and emotion: Perspectives from music therapy'. In P.A. Juslin and J.A. Slobada (Eds.), *Music and Emotion: Theory and Research* (pp. 181-204). Oxford: Oxford University Press.

Curtis, R.A. 2010. 'Australia's capital of jazz? The (re)creation of place, music and community at the Wangaratta Jazz Festival', *Australian Geographies* 41(1): 101-116.

Davies, S. 2001. 'Philosophical perspectives on music's expressiveness'. In P.A. Juslin and J.A. Slobada (Eds.), *Music and Emotion: Theory and Research* (pp. 23-44). Oxford: Oxford University Press.

Driver, C. 2011. 'Embodying hardcore: Rethinking "subcultural" authenticities', *Journal of Youth Studies* 14(8): 975-990.

Duffy, M. 2000. 'Lines of drift: Festival participation and performing a sense of place', *Popular Music* 19(1): 51-64.

Duffy, M., G. Waitt, A. Gorman-Murray and C. Gibson. 2011. 'Bodily rhythms: Corporeal capacities to engage with festival spaces', *Emotion, Space and Society* 4: 17-24.

Edensor, T. 2015. 'Light design and atmosphere', *Visual Communication* 14(3): 331-350.

Fraser, A. 2012. 'The spaces, politics, and cultural economies of electronic dance music', *Geography Compass* 6(8): 500-511.

Geertz, C. 2000 [1973]. 'Thick description: Toward an interpretive theory of culture'. In C. Geertz, *The Interpretation of Cultures: Selected Essays* (pp. 3-30). New York: Basic Books.

Gerard, M. 2004. 'Selecting rituals: DJs, dancers and liminality in underground dance music'. In G. St John (Ed.), *Rave Culture and Religion* (pp. 167-184). London: Routledge.

Haslam, D. 1997. 'DJ culture'. In S. Redhead, D. Wynne and J. O'Connor (Eds.), *The Clubcultures Reader: Readings in Popular Cultural Studies* (pp. 150-161). Oxford: Blackwell.

Hibbett, R. 2005. 'What is Indie Rock?', *Popular Music and Society* 28(1): 55-77.

Jennings, M. 2010. 'Realms of re-enchantment: Socio-cultural investigations of festival music spaces', *Perfect Beat* 11(1): 67-83.

Juslin, P. A. and J.A. Sloboda (Eds.). 2001a. *Music and Emotion: Theory and Research*. Oxford: Oxford University Press.

Juslin, P. A. and J.A. Sloboda. 2001b. 'Music and emotion: Introduction'. In P.A. Juslin and J.A. Sloboda (Eds.), *Music and Emotion: Theory and Research* (pp. 3-22). Oxford: Oxford University Press.

Lefebvre, H. 2004. *Rhythmanalysis: Space, Time and Everyday Life*. London: Continuum.

Malbon, B. 1999. *Clubbing: Dancing, Ecstasy and Vitality*. New York: Routledge.

Nowotny, K., J.L. Fackler, G. Muschi, C. Vargas, L. Wilson and J.A. Kotarba. 2010. 'Established Latino music scenes: Sense of place and the challenge of authenticity'. In N.K. Denzin (Ed.), *Studies in Symbolic Interaction*, vol. 35 (pp. 29-50). Bingley, UK: Emerald Group Publishing.

Overell, R. 2010. 'Brutal belonging in Melbourne's Grindcore scene'. In N.K. Denzin (Ed.), *Studies in Symbolic Interaction*, vol. 35 (pp. 79-99). Bingley, UK: Emerald Group Publishing.

Oz Hip Hop forum. n.d. *Upcoming Oz Hip Hop Shows and Events*. Viewed 16 March 2016. <http://www.ozhiphop.com/forum>.

Peretz, I. 2001. 'Listen to the brain: A biological perspective on musical emotions'. In P.A. Juslin and J.A. Sloboda (Eds.), *Music and Emotion: Theory and Research* (pp. 105-134). Oxford: Oxford University Press.

Probyn, E. 2005. *Blush: Faces of Shame*. Sydney: University of NSW Press.

Rodger, D. 2012. 'Living Hip Hop: Defining authenticity in the Adelaide and Melbourne Hip Hop scenes'. Unpublished PhD thesis, University of Adelaide, Adelaide.

Sloboda, J.A. and S.A. O'Neil. 2001. 'Emotions in everyday listening to music'. In P.A. Juslin and J.A. Sloboda (Eds.), *Music and Emotion: Theory and Research* (pp. 415-430). Oxford: Oxford University Press.

St John, G. 2006. 'Electronic dance music culture and religion: An overview', *Culture and Religion* 7(1): 1-25.

Thornton, S. 1996. *Club Cultures: Music, Media and Subcultural Capital*. Cambridge: Wesleyan University Press.

Turner, V. 1969. *The Ritual Process: Structure and Anti-Structure*. New York: Cornell University Press.

Wall, T. 2006. 'Out on the floor: The politics of dancing on the Northern Soul scene', *Popular Music* 25(3): 431-445.

Washburne, C. and M. Derno (Eds.). 2004. *Bad Music: The Music We Love to Hate*. New York: Routledge.

Wood, N., M. Duffy and S.J. Smith. 2007. 'The art of doing (geographies of) music', *Environment and Planning D: Society and Space* 25(5): 867-889.

4

Pontic dance:
Feeling the absence of homeland

Valerie Liddle

Abstract

Pontic dance originated in the Pontos area of northern Turkey. It survived a genocide and exile of Pontians from that region in the 1920s as well as their migration to Australia thirty to forty years later. In this chapter, I discuss how Pontic dance, in both its choreographic and participatory modes, embodies the loss Pontians feel they have suffered as a result of these ruptures. Pontians assert that it is necessary to have a certain 'feel' in order to dance in an authentic way. Although this 'feel' may manifest itself in the bodily movements of the dance, it is an expression that comes from a sense of loss that Pontians inwardly feel and express through dance, particularly a loss of place and a waning of cultural practice. This loss is referenced in two ways: first, historically, the dances, their execution, costumes and musical instruments embody the loss of the former homeland. Second, the movements of the dance outwardly express the passion the dancers feel about what it means to be Pontian. This chapter explores how the performance space composed of the emotion and sensation of the dance makes present the absence of a way of life in Greece and the loss of the original homeland.

Introduction

Pontic Greeks have a characteristic way of dancing that developed over many centuries in the Pontos area of northern Turkey. The dance practices survived a genocide[1] and their exile from that region in the 1920s as well as their migration to Australia thirty to forty years later. The movements of Pontic dance are different from that of Greek mainland or island dancing. Its dances range 'from the most languid, slow, relaxed, effortless, shuffling steps to the most frenetic, tense, physically demanding and almost violent movement' (Kilpatrick 1975:104), with the dancers' feet covering a small space on the ground. In addition to foot movements, there is 'flexing and rotation of the torso' (105-6), referred to as *shimmying*, which is characteristic of the style of Pontic dance. Almost all dances are performed in a closed circle, with dancers holding hands in particular ways. There is no leader, and any variation in steps can be performed by all in the dance (105-6). All dances have a set number of steps that are repeated over and over again, with the movements of the arms and hands keeping in time to a rhythm that is unique to Pontic dance.

During fieldwork, I observed these dances many times in many different places, performed by members of the whole community or as choreographed routines in front of audiences. I saw them danced at Pontian dinner dances, at other Pontian community functions, at religious festivals, at wider Greek festivals and as part of commemorative events. Pontians also danced at restaurants, in streets as they led the bride and groom to the church, at wedding receptions and at private homes to celebrate birthdays or forthcoming marriages. Of all the different dimensions of Pontic life which I observed, it seemed to me that dance was to Pontians themselves the most quintessential expression of what it means to be Pontian. It was a means by which they displayed their Ponticness, and through which memories were evoked and intense emotions both shaped and expressed.

Pontians assert that, in order to perform dances in a Pontian way, it is necessary to display a specific characteristic, which they refer to as the 'feel' of the dance. One night at a practice session of the senior dance group of the Pontian Brotherhood in Adelaide, I noticed that one dancer did not quite have the same movement as the other dancers,

---

1   The claim of genocide is in relation to the death of approximately 350 000 Pontians out of a population of 700 000 in northern Turkey in the early years of the twentieth century. Around the same time, approximately 1.5 million Armenians were killed in Turkey during World War I. In 1997, the International Association of Genocide Scholars acknowledged that the violence that occurred against Armenians conformed to the 'statutes of the United Nations Convention on the Prevention and Punishment of Genocide' (as cited in Dadrian 2003:80). Other Christian groups, such as the Greek Orthodox Pontians, now contend that their ancestors also suffered in the same genocide. In 2007, the International Association passed a resolution that recognised a genocide against Armenians, Assyrians, and Pontian and Anatolian Greeks (Charny 2011:33).

even though she was performing the same steps. They were dancing *Samsón*, a dance with a particular bounce that comes from the dancers having straight legs and moving swiftly from side to side. When I asked why this dancer was not displaying the same action as the other dancers, Anoula told me that this dancer was new and had not yet learnt to execute the steps, but that, more importantly, she was not yet 'feeling' the dance. She said that this was important for Pontic dance. 'You have to feel the dance inside', she commented, while indicating her heart area (field notes, 10 April 2006).

Similarly, in Greece, I was told about this 'feel' of Pontic dance. At my first interview with Dimitris, he told me that at the Veria Black Sea Club they encouraged dancers to feel the dance rather than just to execute the steps and keep in time or in line with the other dancers. He then demonstrated how the *Omál* should be danced. 'First', he said, 'I will show you how a non-Pontian person dances the *Omál*'. So Dimitris slowly danced the six steps of the *Omál* in anticlockwise fashion, moving around in a circle: 'He can make the moves but he cannot put in the soul'. Then he said, 'Now I will show you how a Pontian person dances the *Omál*'. This time he repeated the same slow six steps but his whole upper torso moved backwards and forwards. At the same time his arms, bent at the elbows, moved in and out from his upper body. The steps of the dance were just as slow and smooth as in the first version, but the movement of the upper torso gave the impression that the dance had increased in vitality. In this way, the incorporation of the upper torso into the dance gave the 'feel' to the dance. But just as I was beginning to think that he was telling me that if I learnt the correct bodily movement, I would be able to get the 'feel' he was demonstrating, Dimitris added, 'Something is happening inside us' (field notes, 10 September 2006).

An inchoate emotion is difficult to describe. The words that dancers may use to express what they feel within the dance are not the same as the experience of it within the immediacy of the dance. Both Anoula and Dimitris could not adequately articulate what they meant by the 'feel' of the dance. Reflecting that they knew 'more than they could tell' (Polanyi 1967:4), both Anoula and Dimitris could only indicate through their bodies what this experience, as expressed in the dance steps, meant to them. They had a 'tacit knowledge' (1967) of the 'feel' of the dance that they could not express verbally. Anoula touched her heart area to indicate the inner feeling that is expressed in the dance. Dimitris, in contrast, had to demonstrate it in his dance steps. It was not just in the way the steps were danced, the way the dancer moved, the turn of the head, the slight pause of body movement or the shimmying of the upper torso. These visible movements were not themselves the 'feel'. Ultimately, for both Dimitris and Anoula, the 'feel' came from an inner experience. The focus of this chapter is on how this inchoate 'feel', experienced in the bodily movements of the dance, is an embodied expression of an emotional sense of being Pontian, which incorporates both a sense of the loss of the place of Pontos through exile as well as an absence of Greece because of migration.

Dance as gesture

Recent theories approach dance from a variety of perspectives. As a cultural manifestation (Kaeppler 1978) and the 'embodiment of cultural memory' (Buckland 2001), dance is seen as a 'rhythmic movement done for some purpose transcending utility' (Royce 1977:5). Other writers study dance from the perspective of 'the moving body' (Farnell 1999), its unique manifestation forming one part of the whole sphere of human movement (Williams 1997; 2004). Hanna describes the multisensory nature of dance and lists its components as 'purpose, intentional rhythm, culturally patterned sequences, and extraordinary non-verbal movement with inherent and aesthetic value' (1979:24). She defines dance as a form of language, an 'extraordinary nonverbal movement' (24) and argues that in the dance these components 'are selected in much the same way that a person would choose sequences of verbal language' (41). All these writers describe the various aspects of dance and its multisensory nature, but none sufficiently explain what the dancers feel when they dance or what the audience feels when they watch them, or how these feelings are produced by dance movements. In contrast to Hanna, Langer (1953) prefers the term *gesture*, in relation to dance, rather than *non-verbal language*, a concept that is linked to a cognitive discursive structure.

> Gesture [in comparison to language] is far more important as an avenue of self-expression than as 'word.' An expressive word is one that formulates an idea clearly and aptly, but a highly expressive gesture is usually taken to be one that reveals feeling or emotion. (180)

Gesture, then, brings us closer to an explication of the 'feel' of the dance.

Langer further argues that any art form has a 'primary illusion' (174). All art is composed of basic materials, but the primary illusion is not to see these but to see the created form. Dance is composed of the rhythmic movement of physical bodies moving through patterned sequences of steps in time and space. This rhythmic motion is what is actually happening, the physical reality or material of the art of dance. The 'primary illusion' of dance is the transformation of the physical movement into the art form of dance as gesture. This transformation, according to Langer, is the 'basic abstraction whereby the dance illusion is made and organized' (174), and it applies to both dancer and those who watch them.

But there is a secondary illusion that comes from a distinction between what the audience sees and experiences, and what the dancers feel and experience. On one hand, the audience sees bodies moving not just in a particular way, but in a way that is out of the everyday way of moving. Seeing these movements or contortions of the body, then, the audience gives meaning to what the movements signify and then responds to the transformation of visible motion into dance gesture, giving a particular meaning to the created art of dance. For the dancer, on the other hand, the ability to perform these movements comes through practised techniques of dance — the basic materials of the dance. The dancer experiences the dance as kinetic energy, whereby the dancers embody the dance that takes them out of themselves into the immediacy of performing (Langer 1953:196).

The third aspect of the illusion of the dance is that a viewer may interpret that the emotion being expressed through the movements of the dance is actually being felt by the dancers at the time. But dance is a 'virtual' gesture. It does not actually exist but appears to do so, and an audience may respond in an emotive way to that perceived display of emotion. The dancers, in contrast, cannot experience the actual intensity of emotion they appear to be portraying and still maintain the actual practised techniques of the dance at the same time without affecting its performance in some way. Giving the example of the ballerina Pavlova performing the 'The Dying Swan', Langer makes the point that the dancer could not actually feel sick, nor could she feel the emotions attached to near death (177). If she did, she would not be able to execute the dance with the dancing expertise it requires. The dancers do, however, experience an emotion in the dance — but this is an inchoate emotion somewhat similar to musicians who experience 'a particular performative kind of emotion' (Dennis 2002:23), which is different from that experienced by the audience. The movements of the dance are gestures that indicate the emotion of dance rather than the immediately experienced emotions of the dancers at the time. What the dancers feel about the dance at the time is *meta-emotion* (Dennis 2007:121) — a performative emotion and thus a generalised emotion.

While the dance illusion might evoke an emotional response in those watching in the same way that the Kaluli dancers arouse intense emotions in their audience (Schieffelin 1977), this is not the aim of Pontic dance. Rather, it is to perform Ponticness. Through the dance illusion, these actual movements of the dance become virtual emotion that gestures to loss, a loss intrinsically tied to the lost former homeland of Pontos. In the execution of the dance steps, in seeing, wearing and feeling the costumes, and in hearing the sound of the musical instruments, the dancer makes the absence of Pontos present. Most of all, the presence of absence is experienced in the 'feel' of the dance, a 'feel' that embodies a multifaceted expression of the emotions of loss. It gestures to the loss of Pontos and, for migrants, to the absence of the life they once had in Greece. Nick Zournatzidis, a well-known Pontic Greek dance teacher and researcher, reflected this idea when he said to me, 'Now Pontos does not exist. It doesn't create dances anymore. But you have to carry the love of Pontos in your heart. You have to love the culture' (field notes, 29 January 2010). Thus, when Pontians dance, either as part of community celebrations or in choreographed routines, the dances they perform shape these emotions and, through them, the physical space created by the formation of the dance becomes Pontian.

The development of two modes of Pontic dance

Pontic dances developed over many centuries in the highly dissected geographical terrain of the Pontos region. Because some isolated villages had little contact with other villages or regions, a variety of distinctive dances evolved that often had slight variations in their steps and way of dance.[2] Not all the dances that were danced in Pontos survived the genocide and exile from Pontos: the knowledge of some dances or their particular mode of execution disappeared when whole villages were destroyed. Those that did survive continued to retain their important place in religious and communal village life in Greece and later in the diaspora. With the waning of some other cultural expressions, such as language and food, dance became an important means whereby Ponticness was preserved and expressed.

After their exile to Greece, in 1923, Pontians tended to be wary of outside political influence and sought to retain their ethnic boundaries despite the pressures to assimilate into mainstream Greek culture. Many 'became ethnicists, actively interested in maintaining their cultural community' and preserving their 'traditional heritage' (Fann Bouteneff 2002:47). By the 1950s, when Pontians started to marry out of their community, teaching dance to the younger generation was seen as one of the important ways in which some aspects of Pontic culture could be retained. While community dance continued, gradually the many clubs and organisations, which were originally formed for Pontian community support, began to teach choreographed routines of Pontic dance to their young people: routines that could be performed by a dance group in front of an audience. Hence, out of the movement to preserve Pontic culture and to pass it on to the younger generation, a second mode of dance began to emerge.

This same development occurred over a twenty-year time span in the Pontian migrant community in Adelaide. Its Pontian Brotherhood was founded in 1958 for mutual support of Pontian migrants. By the 1970s, the need for communal support of the migrant group was not as pressing, and fewer families and young people were involved in the Brotherhood. Some young people whose families did not attend Brotherhood functions grew up without knowing how to dance Pontic dances. For other young people, who were exposed to Pontic dancing through family and community functions, dancing did not now play the same part as it had in the village lives of their parents or grandparents growing up in rural Greece. To counteract these trends, in 1972 a dance group was formed in the Pontian Brotherhood in Adelaide, where Pontic dances could be taught by a specific dance teacher in a more formal setting. From then on, two modes of Pontic dance could be seen at Pontian functions

---

2   Vasilis Asbestas from the Black Sea Club of Veria contends that his research points to the fact that there are about twenty main Pontic dances and that the others are variations. He said that these variations result from the different musical instruments that were used and from climatic, geographical and political conditions (field notes, 5 September 2011).

— dances where the whole community participated, and the newer choreographed ones performed by the dance group.

Folklorists studying the effects of an audience on various ethno-dances note the development of the two modes of dance over time and distinguish between them in various ways. Hoerburger (1968:30) refers to them as 'folk dance in its first existence' and 'folk dance in its second existence'; Shay (1999:33) as 'dance in the field' and dance as a stage performance; and Nahachewsky (1995) speaks of them as 'participatory' and 'presentational' dance. Although Nahachewsky's terms succinctly differentiate between the two, the term *presentational* does not take into account Langer's specific use of the word, where she distinguishes between the '"discursive" symbols of language and the "presentational" symbols of art' (1966:8). In making such a division between a dance that is in front of an audience and one that is not, folklorists such as Nahachewsky fail to take into account the function of dance as a 'perceptible, self-identical whole' (Langer 1966:7), where it formulates and presents the feelings of the inner-life experience, regardless of whether the dance is in front of an audience or not. I will refer to these two modes of dance as *participatory dance*, where the whole community joins in the dance, and as *choreographic dance*, where it is performed in front of an audience, requiring prior planning and rehearsal. However, I understand them both to be within the same art form. Indeed, Pontians themselves do not make a distinction between the two. They never intimated to me that that one was more 'Pontic' than the other or that one had a higher value than the other.

Two modes of dance at a Pontian community event

At one of the first Pontian events I attended, I observed both modes of Pontic dance. This was at a dinner dance held in August to honour Panagia Soumela, patron of the original monastery in Pontos.[3] This particular event, typical of other later Pontian community gatherings I observed both in Adelaide and in Greece, was held at the Polish Dom Polski function centre. On this particular night, the space inside the hall became demarcated as Pontian. It was decorated with balloons in the Pontian colours of yellow and black, and the banner of the Pontian Brotherhood of South Australia hung from the stage. A *lyra* player played and sang Pontian music. The *lyra*[4] is a

---

3   Panagia (*Panayía* in Greek) refers to Virgin Mary, the mother of Jesus Christ, as the all-holy one and the foremost among the saints. A special feast day on 15 August celebrates her death and her bodily resurrection and assumption into heaven. *Soumela* is a contraction of σ σου (*s sou*) in the Pontian dialect meaning 'of the' and Μελά (*Black Mountain*), so the title means *The Virgin of the Black Mountain* (Miller 1926:62). The monastery of Panagia Soumela is set at about 1150 metres above sea level in the mountains, fifty kilometres from the coastal city of Trabzon on the Black Sea in Turkey. Now in ruins, it is still a site of major religious significance for Pontic Greeks.

4   Also known as the Pontic *kementjé*.

three-stringed, bottle-shaped instrument about 45-60 cm in length and about 7-11 cm in width. It is played with a bow by the musician who, either sitting or standing, holds the instrument in an upright position in front of them.[5] Although it was one of a range of musical instruments that were played in Pontos, the *lyra* is now the most recognised and most loved of all the Pontian instruments. Surviving exile and migration, the *lyra* has become the instrument that most encapsulates Ponticness, and hence its sound on this night deemed the space inside the hall to be Pontian.

Many of the 900 people who had purchased tickets sat in groups of ten to twelve at round tables around a central dance floor. This area would be further marked as Pontian once the dancers made the space their own through their dance. The majority of those who attended were of Greek background, with those from the Pontian community predominating. People of all ages attended this function — parents with babies in pushers, young children, teenagers, young adults and grandparents. At our table, there were three generations of the same family. Gradually, people arrived at the hall and, having purchased their meals, brought the food to their tables, where it was shared with other members of their family and friends. At the end of the meal, the compere for the evening, George Donikian, a well-known television presenter who is of Armenian background, described how the traumatic events of genocide have continued to have an effect on him and his family. In conclusion, he said that this night would 'give all people a sense of who Pontian Greeks are, where they come and what it means to be from Pontos'. At the end of his speech, the president of the Brotherhood then asked everyone to stand for a minute's silence to remember those who had died in the Pontian genocide.

Although the Pontian dinner dance was a joyous occasion, a mood of sadness pervaded this segment of the evening. Through the discursive symbols of language, the speaker's ideas and feelings about genocide and exile were made objective. They were transformed into 'things' and 'facts' to 'note, remember, and think about' (Langer 1966:8) in the one minute's silence. But a sense of Ponticness did not only come from words. Although words can describe what happened, the intensity of the feelings attached to the genocide cannot be easily articulated. Through presentational symbols within the art form of dance, the 'idea' of the feelings associated with being Pontian were given form by the dances that followed.

In time with the *lyra*'s introductory notes and the strong *daoúli* beat[6], the junior dancers, ranging in age from five to ten years, slowly danced onto the dance floor. Dressed in the club's black and yellow tracksuits and holding their hands at chest

---

5   I have used the pronoun 'them' to refer to the musician in order to be inclusive of both genders. However, while women are not precluded from playing the *lyra*, during my fieldwork I saw only male musicians.

6   Originating from Pontos, the *daoúli* 'is a two-headed drum played with a stick or the hand' (Kilpatrick 1975: 279). It is used to keep the beat of the dances.

height, they moved gradually around the outside edge of the dance floor and proceeded to dance the slow steps of the *Dipát* and *Omál*, finishing with the dance *Ebbr' Opís* to take them off the dance floor.

An intermediate group of dancers between the ages of eleven and thirteen years straight away moved onto the floor. In contrast to the juniors, these dancers wore traditional Pontic costumes. The girls wore gold satin skirts, with a patterned, fringed scarf draped over them and a short maroon jacket on top. They wore maroon silk scarves over their heads with gold-coloured coins attached. The boys wore black trousers with a black jacket and a black head-covering with bandoliers, containing imitation bullet cartridges, over their shoulders. This group performed a wider range of Pontic dances than the junior group, including a number that were more energetic and required more intricate steps.

The last to perform were the senior dancers, comprising seven men and six women. They entered the dance floor, the women from the right and the men from the left, meeting together in the middle of the floor and joining hands, with men and women interspersed. They, too, wore traditional Pontic costumes, but their dancing steps were much more complicated and performed more expertly than the previous two groups. In one particularly vigorous dance, the *Sherranítsa*, the six women moved forward and performed very spirited movements: their steps were quick and small, their arms moved backwards and forwards and from time to time they stamped their feet. After they had finished this segment, the women moved backward and the men moved forward. Once again, their dance was very energetic, with their hands and arms moving backwards and forwards and then up over their heads. At one stage, they turned to the right and then the left, stamping their feet in each direction, all with a shimmying of their upper torso, characteristic of Pontic dancing. Moving back, they joined the women and moved around the edge of the floor in a circle with their arms interlocked at shoulder level. The men then moved forward and performed another dance with their hands held high, finishing by kneeling on the ground.

To end, they danced a knife dance, known as *Piçak Oyünü*. In this performance, two men wielding knives danced improvised steps of attack and defence. Their steps were small and again there was the shimmying of the upper torso. Although at this event the two men supposedly killed each other, in other versions I saw in Greece, the men pitted themselves against each other in a show of strength, as in preparation for battle, but then at the end they embraced. Throughout all of these performances, the audience members responded by clapping in time to the beat of the rhythms of the dances and, as the intensity of the dances increased and the rhythms and movements became more vigorous, by whistling, cheering and stamping their feet.

When all the dancers had left the floor and the applause had died down, the *lyra* and the *daoúli* started to play again. This time there was no particular announcement by the compere or general invitation to join in the dance, but people knew that this was the time for them to dance together. Many people, men and women, young and old, started to get up to dance, the first dancers forming a circle around the outside of the dance floor. When anyone wanted to join in the dance they moved in between two other dancers, unclasped their joined hands, linked up with the dancers on either side and continued the same hand movements, quickly picking up the rhythm of the dance steps. Similarly, individuals chose when they would leave the dance circle. Soon there were more than a hundred people on the dance floor and three concentric circles had been formed to accommodate everyone who wanted to dance. The *lyra* and the *daoúli* set the pattern and rhythm of the dances. At first, there were the slower dances such as *Omál*, *Dipát* and *Tík*, and then later the faster dances such as *Tík Tónyia* and *Kotsari*, the steps becoming smaller to accommodate the quicker rhythms. Often, a segment of dance lasted up to forty minutes, with the same sequence of steps being repeated over and over again. Late into the night, many people still continued to dance. It was obvious that this participatory dancing and socialising with each other was a most enjoyable experience for all taking part, and it formed the longest part of the evening's entertainment.

The 'feel' of loss in choreographic dance

First, the primary illusion that occurred through the choreographic dances was that the physical movement of the dancers was transformed into the art form of dance as gesture. Secondly, this dance-as-gesture was interpreted and named as Pontic dance. The audience saw not just the dancers 'running around or twisting their bodies' (Langer 1957:5), but 'forces that seem to operate in the dance' (1950:226), which formed a '*dynamic image*' of the dance (1957:5, italics in the original text). The audience saw past the basic materials that were used to create the dances — such as the patterned sequence of the dance steps, the rhythmic movements of the arms and hands, the slight rotations of the torso and the shimmying of the shoulders and upper body — and knew them to gesture to Ponticness. The actual physical movements of the dance were real, but the dynamic image was virtual or an illusion. The gesture the audience saw shaped and gave form to their actual emotion — their idea of the 'feel' of the dance. And, as the actual movements become more in accord with the idea of Ponticness, the perception of the actual movements disappeared and the image of Ponticness became more apparent, and it was this that drew their emotional response.

At the Pontian dinner dance, the dances immediately followed the stories of genocide and the one minute's silence for its victims. Performed against this background, and with the men wearing bandoliers with imitation bullets, some of the more vigorous dances gave form to the feelings that Pontians have about conflicts with the Turks, which have existed for many centuries. In the performance of one of the warrior dances, *Piçak Oyünü*, the movements of the two dancers particularly indicated those of combat, and were a further link to genocide. Pontians believe that this dance, and the other better-known warrior dance, *Sérra*, are derived from ancient war dances called *Pyrrhichios*, thought to prepare soldiers for war by performing in advance the movements that they would use in combat. *Sérra* is most closely associated with Ponticness, and its tempo and movement are particularly aggressive and very physically demanding. Pontian associations worldwide nowadays require that *Sérra* be danced only by men. Although the Pontian Brotherhood dance group allowed women to dance as men in its other dances, it did not have enough men to perform *Sérra* at that time. The performance of *Piçak Oyünü* was the closest they could come to performing one of these warrior dances. But other dances such as *Létchi*, *Letchína* and *Sherranítsa*, which both men and women dance, have come to resemble more and more the combative nature of the warrior dances and always evoke an enthusiastic audience response. The choreographed dances, presented with traditional Pontic costumes and musical instruments, were influential in shaping the feel of the loss of Pontos in a way that language cannot.

> This is reflected in Evagelia's reaction to seeing some of the vigorous Pontic dances:
> I wondered if one source of the 'strength' of the Pontian is from the dance. Both men's and women's dances are quite aggressive and fast-paced in most instances. I know how I feel when I watch them or when I dance some of them. One feels invigorated and energised. It's a much more visceral reaction than just joy of music. It's more about the grunt and the call in the dance, the pound of the foot on the ground, the unified turn and stare of the dancers — a call to action, perhaps? The deep primal drumming of the daoúli. I think that when you put together the stories of the genocide and a strong aggressive dance, perhaps we see that as strength in numbers and community. (Personal communication, 18 May 2009)

While Evagelia could say that these dances made her body feel 'invigorated' and 'energised', she could not completely describe her feelings about them. For her, the 'idea' of the emotion connected to the genocide was presented in the image or virtual entity of the dance. It was expressed by the 'grunt' of the dancers, the 'pound' of their feet and the 'stare' of their eyes. Seeing them as gesture, she gave meaning to them and perceived that the movements signified the loss of Pontos and the genocide of Pontian people. In so doing, they formed and shaped her emotions.

But, because the practised techniques of the dance produce an intense emotional response in Pontians, the audience assumes that the dancers are feeling the emotions that they are expressing through the gesture of the dance. The dancers, however, experience the dance in a different way. For them, it is an embodied form, something they feel within their bodies. Features such as the shimmying of the upper body, the vigorous contortions of the shoulders, the leaps and the stamping, are actual movements and indicate the physicality of Pontic dance, but they are experienced as the spatial patterning and kinetic energy of the dance. In the execution of them, they produce 'a new body-feeling, in which every muscular tension registers itself as something kinaesthetically new, peculiar to the dance' (Langer 1953:203). In experiencing the dance in this way, a body-knowledge is formed that defines the dancer's understanding of what their bodies are capable of doing with others within the dance (Dunagan 2005:31). This may be sensed as a new body-feeling, but the ability to perform the movements comes from practising the techniques of the dance.

The dancers, therefore, cannot experience the actual intensity of emotion they are portraying and still maintain these techniques at the same time. Indeed, if they had been feeling the emotions expressed in the more vigorous dances, it might have been possible to see that intensity displayed in their faces. On the contrary, I noticed that the facial expression of the dancers did not change when they moved from a sedate dance such as *Omál* to the more vigorous ones of *Kótsari, Moscof, Létchi, Letchína* and *Sherranítsa*. Their faces remained composed as they concentrated on the dance itself. The specific emotion of loss that Pontians feel is not experienced by the dancers in choreographic dance: what they say about the experience of the dance is not the same as the feeling of it at the time of the dance.

This is not to say that the dancers do not respond in an emotional way, but rather that it is a performative emotion that comes out of the kinetic experience. After dancing at the monastery of Panagia Soumela in Greece, one of the Adelaide dancers said that she had experienced a feeling that she had not felt before — 'something in me … that … felt good. Like, this is where I should be … It was quite emotional, really'. She could not say what this emotion was, but attributed what she felt to the crowds, to the way the compere introduced them, and the hype about them coming all the way from Australia. She could say afterwards that she felt something, but this is not the same as what she actually felt at the moment of the dance. 'Just to be in this country and to dance on this stage made it surreal', she said (field notes, 20 November 2006). Hence a generalised emotion, rather than actual emotion, becomes the 'feel' for dancers in choreographic dance. The physical movements become virtual gestures that express ideas of emotion connected to the loss of Pontos and the genocide of its people. Whereas choreographic dance is instrumental in shaping the feel of the loss of Pontos, participatory dance, along with the emotions it evokes, shapes the feeling of the absence of the way of life in Greece.

The 'feel' of absence in participatory dance

Functions such as the Pontian dinner dance are attempts in a small way to recreate the celebrations of Greek rural village life, where dance played a key role in the various social events and at important yearly religious celebrations. Despina, who has been in

Australia for over fifty years, recalled how she danced from a very early age in her village in northern Greece. She said:

> At night time, to amuse ourselves my father would sing (we could not afford to have a lyra) and our whole family would dance. We danced the usual dances — Tík, Omál, Dipát, Kótsari and Karsilamá. The neighbours would often say to us how they were happy to see us all dancing. Always during the summer there would be festivals where there would be dancing. We would go to different villages or people would come to ours. I can remember my mother and grandmother dancing on occasions such as weddings. (Field notes, 29 November 2006)

These kinds of village festivals are no longer experienced by Pontians in the diaspora. 'These days are gone and will not come back again', Despina lamented. But when people, like Despina, join with others in participatory dance at Pontian functions, the 'feel' of these remembered dances evokes both a memory of a past time as well as a sense of the absence of Greece. Both memory and a sense of absence become encapsulated in the 'feel' of the dance.

This 'feel' through the dance is transmitted to the next generation in a Pontic milieu. In the past in Greece, children did not learn through formal instruction at a dance school, but in a village setting where the whole community, young and old, took part. While children of the diaspora might be taught the steps and movements of the different dances at formal dance classes, they learn something else when they take part in participatory dances in the social setting of a community gathering. In this mode, children are not segregated from adults but are encouraged to dance alongside them. It was very common to see parents or grandmothers taking the hands of young children and dancing with them in the circle of the dance. Often they were tugged one way and then the other as they tried to keep up. But although no adult was formally teaching them, they were not only learning the steps of the dance but also absorbing the 'feel' of what it means to be Pontian.

As with dancers who perform choreographed routines, dancers in the participatory mode experience the dance as kinetic energy and spatial patterning which not only takes them into the immediacy of performing but also constitutes for them an embodied knowledge of what it is to dance Pontic dance. The sense of touch is fundamental to this process. The dancers attend to the embodied presence of others by dancing in close proximity to each other. They join hands by placing their right hand on top of the left hand of the person next to them and keep their upper arms close to their bodies with their elbows bent, allowing the lower arms to move backwards and forwards. In some dances, the dancers place their hands on the shoulders of the person next to them, intertwining their arms at shoulder level, or, in the more vigorous dances, they raise and lower their arms together in time with the quickened tempo. Here, the sense of touch comes through not only the fingers, where the 'skin mediates between the body and the surrounding environment' (Rodaway 1994:42), but also through a 'haptic sense', which

> ... renders the surfaces of the body porous, being perceived at once inside, on the skin's surface, and in external space. It enables the perception of weight, pressure, balance, temperature, vibration and presence. (Fisher 1997:4-11)

When I was dancing Pontic dance, I became aware of the weights that the dancing bodies support: the pressure brought to bear on the arms and hands by other dancers on either side of me, the sense of balance in relation to various dancing surfaces, as well as the awareness of the rise in temperature of the dancing bodies and the quickness of the breath as the tempo of the dances increased. Most of all, I felt the shimmying of the upper torsos of those next to me. Because shimmying is so characteristic of Pontic dance, the haptic sense is more than corporeal positioning. These movements, therefore, 'are never simply individual ones; they are always associative and therefore communicative, a process in which emotion is ever implicated' (Lyon 1995:256). Thus the body-feeling of dance is experienced as a generalised emotion; it gestures to the sociality of dance, but it is shaped by memory.

Mihalis migrated to Australia from his village in northern Greece in 1960. When I asked him what he feels when he dances, he said:

> As soon as I get into the dance, the first thing that gets into my mind [is] a picture [of] my village where my mother, my father were dancing that simple dance. And then all the memories come of all those people united: they call to each other; they lived together; they suffered together; they helped each other; they shared the happiness and the hard times together; they felt the necessity to exchange with their friends or their neighbours they lived with. So all those memories, they come in my mind and I say first of all what I feel ... er ... er ... something like I'm getting warm; [this feeling] gets into my body and ... and I'm feeling something, something which brings me upside down and I have to concentrate on that picture where I've seen my parents, I've seen my village where they were there, and the picture in there is all those people there in that particular time when they were entertaining themselves and they left everything behind, all the differences if they had any between them, all the difficult times, all the suffering they had through the years. That particular time it was only for the entertainment; they are giving their soul to the dance and with that picture it drags all the history behind it ... What they suffered, where they came from, how they used to live, how hard their life was, what they did. (Field notes, 27 October 2007)

For Mihalis, his emotions were aroused through the memories he had of dance in his village, but he was not able to put these exactly into words. The discursive symbols of language were unable to exactly describe his feelings when he danced. It was 'something like' he was 'getting warm'; it seemed to get into his body and bring him 'upside down'. But what he described were bodily sensations rather than the emotional feeling itself. It was, however, through these senses that the dance 'dragged' into the present the place of his youth. It connected him to the memories of his parents and the way they danced in his village and their struggle to survive in Greece. Rather than a presence of the loss of Pontos, as in choreographic dance, the participatory mode evokes the memories and emotions that are connected to the social nature of Pontic dance. Older Pontians, particularly those who learnt to dance in Greek villages, remember the sociality of physically dancing with their parents and grandparents. It is this remembrance that helps to shape the 'feel' of Ponticness and incorporates into participatory dance the absence of the presence of Greece.

Conclusion

Both the participatory and choreographed modes of Pontic dance play a fundamental role in Pontian community functions. Through the dances, the distinctive costumes and the musical instruments, these dances not only connect Pontians to their social, geographical and historical background, but also gesture to loss that has been shaped prior to the dance as the result of genocide, exile and migration.

In choreographed dance, both dancers and audience might share the same underlying emotion of loss, but there is a difference between how the audience and dancers sense this emotion. In the performance, the dancers are engrossed with the 'actual' bodily movements of the dance, the textures of the costumes and the rhythm and tempo of the music, and they sense this feeling as kinetic energy. Their response is a generalised emotion. The audience response is of a different nature, one where a transposition occurs. Although they see the components of the dance, they 'see', 'hear' and 'understand' the dance to be essentially Pontian. Their energetic applause is in response to this display of Ponticness, which symbolically represents the loss of the place of Pontos.

In participatory dance, the experience of embodied sociality stretches over generations and shapes the feel of what it means to be Pontian. The kinds of festivals in village settings where dance played a key role in social and religious celebrations can no longer be experienced by Pontians who live in the diaspora. Nevertheless, when older members of the migrant community dance the same dances to the same musical instruments as they had in their villages, the movements, rhythms and patterns of the dances not only evoke memories of the past but also express through the dancers' bodies the sociality of dance as a way of expressing the 'feel' of being Pontian. This notion of Ponticness continues to be transmitted to the next generation in a Pontic milieu in the diaspora. Although the children and grandchildren of Pontian migrants might be taught the steps and movements of the different dances for choreographed routines at formal dance classes, when they join with others in participatory dance at community functions, they can 'feel' the sociality of Ponticness as an embodied experience.

Whether the dance is performed by young or old, the image of an inner 'feel' of Ponticness is given an expressive form when time and time again it is performed at Pontian community functions. Formed and experienced through embodied action and the memories and emotions it evokes, Pontic dance becomes an expression of what it means to be Pontian for both dancers and for those who watch it.

References

Buckland, T.J. 2001. 'Dance, authenticity and cultural memory: The politics of embodiment', *Yearbook for Traditional Music* 33: 1-16.

Charny, I.W. 2011. 'The integrity and courage to recognize all the victims of a genocide'. In T. Hofmann, M. Bjørnlund and V. Meichanetsidis (Eds.), *The Genocide of the Ottoman Greeks: Studies on the State-Sponsored Campaign of Extermination of Christians of Asia Minor (1912-1922) and its Aftermath* (pp. 21-38). New York and Athens: Aristide D. Caratzas.

Dadrian, V.N. 2003. 'German responsibility in the Armenian Genocide: The role of protective alliances'. In C. Tatz, P. Arnold and S. Tatz (Eds.), *Genocide Perspectives II: Essays on Holocaust and Genocide* (pp. 79-125). Blackheath, NSw: Bandl & Schlesinger.

Dennis, S. 2002. 'Sensual extensions: Joy, pain and music-making in a police band'. PhD thesis, University of Adelaide, Adelaide.

Dennis, S. 2007. *Police Beat: The Emotional Power of Music in Police Work*. Youngstown, NY: Cambria Press.

Dunagan, C. 2005. 'Dance, knowledge, and power', *Topoi* 24(1): 29-41.

Fann Bouteneff, P. 2002. *Exiles on Stage: The Modern Pontic Theater in Greece*. Athens: Επιτροπη Ποντιακων Μελετων.

Farnell, B. 1999. 'Moving bodies, acting selves', *Annual Review of Anthropology* 28(1): 341-373.

Fisher, J. 1997. 'Relational sense: Towards a haptic aesthetics', *Parachute* 87: 4-11.

Hanna, J.L. 1979. *To Dance is Human: A Theory of Nonverbal Communication*. Austin and London: University of Texas Press.

Hanna, J.L. 2001. 'Language of dance', *Journal of Physical Education, Recreation and Dance* 72(4): 40-53.

Hoerburger, F. 1968. 'Once again: On the concept of "folk dance"', *Journal of the International Folk Music Council* 20: 30-32.

Kaeppler, A. 1978. 'Dance in anthropological perspective', *Annual Review of Anthropology* 7: 31-49.

Kilpatrick, D.B. 1975. Function and Style in Pontic Dance Music. Unpublished Doctoral Dissertation, University of California, Los Angeles.

Langer, S.K. 1950. 'The primary illusions and the great orders of art', *Hudson Review* 3(2): 219-233.

Langer, S.K. 1953. *Feeling and Form: A Theory of Art Developed from Philosophy in a New Key*. London: Routledge and Kegan Paul.

Langer, S.K. 1957. *Problems of Art: Ten Philosophical Lectures*. New York: Charles Scribner's Sons.

Langer, S.K. 1966. 'The cultural importance of the arts', *Journal of Aesthetic Education* 1(1): 5-12.

Lyon, M.L. 1995. 'Missing emotion: The limitations of cultural constructionism in the study of emotion', *Cultural Anthropology* 10(2): 244-263.

Miller, W. 1926. *Trebizond: The Last Greek Empire*. London: Society for Promoting Christian Knowledge.

Nahachewsky, A. 1995. 'Participatory and presentational dance as ethnochoreological categories', *Dance Research Journal* 27(1): 1-15.

Polanyi, M. 1967. *The Tacit Dimension*. London: Routledge and Keegan Paul.

Rodaway, P. 1994. *Sensuous Geographies: Body, Sense and Place*. London: Routledge.

Royce, A.P. 1977. *The Anthropology of Dance*. Bloomington, IN: Indiana University Press.

Schieffelin, E.L. 1977. *The Sorrow of the Lonely and the Burning of the Dancers*. St. Lucia: University of Queensland Press.

Shay, A. 1999. 'Parallel traditions: State folk dance ensembles and folk dance in "The Field"', *Dance Research Journal* 31(1): 29-56.

Williams, D. (Ed.). 1997. *Anthropology and Human Movement: The Study of Dances*. Lanham, MD: Scarecrow Press.

Williams, D. 2004. *Anthropology of the Dance: Ten Lectures*. 2nd edn. Urbana and Chicago: University of Illinois Press.

5 Emotional actors/Affective agents:

Interspecies edgework and sociotechnical networks in the Spanish bullfight from horseback (*rejoneo*)

Kirrilly Thompson

Abstract[1]

Latour (1993) describes an ongoing human preoccupation with 'purification' from categories such as technology from society, nature from culture and human from animal. He identifies a certain irony in that such processes of purification simultaneously enable a proliferation of hybrid states of being: those that fall between the conceptual gaps. One enduring hybrid of Classical Greek mythology is the centaur — half man, half horse. The centaur

---

1   I am grateful to Dr Mike Wilmore, Dr Rod Lucas, Professor Garry Marvin, Professor Adrian Franklin, Professor Drew Dawson, Dr Danielle Every and Dr Alison Dundon for feedback on various versions of this chapter, and to all the humans and animals that shared their lives with me during fieldwork in Andalusia and beyond. This chapter is based on research that was funded by grants from the Department of Anthropology at The University of Adelaide, the Walter & Dorothy Duncan Trust Fund and an Australian Postgraduate Award with stipend.

metaphor is frequently used to describe a state of interspecies intercorporeality referred to in descriptions of horseriders thinking, feeling and moving 'as one' with their horse. However, there is a need to interrogate the centaur metaphor for human-horse intercorporeality by examining the dimensions through which it is generated — not only those of human and animal, but also technology, space and senses. This chapter considers these dimensions by applying an Actor Network Theory approach to the ethnographic example of the mounted bullfight. In so doing, space, technology and emotion (through tension) are acknowledged for having agency alongside and through the horse and rider. Through a careful consideration of the progression of a typical mounted bullfight event, the sociotechnical relations between these 'actors' can be seen to intensify to such an extent that tension cannot be overlooked. In fact, the integral role of tension in the mounted bullfight performance requires a consideration of the agency of emotions in networks. This discussion is framed by the concept of 'edgework' (Lyng 1990), making it possible not only to more fully describe the sociotechnical relations of the human-animal relations in the mounted bullfight, but also to convey how those relationships are felt and experienced by bodies in space, over time.

Introduction

Latour's (1993) early work identified the ironic proliferation of 'hybrids' that arise from, and are made possible by, attempts to purify categories such as 'human' and 'animal'. The centaur is one mythological hybrid that has been used both poetically (Pineda Novo 1988) and academically (Thompson 2011; Game 2001) to describe intercorporeal relationships between horses and riders. However, there has been relatively less interest in the ways in which the bodies of horses and riders relate emotionally and spatially, how those bodies are mediated through technology, and the sensuality of how those bodies 'feel' and feel one another.

The role of technology in social relations has been important to work following Latour — specifically to the approaches known as Actor Network Theory [ANT], or non-representational theory, and the field of Science and Technology Studies [STS]. ANT has become a general premise for some STS scholars, who acknowledge and presume the presence, agency, indivisibility and symmetry of human as well as non-human actors in networks or 'chains of associations'. From this perspective, 'the relation [is] the smallest unit of being and of analysis' (Haraway 2007:165), and effects, affects and properties are generated in, by and through networks of relations. That is, networks are emergent properties of relations.

In relation to spatial analyses, Roe suggests that 'ANT is less interested in time and space, but more in the unique acts of "spacing" and "timing", acts that are conducted through associations of various kinds' (2009:255). In this chapter, however, the spatial dimensions of networks are given consideration. By examining the interspecies, sociotechnical relations of the bullfight, I demonstrate how space is indivisible from bodies, emotions, senses and technology. I go further to suggest that emotion can be considered a legitimate actor in networks, alongside humans, non-human animals and technology. My discussion of emotion as an actor is consistent with explorations of the agency of space (Thrift 1996; 1999) and reminders that agency is not synonymous with intentionality (Whatmore 2007 [1999]).

The Spanish mounted bullfight (*el rejoneo*) is an apt case study for considering the interrelationships between space, senses and emotions. It takes place in a highly structured space imbued with cultural meaning, which is further spatially divided into sub-spaces. The activities that are undertaken within those physical spaces require and remake personal spaces which are made, experienced and shared between technologically mediated human and animal bodies. Below, I explain this by describing the process of the mounted bullfight, focusing on the ways in which relations between human and animal bodies-in-space and time are experienced sensually and emotionally. I describe the ways in which emotion is intensified as horse, rider, bull and technology come increasingly close in spatial and mortal terms. The tension of a 'good' bullfight is materialised in the extent to which human, horse and bull push, nudge or cross 'the edge' of danger, risk, life and death. The rider seeks to create tension by riding the horse dangerously close to the bull's horns, often allowing the bull to butt the horse's tail or rump, but never with the intention of allowing injury to rider or horse. It is a case of: 'How close can you go?' Ultimately, the bull is killed by penetrative technologies used by the rider, and placed through spatial intimacy. This tension arising from spatial proximity and the interpenetration of human and animal bodies via technology is the effect and affect of a 'good' performance.

In this chapter, I adapt an ANT approach to describe and characterise the sociotechnical relations at each stage of the mounted bullfight. I demonstrate the mutual inclusivity of proximity and space with emotion and the senses. To account for the intensifying emotional dimensions that unite those relationships, I draw from Lyng's psycho-sociological concept of 'edgework' (1990), used to describe voluntary risk taking where the stakes are high and the risk of death is genuine. 'Edgeworkers' engage in activities that jeopardise physical or mental wellbeing, thereby requiring that the edgeworker develop and demonstrate the skills required to maintain control over a situation verging on chaos. This requires, and results in, edgework sensations of control, mastery and total absorption in the activity at hand (as with 'flow', according to Csikszentmihalyi 1975). When undertaken successfully, edgework experiences lead to feelings of 'exhilaration and omnipotence' (Lyng 1990:859).

The relevance of edgework beyond its usual application in extreme sports to a 'blood sport' such as bullfighting is clear, albeit unexplored. In this chapter, edgework is significant to my use of tension as a proxy for emotion. Whilst some might argue that tension is a physiological state of response or anticipation, rather than an emotion in the sense of 'ecological phenomena that link us to our environments and enable us to learn from them' (Milton 2005:37), I contend that tension in the bullfight is an emotionally charged and aesthetically experienced quality that is felt, engendered and communicated by bullfighters in relation to very real risk and danger. Bullfighters experience a myriad of emotions when riding 'on the edge', and the word 'tension' conveys the overarching emotional quality they transmit whilst trying to keep the audience members literally 'on the edge of their seats'. By uniting the concepts of 'network' and 'edgework', I attempt to account for the ways in which emotion can be considered a legitimate actor within a sociotechnical network, alongside humans and non-humans. This is a significant advance from an ANT perspective where emotion is more likely to be considered as an *affect* generated by networks than an actor *per se*.

Following Ross's (2004:41) insistence that space/place is constituted through feelings and activities, this chapter demonstrates that the bullring is more than an empty structure designed to be filled with the animate bodies of audience, humans and animals. Through choreographed sociotechnical interactions and intensifying proximity, it is transformed into an intimate space where the feelings and activities of humans, animals and technologies are sensually and emotionally engaged in intensifying ways. The logical conclusion, desire and risk of their spatial and proximal intensification — death — generates the tension at the heart of the mounted bullfight (and underlines the importance of understanding bullfighting as 'edgework' undertaken within, by and through a network). Without this emotional dimension or 'affective atmosphere' (Bissell 2010), the bullfight would be a very different kind of event. However, tension on its own is not enough: it is a particular articulation of tension with bodies-in-space that characterises the mounted bullfight as we know it. Throughout this chapter, I consider the sensual interrelationships and entanglements between space, sociotechnical relations and emotion. Specifically, I consider the ways in which human and animal bodies engage with space in the bullring.

Latour, hybrids and centaurs

Latour was concerned with understanding the demarcation between modern society and a 'premodern' state of being (1993). In the same way that anthropologist Mary Douglas (1966:96) distinguishes primitive and modern cultures respectively as undifferentiated and differentiated, Latour (1993:10-11) argued that modernity is characterised by a fundamental preoccupation with a process of 'purification'. In particular, he identified the purification of society from nature and the human from the non-human. Ironically, purification fuels the proliferation of heterogeneous hybrid mixtures through a process of 'translation' (Latour 1993:12).

The centaur is one particular hybrid that has been used metaphorically to convey the ways in which relationships between rider and horse can generate mutually incorporative states of being which are inseparable from, and more than, human plus horse (Thompson 2011). With the torso and head of a human and the body of a horse, the centaur of Classical Greek mythology elegantly symbolises the intercorporeal relationship that horseriders strive for. However, despite its romanticism and naturalisation, the centaurian relationship is not a *fait accompli* of the riding relationship. It is frequently an unrealised ideal, or at best an intermittent experience (Thompson 2011).[2]

Elsewhere (Thompson 2007), I have demonstrated that whilst there may be a latent 'centaurability' of rider-horse relations, achieving a centaurian relationship is dependent on elements such as riding style, familiarity, time and technology (that is, saddlery). My comparison of mounted figures from footed and mounted bullfighting (Thompson 2011) provides an ethnographic basis to understanding Lagarde, Peham, Licka and Kelso's (2005) observation that 'phase synchronisation' between rider and horse improves with practice. The premise behind phase synchronisation in rider-horse[3] relations has been described in myriad terms, including partnership (Wipper 2000; Thompson & Birke 2014), entrainment, inhabitation or 'embodying the centaur' (Game 2001), 'centaurability' (Thompson 2011), harmony (LeGuin 2005), extension (Latimer & Birke 2009) and attunement or isopraxis (Despret 2004). The Spanish refer to close relations between bullfighters and bulls, as well as riders and horses, with the term *compenetración*, which — of significant interest to this chapter — literally means 'co-penetration'.

Other phenomenological and psychological concepts that can be used to understand and convey 'the centaur effect' of the riding relation include embodiment (Merleau-Ponty 1962), de-differentiation (Stranger 1999), kinaesthetic empathy (Shapiro 1990), habitus/bodily hexis (Bourdieu 1977, applied to showjumping by Thompson & Birke 2014) and flow (Csikszentmihalyi 1990, applied to eventing by Thompson & Nesci 2013). These various terms and concepts can all be employed to describe harmonious states of 'oneness' in riding. They describe affectual states of interbeing and intercorporeality which can convey the sensual dimensions of the rider-horse relations and experience of the centaur. Overall, these concepts tend to romanticise and naturalise the centaur, presenting it as an unmediated interspecies convergence of flesh. However, researchers in the last decade have examined the

---

2   Especially in a post-industrial environment, where horses are seldom used for work.

3   Following Dant's (2004) proposal of the term 'driver-car' to refer to the assemblage of driver and car, I use the term 'rider-horse' to evoke a sense of the unified being of rider and horse. The counterintuitive order of terms in 'rider-horse' also draws attention to the way the role of the horse in the common term 'horserider' is taken for granted. As an anthropocentric phrase, 'horserider' obscures the role that the horse plays in constructing the human as a 'horserider'. 'Rider-horse', on the other hand, draws attention to the transformation of the rider by the horse and the horse by the rider.

important and largely unavoidable role of technology in human-horse relations (Birke 2008; 2007; Latimer & Birke 2009). Whilst technology is often distinguished from human and animal, it is phenomenologically inseparable from those fleshy bodies. In short, technology is fundamentally embodied. As noted by Vergunst,

> [i]n studying technology the role of the body — those who make something, who use it, who are affected by it — is integral. By this reckoning the very distinction between body and tool is blurred and each must be seen in a relationship to the other, in their combination. (2011:206)

Technology is also primarily sensual. Writing about sports equipment, Hockey and Collinson discuss the ways in which sportspeople 'touch, and are in turn touched by the physical properties of terrain and equipment, and so build a two-way, embodied relationship with them' (2007:123). Without suggesting that horses are equivalent to non-sentient technologies, we can also make these same claims about the sensuality and embodiment of human-technology interaction when speaking of human-horse interactions that are also 'two-way': horses sense and embody riders. Moreover, given that riders use tools, that rider-horse relations are technologically mediated, and that riders and horses are mutually embodied (as described above in the centaur metaphor), the interrelationships between human, horse, bull and technology in the mounted bullfight can be understood as fundamentally technologised, embodied and sensual. *Compenetración* therefore does not just involve human and animal bodies; it involves technological actors and technologised bodies in relations of incorporation and, in particular, of extension. Belk (1988; 1996) discusses the ways in which animals (specifically pets) and tools or technology can become special cases of extended human selves. The concept of extended self has been used to explain why humans often risk their own lives to save those of animals during natural disasters (Thompson 2013b; Thompson, Every, Rainbird, Cornell, Smith & Trigg 2014; Thompson 2015). The bullfight, however, provides a clearer example of how the safety of humans and animals is at times profoundly interdependent. I examine below the ways in which this embodiment and sensuality is experienced, performed and transmitted at two levels: the social space of the bullring and the interpersonal space of the actors within.

Rejoneo: Mounted bullfighting

Before I describe the ways in which emotional and embodied relations between humans, animals and technologies are intensified through spatial proximity, it is necessary to describe the mounted bullfight (*corrida de rejones*) and to distinguish it from the more widely known footed bullfight (*corrida de toros*) with its *picador* and *picador*'s horse. Mounted bullfighting is popularly thought to predate the bullfight from foot (Thompson 2007; 2010) and represent a more elite version of bullfighting (Thompson 2012b). It is practised in Spain with variations in Mexico, Portugal, Southern France,

Colombia and California (the latter based on the Portuguese 'bloodless' version). Riders are referred to as *rejoneadores* with women distinguished as *rejoneadoras*.[4]

Rejoneadores combine their skills as horseriders with those of a *torero* (bullfighter) to engage the bull from horseback. Indeed, the horse has been considered by some as being to the mounted bullfighter what the cape is to the footed bullfighter (Arévalo 2001). As with a footed bullfight, a mounted bullfight starts with the *paseíllo* (a procession of performers).[5] However, in the mounted bullfight, this is followed by an equestrian display based on various *alta escuela* ('high school') movements.[6] Three distinct phases are repeated for the six bulls usually killed in each bullfight (the last two bulls are usually killed by a pair of *rejoneadores* when there are four *rejoneadores* on the programme). At each phase of the bullfight, *rejoneadores* ride a different horse, especially selected and trained to address the demands of that particular phase. Sometimes, riders exaggerate the inherent tension in the risk of the horse being gored by the bull by making their mounts 'sit' or 'bow' in the presence of the bull, although many 'classical' riders would disapprove of such 'circus' tricks.

The physical space of the bullring has been understood structurally as urban, human, cultured space, in contrast to the countryside. It has also been described politically as a space in which the audience as 'community' has a rare opportunity to influence the president of the bullfight as 'authority' (Marvin 1994 [1988]). As I demonstrate below, the bullring is also a space in which bodies, senses and emotions cohere in particular, inextricable and intensifying ways.

Fieldwork

This chapter is based on fifteen months of anthropological fieldwork in Andalusia (Southern Spain) from September 2000 to December 2001. I conducted ethnographic fieldwork in Andalusia with *rejoneadores* located on either side of the Guadalquivir River, in Huelva and Cádiz provinces. I interviewed *rejoneadores* (Thompson 2012a), watched them train, attended bullfights and was privileged to travel with a *rejoneador* and his assistants to numerous *corridas* (bullfights) in Spain and thus gain intimate access to the *rejoneo* event and other *rejoneadores* with whom he performed. I recorded these experiences with field notes and a field journal. I also collected and analysed photos, videos, newspaper articles, and bullfighting and equestrian books and

---

4   Whilst women are a minority of mounted bullfighters, it is more acceptable for a woman to become a mounted bullfighter than a footed bullfighter (*torera*). For a detailed exploration of the gendered dimensions of mounted bullfighting, see Thompson (2013a).

5   *Paseíllo* is the diminutive of *el paseo*, from the verb *pasear*, meaning 'a walk or a stroll'.

6   *Alta escuela* is the Spanish translation of *haute école*, a French term for high school training which is commonly used in equestrian discourse to refer to the advanced classical training of horses involving various 'airs above ground' (Tucker 2005; see also Helmberger 1994).

magazines. Whilst I participated in the role of researcher, fan, amateur photographer and assistant, my focus was on the riders rather than on the audience. This was due to my primary research interest in the human-animal relationship in general and in the riding relationship in particular (Thompson 2011).

The three phases of a mounted bullfight

To consider the spatial, emotional, embodied and sensual ways in which humans, animals and technologies interrelate in the mounted bullfight, it is necessary to consider each of the three stages of the bullfight in detail. Doing so provides insight into the ways in which these relationships are spatial, embodied, sensual, emotional, interdependent and, above all, intensified throughout the bullfight.

In fact, the bullfight can be understood as structured specifically to facilitate such intensification. The ethnographic detail or 'thick description' (Geertz 1973) that follows provides a basis for understanding the ways in which the mounted bullfight can be understood as structuring (and being structured by) an intensification of sociotechnical relations, emotions and spaces. This description attends to the humans, animals and technologies which form the physical, tangible elements of the bullfighting network. At the same time, I make clear the agency of emotions, particularly through spatial tension and emotional tension. I will discuss the intensification of the interrelations between physical, spatial and emotional agencies throughout the bullfight later, in relation to boundaries, thresholds and limits, by referring to 'edgework' (Lyng 1990).

First phase: Tercio de salida

The first phase (*tercio*) of a bullfight is known as the *primer* (first) *tercio* or the *tercio de salida* (entrance), as it marks the entrance of the bull to the *plaza*. In this phase, the bull is described as *levantado* (lofty), relating to its high head carriage. The bull is usually fast and energetic, but erratic, unfocused and unpredictable. The *rejoneador* tempers the bull by leading it at a controlled pace around the *plaza*. The typical scene in the first *tercio* is of a horse cantering or galloping close to the inner fence-line of the bullring with the bull in pursuit, its horns butting the horse's tail and very occasionally its rump.

To match the bull's frantic energy and determination to charge in the *tercio de salida*, the *rejoneador* rides a *caballo de salida* (entrance horse).[7] The *caballo de salida* needs to be fast enough to lead the bull in a chase of acceleration and deceleration, whilst maintaining a distance that allows the bull to come as close as possible without

---

7 Horse breeds associated with speed and endurance are typically used at this stage, such as thoroughbreds and Arabians, respectively. Moreno Pidal (2004:252) recommends at least 50 per cent English blood.

injury to horse or rider. A *rejoneador* described the skills required of a *caballo de salida* as follows:

> If the bull's charge is too fast you run alongside it to the right, slowing the horse until you have regulated the bull's charge without ever letting the bull hit the horse. You keep it at the horse's tail, teasing, teasing, teasing [encelando] until the bull gathers its speed and you have controlled its movements. (Interview with *rejoneador*, 4 December 2001)

The verb *encelar* used in this quotation translates literally as 'to make jealous', but it is translated in the context of the mounted bullfight as 'teasing' and provoking — both emotional terms. This terminology evokes the idea of a dangerous attraction between rider, horse and bull. There is a desire for close proximity and intimacy alongside an awareness of the danger in achieving these things, and an intuitive desire to not get (too) close. As a result, considerable risk and daring are involved in riding a horse close to the Spanish bull, which has been selectively bred for its aggression and willingness to charge.

The *rejones* used in the *primer tercio* are the *rejones de castigo* (barbed spears of punishment or 'chastisement'); they are 160 cm in total length. A hollow cylinder of 6 cm in length attaches a double-edged blade to the wooden handle. This *cubillo* has a crossbar affixed, which is also 6 cm long. The blade is 2.5 cm wide and 15 cm long for *novillos* (three-year-old bulls) or 18 cm long for *toros* (bulls aged four years and over) (Ministerio de Justicia e Interior 1996:Article 67.1). Just behind the *cubillo*, the wooden stick is whittled down to a finer 'neck' that breaks away from the long handle when the barb is pushed into the bull and the *rejoneador* pushes against it. As the barb breaks away from the *rejon*, it triggers the unfurling of a coloured flag wrapped around the main handle, which the *rejoneador* can either use to entice the bull to charge or hold high in the air to signal a successful placement. At the same time, these *rejones de castigo* leave a small barb under the bull's skin from which colourful streamers dangle. Even if the streamers fall out, they become, through emotion, memory and language, the first of many visible 'hauntings' and 'passings' (Thrift 1999) of the physical interactions of the actors in the mounted bullfight network.

The entanglement of human, horse, bull and technology in the first phase of the mounted bullfight is clear. It occurs as 'passings' at speed within the confines of the bullring, thus demonstrating the full force and power of the bull. This stage establishes the risk which is inherent in the bullfight and which gives rise to the emotional quality of tension that in turn is reliant on space. In this first phase, human, horse, bull and technology create a particular kind of space imbued with particular emotions, qualities and sensory capabilities. Throughout the bullfight, space takes on increasing intimacy and intensity, thereby continuing to shape the embodied and emotional relations of the bullfighting network.

Second phase: **Tercio de banderillas**

The second phase, or *tercio de banderillas*, is named after the gaily decorated barbs that are used, which are considered to *adornar* (decorate) and *animar* (enliven) the bull. In the *tercio de banderillas*, the bull is less interested in following the horse and is thus described (Arratia 1988:288) as '*parado*' (fixed or stationary). The bull often stands still and may be reluctant to charge, especially if it is standing in a space referred to as its *querencia*. The *querencia* is a location in the bullring identified as a place to which the bull frequently returns and where it is considered to feel most comfortable (de Cossío 2000:27; Arratia 1988:287). The *rejoneador* tries to keep the bull out of its *querencia* and avoids being positioned between it and the bull. This is for reasons of safety and aesthetics, as the bull is more confident and less active in its *querencia*. The *querencia* is an elegant example of a zoo-centric 'emotional geography'. It is a space which attracts, and is constructed by, the bull, and which the bull characterises emotionally as a place of confidence and control. Moreover, humans construct the bull's *querencia* as a particularly high-risk area in which to engage with the bull.

The *tercio de banderillas* is considered by many to be the most *vistoso* (eye-catching) phase of the mounted bullfight because the *banderillas* are considered decorations or adornments (*adornos*), adding to the beauty of the bull and the spectacle of the bullfight.[8] This *tercio* is also considered the most important in terms of securing 'trophies'[9], (notwithstanding the importance of the kill in the final phase). The horse used in the *tercio de banderillas* is referred to as the *caballo de banderillas*.[10] It should be *vistoso* itself and, according to Moreno Pidal (2004:256), no less than the *rejoneador*'s best horse. The *caballo de banderillas* must have the confidence to remain within close proximity to the 'fixed' bull, being attentive to the bull and ready to follow its intuition, whilst simultaneously being attentive to, and responding to, signals from the rider.

---

8   *Banderillas* are decorated with brightly coloured tissue, typically in three segments and often balanced with the same colour at each end and a contrasting colour in the middle. The colours are usually symbolic of a particular stud or a region. For example, blue-white-blue is a combination favoured by *rejoneadores* from *Jerez de la Frontera*, as these are the town colours. Green and white are the colours of Andalusia, whilst red and yellow refer to the colours of the Spanish flag. Similar colour combinations are often reflected in the ribbons woven into the manes of the *caballos toreros*.

9   These trophies are the ears and tail awarded to the *torero* [bullfighter] according to the quality of the performance, on a scale of one ear, two ears, or two ears and a tail.

10 The Iberian horse (the Spanish *Pura Raza Española*, or 'pure race') and its Portuguese relation (the *Lusitano*) are the preferred breeds for this *tercio* due to an innate 'capacity for collection, for training, for its beauty, its valour and its capacity to "moderate" [*templar*] the bull [its direction and speed]' (Jiménez Benítez 1994:102).

The *rejoneador* aims to engage the bull's attention, which can move quickly from the horse to the crowd or elsewhere. The *rejoneador* calls 'Eh!' to the bull, makes the horse move or raises a *banderillo* or *rejon* in the air. The rider will advance towards the bull unless it is moving, and should only place a *rejon* or *banderillo* into a bull that is moving towards the horse. Moments of tension precede each 'charge', where the horse rapidly accelerates or swerves to avoid a goring. When in pursuit, rider and horse otherwise remain as close as possible to the bull. All the while, the horse maintains a heightened state of sensory arousal (in many ways, the bullfighting horse acts against its herd-based flight instincts, but at the same time it could be seen to draw from its instincts of fighting with other horses to assert dominance).[11] Paralleling the human *banderillero* in the second phase of the footed bullfight, rider and horse perform one or more full pirouettes in front of the bull's oncoming horns. The telepathic timing and co-ordination required to safely perform these pirouettes illustrates the centaurian relation in action. This is exemplified *par excellence* when the *rejoneador* rides *sin manos* (without hands) to place a pair of *banderillas* simultaneously. The reins are attached to the *rejoneador*'s belt and the horse is guided using the rider's seat, legs and weight.

There are two kinds of *banderillas*: *largas* and *cortas* (long and short). The *banderillas largas* are 80 cm in length with a harpoon 6 cm long at one end (Ministerio de Justicia e Interior 1996:Article 63.1). The *banderillas cortas* have the same harpoon as the long *banderillas*, but are between 20 cm and 35 cm in length. The *banderillas cortas* that are 20 cm long are often decorated with green and red tissue paper or with artificial flowers to resemble *rosas* (roses), by which name they are then referred to.[12] The function of the *banderillas* is to excite the bull. The verb *alegrar* (Gargantilla Rodríguez 2005:36) is used to convey this, which means 'to enliven', from *alegría* for happiness. However, the use and placement of the *banderillas* engender emotion that is distributed amongst the sociotechnical network of rider and horse. For many *rejoneadores*, the intensity of this emotion is so profound as to be ineffable, although they are able to describe the physical impact of such emotion on the body. As one *rejoneador* explained:

> Well, if you place them [the banderillas] properly, in the right place and if the bull is very bravo, it produces an indescribable emotion and gives you goose bumps. Me, for example, I'm often criticised for not smiling enough, for being too serious. But I believe that when you do something beautiful, instead of laughing you feel like crying, because the emotion is very intense. (Interview with a *rejoenador*, 26 September 2001)

---

11 The idea of the horse as a fearful animal is discussed by LeGuin (2005:181).

12 The invention of the *rosas* is credited to the *rejoneador* Angel Peralta (Abarquero Durango 1984:107).

The emotion described by this *rejoneador* arises from the tension in getting closer and closer to a bull, necessitated by the decreasing length of barbs. Successfully taking the maximum risk by sharing the most intimate space possible with the bull results in heightened, ineffable emotions. Rider, horse, bull and technology not only share increasingly intimate space within the *plaza*, but they also become increasingly co-penetrated. This impending implosion of bodies, senses, emotions and space is predicated upon the mortal, 'edgework' threshold of life and death which takes on most significance in the final phase of the bullfight.

Third phase: Tercio de muerte

The third *tercio* is known as the *tercio de muerte* (*tercio* of death) or *último tercio* (last *tercio*). The bull at this stage is described as *aplomado*, meaning heavy or weighed down (Arratia 1988:288), and, although it retains some strength, its movements are most 'fixed' in space. The *rejoneador* selects a horse with specific abilitiy and training to match the requirements of this *tercio*. The *caballo de muerte* or *caballo de matar* (literally 'the horse of death') is required to be *noble* (noble)[13] and *valiente* (valiant), and to perform difficult movements in tight spaces, such as pirouetting in the face of the bull, thereby exposing its chest and rump close to the bull's horns.[14] It ideally moves smoothly and comfortably to aid the rider's accurate and effective placement of the *rejon de muerte* (*rejon* of death). The more precise the placement, the greater the chance of a quick kill, which will enhance the *rejoneador*'s overall performance and give a greater likelihood of being awarded trophies.

The *rejon de muerte* (*rejon* of death) delivers the *coup de grâce*.[15] It is a sword 1.6 m long with a double-edged blade that is 2.5 cm wide and either 60 cm in length, for *novillos*, or 65 cm long, for *toros* (Ministerio de Justicia e Interior 1996:Article 67.3).

13 The description of good horses as 'noble' is common in Spain, especially in reference to the indigenous *Pura Raza Española*. It is a fascinating adjective to apply to a horse, given that it refers to horses which retain their symbolism of freedom and wildness whilst allowing (offering?) their services to be used for human purposes. In this way, the idea of the noble horse is not unlike the idea of the noble savage. As LeGuin comments, 'characterization of horses as noble and quasi-human may have something to do with [an] extremely resourceful resistance to subjection, a quality long associated with moral integrity in humans' (2005:184).

14 Iberian breeds similar to those preferred for the *tercio de banderillas* are preferred for this *tercio*.

15 During the numerous *corridas* that I travelled to with a *rejoneador* and his *quadrilla* (team), I did not hear the *mozo de espadas* (sword handler) use the words *rejon de muerte*. He always referred to the *rejon de muerte* as an *espada* (sword) and everything else as *cuchillos* (knives), which he differentiated with the words 'long' or 'short' (*larga* or *corta*).

The blade is sheathed in red tissue paper.[16] Like the *rejones* and *banderillas*, it is used from horseback, at least initially.[17]

After placing the *rejones de castigo* in the first *tercio*, the *banderillas largas* and the *banderillas cortas* and *rosas* in the second *tercio*, the bull is considered *parado* (fixed/grounded). The *banderillas* bend outwards from its shoulder blades parallel to the ground, flapping up and down in time to the bull's panting. Its mouth is open and its dry tongue sticks out in the style of a jagged Picasso sketch. The *rejoneador* needs to place the *rejon de muerte* amongst all the *banderillas* and barbs that adorn the bull, the 'hauntings' of its relational intensification throughout the preceding phases of the bullfight. If the bull is killed by the first *rejon de muerte*, the 'sugar on top' to a sweet kill will be the handle of the *rejon* sitting squarely between its shoulder blades. Killing the bull is an intense emotional experience, as explained by Chilean rider Conchita Cintrón (Concepción Cintrón Verrill), the most famous female mounted bullfighter, who fought from the late 1930s until 1950[18]:

> Only a person who has experienced it can understand the indescribable moment when the bull falls; the mixture of respect a torero feels before an adversary who has stood his ground and fought honourably and well. As the bull struggled against the unsteadiness which overcame him, he was worthy of admiration. Drunkenly he took a step in my direction. Then one more. I stood firmly in place. The animal was now very close. There was no muleta or cape between us. Just one strong effort, and he would get the best of me. The tension kept me petrified. One of us had to give. A silent duel occurs often in the arena, but this was my first experience of it. When the bull finally let go of life and fell at my feet, I would not have traded my place for any other in the world. (Cintrón 1968:105)

Cintrón provides an evocative demonstration of the ways in which space, emotion and the senses are not only inseparable in the bullfight, but are also intensified in relation to the kill, where the edge between life and death has been crossed by the bull and successfully navigated by the bullfighter. Spaces, emotions and senses are thus

---

16 Álvaro Domecq y Díez (a *rejoneador* who faced bulls from horseback in the 1930s and 1940s) killed bulls using the *estoque*, the same sword used by *toreros* on foot (Fifield 1978:108).

17 The *rejoneador* must make a minimum of two separate attempts with the *rejon de muerte* before being allowed to dismount to kill the bull from the ground (Ministerio de Justicia e Interior 1996:Article 85.5). After two warnings from the president, the *rejoneador* must dismount. The first warning comes if the bull has not been killed within five minutes of the start of the *tercio de muerte*, and the second warning comes two minutes after the first (Ministerio de Justicia e Interior 1996:Article 88.6). The *rejoneador* can substitute a qualified understudy to complete the kill.

18 For a more detailed discussion of Conchita Cintrón, see Thompson (2013a).

enmeshed in a network comprising the bodies of humans, animals and technology. The omnipresence of death heightens their intensification and provides a reminder that affording agency in symmetrical network terms does not necessarily entail a homeostatic rendering of network interactions or interrelations. I discuss this below in relation to 'edgework', in order to acknowledge the textures of different networks which can be evidenced through bodies, spaces, emotions and senses.

The *rejon* used in the final *tercio* is as long as the *rejones de castigo* used in the first *tercio*. However, its length is comprised mostly of blade, whereas the length of the *rejones* and *banderillas* used in the previous phases is primarily staff. Placing the *rejon de muerte* presents the greatest risk to the rider-horse being gored as the rider reaches between the bull's horns to thrust it 'to the hilt'. This provides the deepest penetration of the bull, otherwise understood as the greatest intensification of space between rider-horse-technology and bull.[19]

During my fieldwork, it was typical for *rejoneadores* to dismount and stand before the bull as it died, even if the *coup de grâce* came from horseback. At the mounted bullfight of the *Feria del Caballo* in 2001, Luis Domecq paraded to and fro in front of the bull in the style of a *flamenco* dancer, with proud bearing and deliberate turns that incorporated bending down on one knee and stretching a hand poignantly towards the bull. As with other occasions where I observed this kind of *flamenco*-inspired performance, the crowd greeted each turn with enthusiasm, calling out, 'Olé'. This dance of, and with, death contributed to the theatrics, affective atmosphere and performance tone of the mounted bullfight, engendering a profound emotion of reverence to the space of the bullring — an emotion that spread through the stands as the crowd waited together with the bullfighter for the moment of the bull's death.

Once the bull's expiration was secured, *rejoneadores* walked to the centre of the ring to salute the crowd and accept applause. On other occasions, where the final kill had been 'messy' and involved a number of attempts, *rejoneadores* often walked directly to the barrier, too ashamed to greet the crowd. No matter how well a *rejoneador* performs in the other stages of the *corrida*, difficulties with the kill can spoil a performance.

At this point, it is worth summarising the features of the *corrida* central to my argument. In the preceding sections of this chapter, I detailed the three phases in

---

19 The sexual undertones here (and in the description of Table 5.1) have not gone unnoticed. 'Among the layered semiotics of the bull-fight, the sexual connotations are the most intriguing' (Cornwell 1997:17). Attention has been given to the sexual psychology of the *corrida* and psychoanalytic interpretations, mostly based around Freud's concept of the Oedipal drama and notions of patricide (see, for example Desmonde 1952; Paniagua 1992; Grotjahn 1959; Hunt 1955; Ingham 1964; Kothari 1962; Pollock 1974) or of the expression of repressed anger towards male authority (Conrad 1957). For further discussion on the sexual and gendered dimensions of the mounted bullfight see Thompson (2013a).

the mounted bullfight according to the qualities and activities of the bull, horse and technology and the emotions experienced by the bullfighters. In the first phase, the *rejones* are relatively long. They are used to tease the bull, to begin to breech the spatial boundary between rider-horse and bull, to test boundaries between grabbing the bull's attention, enticing it to charge and pushing the horse's tolerance for staying within the bull's space. The *rejones* in this stage are used to 'tease', 'chastise', 'punish' and flirt with the danger presented by the bull's horns and the rider's barbed and piked technologies. This act of establishing limits continues into the second phase, when the bull may lose interest in the rider-horse and *rejones*. *Banderillas* are used in this phase to 'enliven' and 'excite' the bull and to renew its interest in a dangerous liaison. As the *banderillas* decrease from 80 cm to 20 cm in length, enlivening the bull with them entails simultaneously entering its space and drawing it out from that space. All the while, rider-horse and bull are required to share increasingly intimate space.

In the final phase, a logical conclusion comes to the flirtatious and provocative relationship initiated between dangerous partners. If the risk pays off, the rider-horse emerges from the encounter unscathed, and tension has reached a maximum. (If the risk does not pay off, then the rider-horse has most likely been unable to successfully heighten and manage the risks of sharing increasingly intimate spaces with the bull.) The death of the bull is experienced emotionally as profound beauty: the kind that can make someone want to cry (as quoted above). Some *rejoneadors* are so moved by the beauty of this deathly encounter that they are inspired to dance and posture before the bull during its final living moments.

The decreasing length of the technologies is central to my argument about intensifying intimate spatial relations between rider-horse and bull. Table 5.1, below, illustrates the different tools used at each of the three stages of the mounted bullfight, showing the name/type of barb, maximum number that can be used, length of the shaft of the tool and the length of the blade. The maximum number of barbs that can be used at each stage represents the maximum number of deliberate penetrative encounters between rider-horse and bull (the bull may seek more encounters of its own accord). The length of the blade is synonymous with the depth of physical penetration of the bull's corporeal boundary, whilst the length of the shaft suggests how close the *rejoneador* has to be to place the barb into the bull. Of most importance to this chapter, the *rejones* become shorter throughout the first two *tercios*, decreasing in length from 160 cm (or 250 cm on the less common occasions when the *garrocha*[20] is used) to the *rosa*, which is 20 cm in length (see bold text in Table 5.1).

---

20 The *garrocha* is a wooden pole around 2.5 m long and 5 cm thick, which is used in the countryside to control the movements of bulls at liberty, or to knock them over in order to be able to attend to them. There are no official regulations regarding the usage of the *garrocha* in the mounted bullfight, as its use in the bullfight is an infrequent innovation.

Tercio	Name of tool	Number	Length of tool	Length of blade
Prior	Divisa	1	8 cm	3 cm
Primer tercio	Rejon de castigo	Max. 3	**160 cm**	15 cm novillos 18 cm toros
	Garrocha	n/a	250 cm	n/a
Segundo tercio	Banderillas largas	2-3 pairs	80 cm	6 cm
	Farpa		80 cm	7 cm
	Banderillas cortas		20-35 cm	6 cm
	Rosas		**20 cm**	6 cm
Tercer tercio	Rejon de muerte	Min. 2 before dismounting	160 cm	60 cm novillos 65 cm toros
	Descabello	Max. 3	88 cm	10 cm max. penetration

Table 5.1: Description of technology according to *tercio*. (Source: Author.)

In order to place the *rejones*, the *rejoneador* needs to manoeuvre his horse perilously close to the bull's horns in each phase. Adopting the theories of technology as fundamentally sensual and embodied as outlined earlier (Hockey & Collinson 2007; Vergunst 2011), together with an ANT emphasis on relations, we can understand the bodies of humans, animals and technologies as folding onto, into and unto one another throughout the mounted bullfight. This spatial, sensual and embodied folding is intensified through the progressive shortening of technology. Moreover, it is experienced emotionally as tension, since it simultaneously entails escalating risk to horse, human and bull. After all, three sentient bodies will enter the bullring and at least one will die.[21] In this way, technology, space, emotions and intercorporeality are utterly indivisible in the mounted bullfight.

The following scenario illustrates the importance of communicating emotion and the relationship between space, bodies and technology in developing the tension required of an emotive mounted bullfight. At a *corrida* in *Talavera de la Reina* in 2001, I watched a *rejoneador* whose style would be described as *valiente*, as opposed to *artista* (artistic). This young and daring *rejoneador*, astride horses scarred with old *cornadas* (horn wounds) and bleeding mouths and sides (from inelegant use of bit and spur),

---

21 There are exceptions where the bull lives, known as an *indulto*, where the kill is feigned by the *torero*, using a *banderilla* (the gaily decorated barbs placed into the bull in the early stages of the *corrida*) in place of an *estoque* (sword).

showed the audience just how close he was prepared to get to the bull and how much risk he was prepared to take and expose the horse to. This included making his horse sit down on its rump vulnerably in the presence of the bull. On one occasion, he held a *banderilla* out to the crowd (dedicating it to them), rode to the inner fence of the bullring (*barrera*) and cracked the *banderilla* against the rail, snapping it in halves and sending wooden splints ricocheting dangerously into the crowd. In doing so, he communicated his desire and ability to get closer to the bull sooner than required, and his daring in taking maximum risk to do so.

However 'rough' his style was, his actions can be understood as a performance of his willingness and desire to accelerate the spatial, emotional and embodied intensification of the mounted bullfight network. This scenario also demonstrates that the emotional basis of the bullfight is about being close, getting closer, and how close one can get to 'the edge' — in this case the edge of life and death. In short, his actions illustrate that while relations can be analysed symmetrically, they are often experienced with the highly emotional texture of thresholds, tipping points, boundaries and limitations — or, in other words, the edgework of bullfighting. In the remainder of this chapter, I discuss the 'edgework' inherent in the mounted bullfighting network in order to underline the ways in which space, emotions and the senses come together to bring together the bodies of humans, animals and technology.

Edgework: Relational intensification, thresholds and risks

The shortening of technologies in the mounted bullfight demands an increased spatial intimacy between human and animal bodies. This intensifying intimacy is experienced emotionally — teasing the bull, tempering it, controlling it, putting human and horse at risk and, indeed, in mortal danger, but (ideally) just short of an injury. The rider-horse must ascertain how close the bull can get to the horse without a fall or goring to rider or horse. By adopting an ANT approach to the mounted bullfight in this chapter and considering the agency of animals and technologies alongside that of humans, I have been able to identify the role of technology in the spatial, sensual and emotional intensification of bodies. In particular, by identifying the critical role of tension in the construction, experience and communication of mounted bullfighting, I have been able to demonstrate the agency of emotion within the bullfighting network alongside human and non-human actors.

Because of the inherent danger and risk in the case study of bullfighting, I have paid particular attention to the role of thresholds, boundaries and edges within the bullfighting network and sociotechnical relations. The character of such textural networks and relational timbres are often considered to be somewhat sacrificed in ANT approaches in order to sustain the principle of symmetry (Pink 2011). However, I explore them in the remainder of this chapter by overlaying Lyng's (1990) concept of 'edgework' to the network approach used above. This enables a consideration of the ways in which space does more than put networks in their place, and emotion and the senses are more than effects of network relations. Rather, they relate as actors in relational networks, alongside humans, non-human animals and technology.

As I have already discussed, a 'good' mounted bullfight is one in which the rider and horse have gone as close as possible to 'the edge' and been able to return. The edge is characterised primarily at a spatial, embodied level, which is experienced with emotions that are intense, if not primal, given the real chance of death to rider and horse. The closer the horse and rider come to the bull's horns, the more intimate their use of space, and the shorter the penetrative technologies, the greater the risk. Danger and risk are essential to the emotion of tension which characterises a good performance. Not only does tension intensify the relations between human, horse, technology and bull, but it also joins them with an audience who cares which physical, embodied boundaries are being crossed.

To more fully understand the limitations and thresholds around which tension arises and effects network relations, the bullfight can be considered a form of 'edgework', and bullfighters as 'edgeworkers'. Lyng (1990) offers the sociological concept of edgework to overcome the psychological reductionism that dominates the literature on voluntary risk taking.[22] Whilst different edgework activities can be characterised by varying skills and sensations, Lyng outlines a 'general principle of edgework — the commitment to get as close as possible to the edge without going over it' (1990:862). The edge that he refers to is the boundary 'between chaos and order' (855) and, at the highest level, that of life and death. The line between life and death is salient in bullfighting, especially as an activity oriented around a human putting his or her life at risk to bring about the death of the bull. In the reminder of this article, I 'flesh out' the edge in relation to bullfighting.

Lyng examines edgework activities, skills and sensations in relation to 'modern'[23] sports such as skydiving, but translates edgework to mounted bullfighting. Bullfighting, Lyng states, involves 'a clearly observable threat' to the bullfighter's 'physical and mental wellbeing' which can result in death or injury to rider or horse (857). Mounted bullfighting is a 'skilled performance' requiring the rider (and horse) to not only be proficient with the skills and technologies required of bullfighting, but also to control their fears and anxieties, to be instinctual and, ultimately, to survive. Uppermost is the bullfighter's 'general ability to maintain control of a situation that verges on total chaos' (871). Finally, bullfighting provides sensations of a heightened sense of self and

---

22 Lyng's secondary motivation for developing edgework is to consider voluntary risk-taking behaviour through a synthesis of Marxian and Meadian frameworks in social psychology. This involves micro- and macro-structural analysis in the consideration of risk taking.

23 I have used the word 'modern' in quotation marks here because the bullfight is a symbol of modern, civilised Spain for many (Pink 1996).

self-mastery, control (or the illusion of control) and immersion in a highly focused and narrow field of perception.

These sensations are tied to the emotional achievement of overcoming fear, which leads to 'exhilaration and omnipotence' (859).[24] Edgework sensations gained from the bullfighting experience were poetically illustrated by a *rejoneador* who told me that killing bulls was 'the most beautiful thing' because killing a bull in that way could only be carried out by a select, skilled few, of which he was one. For him, the edgework sensations of bullfighting were completed by the fact that the experience and skill required were rarely experienced by others; it was an exclusive experience (Thompson 2012a).

At the micro-level, edgework presents the risk taker largely in a social vacuum. Any mention of dependence or trust is made in relation to non-sentient objects (climbing ropes, helmets, and so on) or technologies (GPS, weather forecasting devices and so forth). In contrast to ANT principles and network approaches that consider the agency of the inanimate and the mutual influence of human-technology relations (such as Beckmann 2004), the human-technology relation in edgework and similar approaches is typically construed as one of subject-object. For example,

> [i]n many cases, edgeworkers explore the performance limits of both themselves and a material form; with the increasingly sophisticated nature of modern technology, individuals must sometimes push themselves to the outer limits of human performance in order to reach the performance limits of the technology under their control. (Lyng 1990:858)

Indeed, a particular sensation associated with edgework is 'a feeling of "oneness" with the object or environment' (861), something Stranger (1999) describes as 'de-differentiation'. This feeling translates readily to human-horse relations. Whilst the *rejoneador*'s mastery of technology such as *rejones* is clearly required, mastery of the human-horse relationship is paramount to the safety of horse and rider. This mastery can be understood as the ability for horse and rider to build an interspecies relationship where 'horse and rider appear to be moving and thinking as one'. This de-differentiation is reflected in Lyng's comment that,

> [n]o longer capable of distinguishing between self and certain environmental objects, edgeworkers develop a sense of oneness with these objects or, in the most extreme form, feel as if they could mentally control them. (1990:882)

---

24 Bullfighting can be considered an edgework experience in all dimensions of the concept, with the exception that 'true edgework involves completely novel circumstances' (Lyng 1990:878). The bullfight is not strictly novel. Rather, it is a highly structured activity within which variations are expected and novelty is common (for example, in relation to the behaviour of the bull, horse and audience). In any case, the extent to which any activity pre-selected by a participant can be 'completely' novel is debatable.

Moreover, the oneness of human-object, or human-horse relations, can, as I have demonstrated above, be understood as 'more than' edgework, in that the edge or boundary between human, animal and technology has been made redundant or has been reabsorbed in a state of oneness or de-differentiation. The edge between human and horse is transgressed and transmuted, whilst the edge between life and death must be challenged but carefully maintained.

In the case of mounted bullfighting, the limits of networks relate not only to their intensification but to the attenuation of emotional and corporeal sociotechnical relations. For example, the intensification of the rider-horse-bull network is intended to result in the death of the bull. However, if the relationship between the rider and horse attenuates, their inability to move harmoniously and instinctively 'as one' may result in their own deaths from a goring or fall (Thompson 2012b, 2013a).

Considering the fleshy human-horse relationship using concepts such as edgework which have been most concerned with human-object relationships provides a more social understanding of voluntary risk-taking behaviours, in that the *rejoneador* places trust in, and develops a partnership with, an animate and sentient being. After all, horseriding is irrevocably a team sport, even when done individually (Thompson & Nesci 2013; Thompson & Birke 2014). This consideration of mounted bullfighting in my chapter has implications for recognising the sociality of animals and technologies in general, whilst also considering the social and shared dimensions of voluntary risk taking in human-human paired activities, such as tandem skydives.

The concept of edgework not only provides an alternative means of considering centaurian oneness between horse and rider, but also highlights the emotional dimension to activities centred upon risk, danger and 'getting closer'. Edgework adds an emotional dimension to attempts to categorise the bullfight as ritual, performance, art or sport (for example, Arratia 1988). That is, rather than asking what bullfighting is, one can ask how bullfighting *feels* and how that feeling interrelates with space and bodies. In this way, edgework complements the network approach taken above by underscoring the importance of emotion. The edgework concept readily applies to a case study such as the mounted bullfight, where the limits of life and death are plain and the question of what is at stake is easily answered. However, by referring to mounted bullfighting in this chapter, my intention has been to prompt questions of what is at stake in more mundane networks and activities. If, following Foucault (1978:121-2), power is everywhere, comes from everywhere and is located in every relation, then surely there is always something at stake.

Conclusion

Acknowledging the agency of non-human beings such as animals and technology is an important redress to anthropocentric claims to agency, and a gesture of deference to the importance of relations (interpersonal, interspecies, sociotechnical and human-animal).

However, there has been little acknowledgment and consideration of emotion and space as important and arguably unavoidable actors in networks. In this chapter, I have taken a more traditional network approach by considering the interrelationships between humans, animals and technology. In the case of the mounted bullfight, these relationships are increasingly intensified in two fundamental ways: spatially and emotionally. The 'ability' in centaurability, it seems, is dependent on space, technology *and* emotion.

The co-penetration of human and non-human bodies that precedes but is intensified throughout the bullfight can be understood as a form of increasing spatial intimacy. However, this intimacy does not follow the regular and regulated patterning that can be evoked by a network approach (as critiqued by Pink 2011). Rather, this intimacy ebbs and flows with a rich emotional texture. In the extreme drama of the mounted bullfight, spatial intimacy evokes heart-stopping tensions surrounding touch-points and mortal thresholds of life and death. The mounted bullfight exemplifies the emotional texture and character of networks and illustrates the ways in which networks have natural, social and cultural edges, punctuations, fringes, limits and liminalities. Using the ethnographic detail of the mounted bullfight and the experiences of mounted bullfighters, I have been able to demonstrate the value of combining Lyng's (1990) concept of edgework with ANT approaches as well as interspecies relations. An edgework focus on sensations and motivations presupposes the importance of emotion in voluntary risk-taking activities. More importantly, the concept of edgework advocates a role for emotion in sociotechnical networks not only as an agential effect, but also as an affective agent.

References

Abarquero Durango, R. 1984. *El Toro, El Caballo y El Hombre Como Interpretes de la Fiesta Nacional: Control de la agresividad, del dolor y de la conducta.* Madrid: Consultores Editoriales, S.A.L.

Arévalo, J.C. 2001. 'Hermoso De Mendoza: '"El caballo es un capote, el caballo es una muleta"', *6Toros6*. Viewed 31 July 2001. <http://www.hermosodemendoza.com.htm/prensa01%20julio.htm>.

Arratia, M.-I. 1988. 'Bullfights: Art, sport, ritual', *Play & Culture* 1: 282-290.

Beckmann, J. 2004. 'Mobility and safety', *Theory Culture Society* 21 (4-5): 81-100. DOI: 10.1177/0263276404046062.

Belk, R.W. 1988. 'Possessions and the extended self', *Journal of Consumer Research* 15(2): 139-168.

Belk, R.W. 1996. 'Metaphoric relationships with pets', *Society and Animals* 4(2): 121-145.

Birke, L. 2007. '"Learning to speak horse": The culture of "Natural Horsemanship"', *Society and Animals* 15: 217-239.

Birke, L. 2008. 'Talking about horses: Control and freedom in the world of "Natural Horsemanship"', *Society and Animals* 16: 107-126.

Bissell, D. 2010. 'Passenger mobilities: Affective atmospheres and the sociality of public transport', *Environment and Planning D: Society and Space* 28(2): 270-289.

Bourdieu, P. 1977. *Outline of a Theory of Practice*. Cambridge: Cambridge University Press.

Bourdieu, P. 1990. *In Other Words: Essays towards a Reflexive Sociology*. Stanford: Stanford University Press.

Cintrón, C. 1968. *!Torera! Memoirs of a Bullfighter*. London: Macmillan and Company Ltd.

Conrad, J.R. 1957. *The Horn and the Sword*. Westport, CT: Greenwood Press.

Cornwell, J. 1997. 'Beauty and the beastly', *The Australian Magazine*, June 21-22, pp. 14-20.

Csikszentmihalyi, M. 1975. *Beyond Boredom and Anxiety: The Experience of Play in Work and Games*. London: Jossey-Bass Limited.

Csikszentmihalyi, M. 1990. *Flow: The Psychology of Optimal Experience*. New York: Harper Perennial.

Dant, T. 2004. 'The driver-car', *Theory Culture Society* 21(4-5): 61-79. DOI: 10.1177/0263276404046061.

de Cossío, J.M. 2000. *El Cossío*, vol.1. Madrid: Espasa Calpe, S.A.

Desmonde, W.H. 1952. 'The bullfight as a religious ritual', *American Imago* 9: 173-195.

Despret, V. 2004. 'The body we care for: Figures of Anthropo-zoo-genesis', *Body & Society* 10(2): 111-134.

Douglas, M. 1966. *Purity and Danger: An Analysis of Concepts of Pollution and Taboo*. London: Routledge and Kegan Paul.

Downey, G. 2010. '"Practice without theory": A neuroanthropological perspective on embodied learning', *Journal of the Royal Anthropological Institute* 16: S22-S40. DOI: 10.1111/j.1467-9655.2010.01608.x.

Fifield, W. 1978. *The Sherry Royalty*. Jerez, Spain: Sexta, S.A.

Foucault, M. 1978. *The History of Sexuality*, vol. 1: *An Introduction*. Trans. R. Hurley. New York: Pantheon.

Game, A. 2001. 'Riding: Embodying the centaur', *Body & Society* 7(4): 1-12.

Gargantilla Rodríguez, A. 2005. *Diccionario Taurino*. Madrid: Biblioteca DM.

Geertz, C. 1973. *The Interpretation of Cultures*. New York: Basic Books.

Grotjahn, M. 1959. 'On bullfighting and the future of tragedy', *International Journal of Psycho-Analysis* 40: 238-239.

Haraway, D. 2007. *When Species Meet*. Minneapolis: University of Minnesota Press.

Helmberger, W. 1994. *The Spanish Riding School in Vienna*. 5th edn. Barcelona: Editorial Escudo de Oro, S.A.

Hockey, J. and J. Allen Collinson. 2007. 'Grasping the phenomenology of sporting bodies', *International Review for the Sociology of Sport* 42(2): 115-131. DOI: 10.1177/1012690207084747.

Hunt, W. 1955. 'On bullfighting', *American Imago* 12: 343-353.

Ingham, J. 1964. 'The bullfighters', *American Imago* 21-22: 95-102.

Jiménez Benítez, M. 1994. *El Caballo en Andalucía: Orígenes e Historia; Cría y Doma*. Madrid: Ediciones Agrotécnicas, S.L.

Kothari, U.C. 1962. 'On the bullfight', *Psychoanalysis and the Psychoanalytic Review* 49(1): 123-128.

Lagarde, J., C. Peham, T. Lick and J.A.S. Kelso. 2005. 'Coordination dynamics of the horse-rider system', *Journal of Motor Behavior* 37(6): 418-424.

Latimer, J. and L. Birke. 2009. 'Natural relations: Horses, knowledge and technology', *The Sociological Review* 57(1): 2-27.

Latour, B. 1993. *We Have Never Been Modern*. Trans. C. Porter. Hemel Hempstead, UK: Harvester Wheatsheaf.

LeGuin, E. 2005. 'Man and horse in harmony'. In K. Raber and T.J. Tucker (Eds.), *The Culture of the Horse: Status, Discipline, and Identity in the Early Modern World* (pp. 175-196). New York: Palgrave Macmillan.

Lyng, S. 1990. 'Edgework: A social psychological analysis of voluntary risk taking', *The American Journal of Sociology* 95(4): 851-886.

Marvin, G. 1994 [1988]. *Bullfight*. New York: Basil Blackwell Inc.

Merleau-Ponty, M. 1962. *Phenomenology of Perception*. Trans. C. Smith. London: Routledge.

Milton, K. 2005. 'Meanings, feelings and human ecology'. In K. Milton and M. Svasek (Eds.), *Mixed Emotions: Anthropological Studies of Feeling* (pp. 25-42). Oxford and New York: Berg.

Ministerio de Justicia e Interior. 1996. 'Reglamento de espectaculos taurinos'. In Unión de Criadores de Toros de Lidia (Ed.), *Legislación Vigente en Materia Taurina* (pp. 13-62). Madrid: Boletón Oficial del Estado.

Moreno Pidal, M. 2004. *Método de Doma de Campo y Rejoneo*. Sevilla: Grupo Lettera, S.L.

Paniagua, C. 1992. 'Bullfight: The torero', *International Review of Psycho-Analysis* 19: 483-489.

Pineda Novo, D. 1988. *Centauros de la Marisma*. Sevilla: Gráf. Santa Maria, S.C.A.

Pink, S. 1996. 'Breasts in the bullring: Female physiology, female bullfighters and competing femininities', *Body & Society* 2(1): 45-64.

Pink, S. 2011. 'Sensory digital photography: Re-thinking "moving" and the image', *Visual Studies* 26(1): 4-13.

Pollock, R. 1974. 'Some psychoanalytic consideration of bull fighting and bull worship', *Israel Annals of Psychiatry and Related Disciplines* 12: 53-67.

Roe, E.J. 2009. 'Human-nonhuman'. In K. Rob and N. Thrift (Eds.), *International Encyclopedia of Human Geography* (pp. 251-257). Oxford: Elsevier.

Ross, F.C. 2004. 'Sense-scapes: Senses and emotion in the making of place', *Anthropology Southern Africa* 27(1/2): 35-42.

Shapiro, K. 1990. 'Understanding dogs through kinesthetic empathy, social construction, and history', *Anthrozoös* 3: 184-195.

Stranger, M. 1999. 'The aesthetics of risk: A study of surfing', *International Review for the Sociology of Sport* 34(3): 265-276. DOI: 10.1177/101269099034003003.

Thompson, K. 2007. 'Le Voyage du centaure: La Monte à la lance en espagne (XIVe-XXIe siècles)'. In D. Roche and D. Reytier (Eds.), *À cheval! Écuyers, Amazones & Cavaliers du XIVe au XXIe Siècle* (pp. 195-209). Paris: Association pour l'Académie d'Art Équestre de Versailles.

Thompson, K. 2010. 'Narratives of tradition: The invention of mounted bullfighting (*rejoneo*) as "the newest but also the oldest"', *Social Science History* 34(4): 523-561.

Thompson, K. 2011. 'Theorising rider-horse relations: An ethnographic illustration of the centaur metaphor in the Spanish bullfight'. In N. Taylor and T. Signal (Eds.), *Theorising Animals* (pp. 221-253). Leiden and Boston: Brill.

Thompson, K. 2012a. 'Bloodlust: In the blood of bulls, horses and bullfighters'. In S. Boccalatte and M. Jones (Eds.), *Blood* (pp. 15-16). Sydney: Boccalatte Pty Ltd.

Thompson, K. 2012b. 'Classy performances: The performance of class in the Andalusian bullfight from horseback (rejoneo)', *Journal of Spanish Cultural Studies* 13(2): 167-188.

Thompson, K. 2013a. '*Cojones* and *rejones*: Multiple ways of experiencing, expressing and interpreting gender in the Spanish mounted bullfight (*rejoneo*)'. In M. Adelman and J. Knijnik (Eds.), *Gender and Equestrian Sport* (pp. 127-147). New York: Springer.

Thompson, K. 2013b. 'Save me, save my dog: Increasing natural disaster preparedness and survival by addressing human-animal relationships', *Australian Journal of Communication* 40(1): 123-136.

Thompson, K. 2015. 'For pets' sake, save yourself: Motivating emergency and disaster preparedness through relations of animal guardianship', *Australian Journal of Emergency Management* 30(2): 43-46.

Thompson, K. and L. Birke. 2014. 'The horse has got to want to help: Human-animal habituses and networks in amateur show jumping'. In J. Gillett and M. Gilbert (Eds.), *Sport, Animals, and Society* (pp. 69-84). New York: Routledge.

Thompson, K., D. Every, S. Rainbird, V. Cornell, B. Smith and J. Trigg. 2014. 'No pet or their person left behind: Increasing the disaster resilience of vulnerable groups through animal attachment, activities and networks', *Animals* 4(2): 214-240.

Thompson, K. and C. Nesci. 2013. 'Over-riding concerns: Developing safe relations in the high-risk interspecies sport of eventing', *International Review for the Sociology of Sport*. DOI: 10.1177/1012690213513266.

Thrift, N. 1996. *Spatial Formations*. London: Sage.

Thrift, N. 1999. 'Steps to an ecology of place'. In D. Massey, J. Allen and P. Sarre (Eds.), *Human Geography Today* (pp. 297-322). Cambridge: Polity Press.

Tucker, T.J. 2005. 'Early Modern French noble identity and the equestrian "airs above the ground"'. In K. Raber and T.J. Tucker (Eds.), *The Culture of the Horse: Status, Discipline, and Identity in the Early Modern World* (pp. 273-309). New York: Palgrave Macmillan.

Vergunst, J. 2011. 'Technology and technique in a useful ethnography of movement', *Mobilities* 6(2): 203-219. DOI: 10.1080/17450101.2011.552900.

Whatmore, S. 2007 [1999]. 'Hybrid geographies: Rethinking the "human" in human geography'. In L. Kalof and A. Fitzgerald (Eds.), *The Animals Reader: The Essential Classic and Contemporary Writings* (pp. 336-348). Oxford: Berg.

Wipper, A. 2000. 'The partnership: The horse-rider relationship in eventing', *Symbolic Interaction* 23: 47-72.

6 | Sensual feasting:
Transforming spaces and emotions in Lihir

Susan R. Hemer

Abstract

This chapter explores how shifts between differing emotions are mediated spatially and sensually. Drawing on Hochschild's (1979) concepts of 'feeling rules' and 'emotion work', the chapter questions how spatial and sensual aspects of social events may evoke particular emotions and, in turn, how feeling rules for social situations may be transformed in the process. I focus on the case of events surrounding a project for women's development in Lihir, Papua New Guinea, in the early 2000s. One form of anger, a simmering withdrawal, was changed to open conflict following a large feast to mark the opening of a sewing centre. The sensuality of feasting, with its sounds, smells, tastes and crowds, allowed women to take ownership of the centre and of their right to openly express hostility. This case allows for critical reflection on the concept of feeling rules in a setting that places less emphasis on individual emotional management and more on social relatedness.

Introduction

In April 2002, the small boat harbour at Londolovit in Lihir, Papua New Guinea, came alive. Lihirian women took over the normally empty space with its yellow coronous road, green grass and large white metal building, and changed it into a bustling, noisy area. Thousands of people packed into the space to eat hot tubers and meaty pork, to watch dancers arrayed in neat lines moving to the sounds of beaten bamboo and *kundu* (hour glass) drums, to smell the scent of herbs adorning the dancers and hosts. They watched fashion parades with newly made garments and white wedding dresses, and listened to speeches by dignitaries and songs proclaiming women's togetherness.

This unprecedented event was planned and executed by Lihirian women's leaders to celebrate gaining their own space in Londolovit township. Yet this event was preceded by simmering conflict and followed by open conflict. In this chapter, I unravel this event through an understanding of its emotional, sensual and spatial dimensions. In doing so, I critically comment on the concepts of feeling rules and emotion work.

Senses, spaces, emotions

The last two or three decades have seen an outpouring of interest in emotions, the senses and embodiment in disciplines such as anthropology, geography and sociology. Sometimes these interests have been paired with an attention to space and place and have led to discussions and concepts such as emotional geographies (Davidson & Milligan 2004), topophilia (Tuan 1977; Hastrup 2011), sensuous geographies (Rodaway 1994; Paterson 2009), sense-scapes (Ross 2004) and Feld and Basso's collection *Senses of Place* (1996). These discussions and key concepts all aim, in their various incarnations, to draw attention to the ways senses or emotions are implicated in, evoked or constrained through places.

A few contributions to this area have discussed the ways that people can transform the emotional and sensual spaces they occupy. Matthee (2004) argues that women's engagement in the sensual practice of cooking and eating can reorientate gender relationships and allow women to reappropriate space in the context of Western Cape in South Africa. Wood and Smith (2004) describe the 'sound-space' of music as powerful and transformative of emotions, and they explore the ways it can be actively harnessed through music therapy. This chapter draws on these general understandings of not only the ways that spaces may evoke or shape emotions, but also the ways in which the sensorial and emotional qualities of spaces may be challenged or changed.

A key sociological contribution to this area is Hochschild's (1979; 1983) notion of 'feeling rules', and the 'emotion work' that may be needed to ensure that the rules associated with particular situations, or social spaces, are met. She argued that social situations are characterised by unwritten feeling rules, of which people are consciously aware. Situations have a conventional frame and a sense of what should be felt. Feeling rules specify the extent of feeling, the type of emotion and the duration of feeling (1979:563-4).

> We assess the 'appropriateness' of a feeling by making comparison between feeling and situation ... This comparison lends the assessor a 'normal' yardstick — a *socially* normal one. (1979:560, italics in the original text)

When this assessment of feeling suggests that there is a mismatch, then people engage in 'emotion work' to change their feelings. This work is not aimed at simply appearing to feel appropriately — better known as 'impression management' (Goffman 1971) — or 'display rules' (Ekman & Friesen 1975; Matsumoto 1996), but at actually *feeling* appropriately. Hochschild argues that this occurs through deep acting, and efforts to evoke, shape or suppress particular feelings (1979:561-2). In particular, the techniques of emotion work include cognitive efforts to change images, or thoughts to change feelings associated with them; bodily efforts to change somatic or other physical aspects of emotion; and expressive emotion work to shape the expressive gestures of emotion in attempting to change the inner feeling (562).

Hochschild's concepts of feeling rules and emotion work rely, first, on an individual, conscious actor working on their own or someone else's feelings. Second, Hochschild also focuses on feeling rules as given for a particular situation. Both of these assumptions are problematic. What I would like to question here is how the feeling rules for a situation may be actively challenged or changed, and how emotion work may be accomplished at a social rather than individual level. If, in Hochschild's terms, cognitive, bodily and expressive techniques can work to change individual feelings, it would seem that certain aspects of situations would need to be altered to transform the feeling rules of the situations. Here I would suggest that sensorial and spatial characteristics of situations are crucial to their feeling rules, and shifts in these characteristics are key to the social emotion work needed not only to challenge feeling rules but also to transform the emotions of groups. This chapter aims to explore the possibilities for such an analysis through the case study of women's associations in Lihir.

Mining and Lihirian women

The four Lihir islands are home to some 15 000 Lihirians with a clan-based matrilineal society. Prior to the 1990s, Lihirians relied on subsistence production of root crops and other vegetables, particularly yams, as well as some fishing, cash cropping of coconuts, and remittances from labour. Despite matrilineal inheritance, leadership and land management was generally men's domain, with women having few opportunities for control of land or ritual exchanges in their own right (Hemer n.d.; Macintyre 2003). A large gold mine was constructed on the main island of the group in the mid-1990s and began production in 1997, managed by the Lihir Management Company [LMC]. With the mine have come numerous changes, such as improved health and education facilities, a ring road around the main island, opportunities for employment and business activities, cars, alcohol and migrants from outside Lihir. Despite these many changes, most Lihirians continue to rely on subsistence production from gardens, and this heavily depends on women's labour.

Before mining, women were organised into village-based women's church groups — generally *Katolik Mamas* ('Catholic Mothers') or United Church Women's Fellowship, depending on the affiliation of the village. In the early 1990s, it was decided that an overarching women's organisation was needed to provide a representative body for Lihirian women in negotiations with the company planning to mine gold.[1] Women had very little input into negotiations or political processes on the islands (Macintyre 2002; 2003). So at this early stage the Petztorme Women's Association was begun.[2] A female consultant to the Community Relations Department of the mine, Suzy Bonnell, worked with Lihirian women to set up the organisation, which could then liaise with the Women's section to address issues affecting Lihirian women. Under Petztorme, the leaders for village church groups became part of the general committee, and all Lihirian women were nominally part of Petztorme.

From as early as 1992, Lihirian women were calling for an area in which they could hold meetings and conferences, and where they could learn new skills. As Petztorme began with little assistance from the mining company or externally, it had no funds with which to construct such a building or space. Instead, it started with the idea of self-help and incremental change (Macintyre 2003:124), with a number of relatively small income-generating projects in the late 1990s and early 2000s. Given the pace of change and development due to mining in Lihir, criticisms arose that Petztorme was 'doing nothing' for Lihirian women.

A new project for women began in 2000 with the inception of a program of sewing training for Lihirian women. An expatriate woman trained as a dressmaker began offering training in sewing with the help of seed funds raised through a cultural exchange program and craft fair held in the mining township. This training program was soon named Tutorme, and had an Advisory Committee set up to manage the programs and funds.[3] At the time, I was working on a community health research project for the mining company, and I was invited to become a member of the Advisory Committee, with other expatriate and Lihirian women. Over time, Tutorme provided sewing and home safety training to dozens of Lihirian women, and it outgrew its small building in early 2001. This need for a new space for Tutorme precipitated the

---

1   At the time, the company in question was Kennecott, then Davey Kinhill Four Daniel. During construction, it was the Lihir Management Company, a wholly owned subsidiary of Rio Tinto; then it was Lihir Gold Limited; finally, more recently, the company is Newcrest Mining.
2   *Petztorme* means 'work together' (*petz* — work, and *torme* — together).
3   *Tutorme* means 'stand together' (*tu* — stand, and *torme* — together). It does not mean 'tutor me' as was the common assumption and mispronunciation by expatriates.

growing conflict between Petztorme and Tutorme, and between expatriate and Lihirian women's views of development. This simmering conflict became the subject of work and transformation at the feasting held to celebrate Lihirian women gaining a space in Londolovit township.

Pre-feasting simmering conflict: *Sa mus*

One of the key desires (*a le*) of Lihirian women was a space in which to conduct meetings, workshops and other activities. *A le* can be translated as a desire, a want or a need, and is etymologically related to the term *leimuli*, meaning to love or desire. Lihirians do not linguistically distinguish between requiring something and simply wanting it. Hence their desire was also understood as a requirement or a need. Their desire or need was for the space to be centrally located for women's access, to have a good-sized area, and to have all groups working for women co-located. Instead, spatially, women were both separated and cramped. In 2000, Petztorme was functioning out of a rusted shipping container in one part of Londolovit township, Tutorme was located in a small building atop the hill near the residential area of the township, and there was also a 'Women's section' located in the Community Relations Department of LMC. None of the groups working for women felt secure, as all buildings were borrowed and on the Lease for Mining Purposes [LMP]. Communication was difficult, with neither Petztorme or Tutorme having a telephone line or vehicle.

The spatial and communication difficulties made co-operation essential to the functioning of the women's groups. Initially, the relationships between the two women's organisations in Lihir had been positive. Petztorme provided some funds for refreshment for the Tutorme training classes, and acted as the means by which information was distributed to women in villages about the training courses on offer. Women's church groups in villages also cooked lunches for training sessions for a fee. In turn, Tutorme provided the Petztorme Executive with information about the progression of classes.

In 2001, LMC offered to find a large building, and donate it for the use of Lihirian women, as they were keen on supporting Tutorme. This seemed the ideal opportunity for Lihirian women to co-locate those working for women's development. LMC offered a spacious unused building near the small boat harbour in Londolovit township. Located in a place that had excellent boat and road access, this seemed the answer to women's needs and desires. Yet LMC appeared to see this as an opportunity to provide Tutorme with the space and resources to make a successful sewing and training centre, rather than a general centre for women. They did not want to co-locate Petztorme and the Women's section of LMC with Tutorme.

Relations between Lihirian women and LMC deteriorated. Petztorme withdrew support from Tutorme, and some women talked about boycotting the Centre.

Eventually, the women agreed with LMC that Petztorme could choose either to have an office space within the Tutorme building, or have a small building constructed where they chose.[4] Petztorme chose the latter option, and positioned their new building in front of the new Tutorme building, hence achieving the desired co-location of women's organisations, and their accessibility to Lihirian women in a prominent public site.

Yet despite this apparently amicable solution, relationships between Lihirian women's leaders and LMC remained strained. What ensued was what can be termed *mus*, a form of withdrawal and a simmering silence. Lihirian women would either not attend Tutorme Advisory Committee meetings, or would attend but not oppose moves instigated by expatriate women on the committee. Seeing the meetings as particularly formal and public, chaired by an expatriate woman and with minutes formally taken by myself and distributed later, Lihirian women felt only able to voice their opinions in the Advisory committee meetings when matters were raised as questions or suggestions. When matters were raised more forcibly by expatriates, Lihirian women would show little sign of dissent and would certainly not publicly disagree. For example, the value of the Advisory Committee was questioned in February 2001 and again in August that year, and on both occasions Lihirian women suggested that the committee was still needed. Yet when the Chair of the Committee announced the abolition of the Committee in February 2002, Lihirian women acceded. Privately they were furious.

Mus is a behaviour seen as arising from anger (*lil tua*), and is understood to be a common and appropriate response of women to slights from another party (Hemer 2013). It is often not seen as appropriate for women to express anger in more open forms such as verbal or physical aggression, particularly when there may be differentials of status. In the case of *mus*, the person who is the cause of the *lil tua* needs to rectify the injury rather than apologise for wrongdoing. If this cannot be done, then the *mus* will just gradually disappear with the passing of time, or, alternatively, it can be indicative of a more long-term breach in social relations. In the case here, neither LMC nor the expatriate women on the Advisory committee seemed willing to be more accommodating of Lihirian women's desires for development in the particular way that they understood it.

This withdrawal by Lihirian women was taken by expatriate women on the committee either as disinterest or tacit agreement with whatever plans were put forward. There appeared little understanding of the ways by which Lihirian women might negotiate through informal and lengthy meetings in order to resolve issues of contention. It appeared to me that the likely course of action from this point was further withdrawal of Lihirian women from the role of organising the work of Tutorme.

---

4   This was to be based on the design of houses built by LMC within villages as part of their village development scheme. These houses are high-set wooden constructions, with a number of internal rooms, but no bathroom facilities.

It was at this point, in early 2002, that the opening ceremony for the Petztorme and Tutorme buildings began to be planned, through the Advisory Committee of Tutorme and the Executive of Petztorme. Even in the weeks leading up to the opening celebration, relations were poor, and the expatriate manager of Tutorme was concerned that the celebrations were going to be a complete failure. Instead, the opening was one of the more memorable occasions in Londolovit township.

Sensual feasting and *sa ngat*

The opening celebration for the Petztorme and Tutorme buildings was no small affair. Lihirian women's leaders, following Lihir custom, planned the opening as a *karot*, a major event comprising the gathering of many people, the contribution of dances by those coming to the feast, and the consumption of pork. Each ward on Lihir had provided feasting food for the opening including pigs, and, as is the custom on Lihir, each contribution of a pig was accompanied by a dance (*a ngues*, or, in Neo-Melanesian Tok Pisin, *singsing*). *Karot* are typically the scene for the transformation of relationships. The various mortuary rituals (*Mbiektip, Pkepke, Tunkanut*), opening of new men's houses (*Tmaziarih*), and major church celebrations (such as confirmation; see Hemer 2011) are all *karot*, and perform a shift in relations, such as the movement of a person from childhood to adulthood, from life to death, or the transference of rights in land (Hemer 2013).

The sensorial aspects of this feast link it to previous *karot*, and hence provide participants with the situational guides for feeling rules. Some *karot*, such as *Pkepke*, are characterised by the singing of the sad *yiargnen* songs that mark mourning, and either slow dances or none at all. This *karot*, however, had much more in common with the noisy, bustling *Tunkanut*, where debts to the deceased are finished, people feel relieved, and new relationships between young people are kindled. The feeling rules for *karot* such as this are to be happy (*sa ngat*), evoked by the vigorous dancing, the upbeat music and colourful decorations.

Like many *karot*, this event was spread over two days. The first day, a Friday, was the more low-key, with tours of the two buildings, a fashion parade of garments made by Tutorme, speeches by the President of Petztorme and by the President of the New Ireland Women's Council, and singing by many choirs. Lunch was provided by the local catering company, NCS [Niolam Catering Services], paid for by Petztorme Women's Association. This first day was particularly aimed at the Seventh Day Adventist members of Petztorme and Tutorme, who would not be able to attend the final day due to religious restrictions.

The final day was a sensual feast. Thousands of people attended, crowding the area at the small boat harbour. Security working for the mining company had hoped to control the area with both barricades and their presence, with dances carefully organised to occur on the field area behind the buildings one at a time. Yet instead the day took on a life of its own, with two or three dances on at any one time, positioned between the buildings or on the road in front of them, and none in the field. In the afternoon, the area was packed tightly with people surrounding these dances, as new dancers marched into the area to begin, and women of the organising committee walked around each dance to welcome it with shell money and calls of '*A ginas!*' ('Happiness!') or '*Berksien!*' ('Sisters!'). This movement and crowding is in sharp contrast to the empty stillness of the area normally, and is characteristic of feasting in Lihir.

Visually, the day was a spectacle, and Lihirian women were on show. During the tours, visitors were treated to a visual history of Tutorme in photographs, and displays of the clothes and goods they had made. Once again there was a fashion parade of garments made by Tutorme, modelled by Lihirian women and members of the township. Then there were the dance performances: the male Lipuko culture group were painted half in red and half in white, with beaten bark pants; other dance performances were by groups in brightly coloured *meri*-blouses, or dressed in matching *laplaps* with colourful decorations of dyed feathers. There was a total of twenty-nine performances across the two days by men's and women's groups, marking the significance of this event.

The smells of feasting are quite distinctive, and arise from a mixture of cooked yams and sweet potato, cooked pork, the wilted leaves used to cover the ground ovens, and the heady scents of the herbs used by people for decoration.

> Odors lend character to objects and places, making them distinctive, easier to identify and remember. (Tuan 1977:11)

These scents are in the air before the food is fully cooked, but strengthen as the ground ovens are opened. *Karon* (*Euodia hortensis*) and *zingil*, a local herb that smells like a cross between basil and marjoram, are used for decoration, and give off strong scents as people brush against one another in the crowded feasting area. For this feast, *karon* was worn by members of the organising group including myself; it is said to demonstrate that one is *sa ngat*, or happy. For people at the feast, these scents link this event to ones they have attended in the past.

Food is crucial to the definition and transformational aspects of a *karot*. As for most *karot*, for this feast, groups that provided a traditional dance (*a ngues*) also brought at least one pig. These groups tended to be either male or female, and were village-based, rather than clan-based as is the case for many feasts. Each ward in Lihir also provided a range of vegetable foods, mostly yams, mami and sweet potatoes. This food was cooked in large ground ovens, and during the final day was distributed to all ward groups, who then subdivided the food for all those attending. There was plenty of food, a crucial sensorial aspect for creating a memory of this feast as an efficacious event (Eves 1996).

Like many *karot*, this feast was characterised by the sounds of music and song. There were many choirs for the two days, and the organising committee sang a song specifically written for the event, which contained a line stating: 'Petztorme, Tutorme, arise and join together; to raise the name of Lihir, we will be happy'. One of the choirs sang condemning domestic violence. The music was generally upbeat, with the use of *kundu* drums, bamboo clappers, and even electric guitars in one performance. The use of conch shells was avoided, as these signal sadness. As Wood and Smith state, 'musicians actively create emotionally charged contexts' (2004:537). This *karot* was clearly a time for celebration: this was a distinct break with the anger and withdrawal that had characterised the previous months.

In key sensorial ways, this event was a *karot*, and one which was celebratory. The crowds, smells, feast food, dances, songs and music evoked *sa ngat*. People's behaviour reflected this feeling: towards the end of the final day of feasting, there were shouts and laughter as members of the organising committee started a spontaneous dance. This included both Lihirian and expatriate women who had been at odds for months and even in the days leading up to the feast. The sensorial aspects of the feast had accomplished the social emotion work needed to evoke feelings which were appropriate to this event. I also joined in and we all boogied around between the Petztorme and Tutorme buildings to some music while the crowd watched. We were elated at how well the event had gone, and partially exhausted after months of planning.

While clearly linked to other *karot*, this feast was in other ways unique and prompted new understandings of Lihirian women. In verbal terms, in speeches, this event was on the one hand dedicated to a celebration of Christian togetherness and blessing; on the other hand, it was a platform for talking about women's roles, and the relationship between women and men. Hence Bishop Ambrose Kiapseni of New Ireland Province held an outdoor church service, and then blessed both buildings while we sang *Bless this House*. There was a speech by a Lihirian woman who thanked God for this opportunity, and then argued that Lihirian women could contribute more to communities than just housework. Sir Anthony Siaguru, Papua New Guinea statesman and member of the Board of Lihir Gold, gave a speech arguing that men should be more supportive of women. Margaret Elias, secretary for the Department of Labour and Employment, talked about women's role at the National level in Papua New Guinea and argued that men should not beat their wives, and then she cut the ribbon to officially open the buildings. Such public statements about women's roles and domestic violence were unprecedented in Lihir, and clearly marked this out as a women's feast. All the organisers, or *hukarot*, were women, a distinguishing feature of this feast.

Many sensorial aspects of this *karot* linked it to past *karot* and to feeling rules which evoke *sa ngat* or happiness; however, particular verbal and organisational aspects challenged accepted understandings of Lihirian women. On the final day itself, it was clear that there was some process of transformation underway: that is the core work of all *karot*, and is particularly highlighted through the killing and consumption of pigs. Feasting in Papua New Guinea is well understood to be more than simply a gathering with food, and scholars have consistently noted the work that feasts do in processes of social reproduction and transformation (for the New Ireland context, see Bolyanatz 2000; Brouwer 1980; Eves 1996; Foster 1995; Wagner 1986). Sensorial aspects of feasting are crucial to these transformations, as Eves argues, particularly in terms of the sense of fullness and overeating for the Lelet area.

Just what aspect of social relations was being changed in this context was unclear, however. At the feasting, Lihirian women clearly demonstrated their capacity to be united and organise a major event. This directly contradicted the accusations often levelled at women by Lihirian men that they cannot co-operate. They were supported at this event by both the mining company through its presence, including the Board of Lihir Gold, and by Lihirian men through both their presence and their contributions of dancing and food. These factors, and the open statements about male-female relationships, suggested to me that there might be a transformation of gender relationships in Lihir following this event. It was only in the months following this event that it became apparent that this was not the case.

Post-feast open conflict

In the weeks following the opening celebrations, there seemed to be a shift from the former state of *mus*, or simmering withdrawal, to one of engagement. Things appeared to be functioning well. Petztorme and Tutorme were located near each other at the small boat harbour. The committee that had functioned to plan the celebrations was retained as the Advisory committee to Tutorme. Women continued to attend training at Tutorme, with some 200 being trained on domestic or industrial sewing machines in 2000-01. Some women gained employment with Tutorme, and were filling contracts for the public or for LMC (for example, making curtains or embroidering names on shirts). Petztorme, meanwhile, was busy with its income-generating projects, such as the market in Londolovit town, and by mid-2002 had some PNG K50 000 in the bank. With the spatial linking of Petztorme and Tutorme, there was an expectation that social relations would mirror this.

Yet all was not well (Macintyre 2003:130). The Women's section of LMC remained located in the Community Relations office away from the small boat harbour. While it had occasional access to a car, both Petztorme and Tutorme did not, which hampered their efforts to work together. Although Petztorme and Tutorme had been co-located, this did not seem to signal similar shifts in relationships. Petztorme leaders continued to feel that they did not have a significant input into organisational issues in Tutorme.

While the Advisory Committee of Tutorme had once functioned as a decision-making entity to which the Co-ordinator reported, from 2002 the Advisory committee only provided general advice on cultural matters related to training and sewing, such as the days or hours that women were available. It became an informal committee, with no Chair, no Secretary and no minutes recorded. In the four months following the opening celebrations, there was only one meeting. Instead, decision-making powers from 2002 were held by a Financial Management Committee largely composed of LMC representatives and the Co-ordinator of Tutorme, with two Lihirian women present in their roles as employees of Tutorme or of the LMC Women's Section.

Lihirian women privately spoke of their anger (*lil tua*) at the direction that Tutorme had taken. *Lil tua* is the expected response to what is perceived as the denial of social relationships and mutual obligations (Hemer 2013). In this case, women felt that there was an obligation for LMC representatives and expatriate members of the Financial Management Committee to share knowledge and decision-making powers about Tutorme. Instead, women felt excluded from knowing about the financing of the Centre and about its plans for the future, despite it being expressly for their benefit. Unlike with the situation before the opening celebrations, however, this *lil tua* did not result in *mus*: instead, it became open conflict.

Lil tua can lead to a number of courses of action. Some of these actions seem indirect, and *mus* is one of these, as was seen before the opening celebrations for the Petztorme and Tutorme buildings. Other somewhat passive actions associated with *lil tua* are *eretek*, a form of barbed joking at someone else's expense, and *tetnge piel*, or gossip. Both *eretek* and *tetnge piel* are ways of expressing anger such that the object of the anger may become aware of a critique of their behaviour without being directly confronted. While there was some gossip about the state of Tutorme and the actions of the Co-ordinator prior to the opening celebrations, most angry action was in the form of *mus*. What was seen after the feasting, however, were more direct forms of angry action. This was not in the form of violence (*eresas*), which is one possible way of expressing *lil tua*, but instead was a public critique.

About two months after the opening celebrations, Lihirian women held a meeting at the Petztorme building and discussed courses of action. They resolved, at that meeting, to call for the sackings of both the expatriate female Co-ordinator of Tutorme, and the Lihirian male Manager of the Business Development Section of LMC. They believed that both were not working in a frank and sincere manner in the best interests of Lihirian women. There was concern that the current status and future of Tutorme was being concealed, and that there was a lack of input into decision making about the Centre. They drafted the letters, a group of women present signed them, and they sent them to the mining company.

At the same meeting, the option of placing a *golgol* (or, in Tok Pisin, *gorgor*) on the gates of the Tutorme building was discussed. This would effectively shut down the operations of the Centre. In Lihir, a *golgol* is a ginger plant that is tied onto or around objects to prohibit use or action of those objects. While when tied to things that are in the process of being made or built it signals the need to stop work and negotiate, when tied to trees it prohibits use of their fruit. There is a clear understanding in Lihir that, in order to be able to place a *golgol* on a tree, garden or building, one needs to believe that one is the rightful owner of the these things; if that is not the case, one is liable to a fine of a pig. Hence the women discussing the possibility of placing a *golgol* on the Tutorme building were making a clear ownership claim — ownership that was earned through the performance of *kastam* work at the opening celebrations. These two forms of public critique were aimed at clearly expressing the women's anger, while trying to change the situation or gain some level of control over it.

Despite the shift from simmering withdrawal to actions of open conflict, there was no satisfactory resolution of the conflict surrounding Tutorme. The *gorgor* was placed on Tutorme, and remained for some four months. During this time, LMC investigated the role of the Lihirian female leader of the Women's section in potentially instigating and encouraging the conflict. It did not remove either the Co-ordinator of Tutorme or the Manager of the Business Development section; nor did it engage more with Lihirian women. Eventually, the leader of the Women's section resigned to more fully support Lihirian women. Hence, as a strategy, open conflict was a failure due to the lack of political power of Lihirian women in the face of a multinational mining company. Yet this does not detract from the analysis of the role of sensual feasting in transforming Lihirian women's relationship to the space at the small boat harbour, and the emotional tone and actions of Lihirian women.

Conclusion

Prior to the sensual feasting commemorating the opening of the Petztorme and Tutorme buildings, it was clear that relationships among Lihirian women, and between them and mining company representatives, had particular spatial and emotional dimensions. Spatially, there was separation among the different women's groups, Petztorme, Tutorme and the Women's Section, and this separation caused concern. Emotionally, there was considerable anger expressed in the form of *mus*, or simmering withdrawal. *Mus* is, in fact, a lack of sensorial engagement with the target of the anger, and hence the spatial, emotional and sensorial aspects of relationships at this time were characterised by separation.

With the opening celebrations, there was a clear shift in spatial and sensorial organisation, with a bustling and crowded small boat harbour that was sensorially enriched by the sights, smells, sounds and tastes of feasting. These changes evoked transformations in the emotions of Lihirian women, particularly those women of the Advisory or organising committees. Happiness — *sa ngat* — was expressed through statements, through decoration and through spontaneous dance. The feast was highly successful in achieving this emotional shift, and in the recognition of the efforts of Lihirian women through Petztorme and Tutorme.

While the sensorial and spatial transformations inherent in the feast passed — the area became quiet and uncrowded once again — the effects of this shift remained. Lihirian women did not return to their former state of *mus*. Instead they held greater expectations of co-operation and control; when this was not forthcoming they were able to express their anger in more direct forms, having earned this right through the transformative spatial and sensual properties of their *karot*.

Feeling rules are not just relevant to an individual's emotional state in particular situations. While for Hochschild, her focus was on an individual measuring their feelings against a set of rules, and then individually working to shape appropriate emotion, in the case above, feeling rules constrained women's ability to directly express anger to people in positions of power or with greater social status. Advisory Committee meetings were formal spaces with a subdued atmosphere. Women needed to follow the often unspoken rules regarding addressing a meeting through the Chair. This constrained their ability to disagree, and encouraged the experience of anger as *mus*. The sensual feasting, once again, carried its own feeling rules regarding the requirement to be, and express, happiness. The feasting also worked as a social form of emotion work not only to produce this happiness, but also then to allow women to express anger more directly in the months following by changing women's status through ownership of space.

Rather than rely on cognitive, bodily or expressive means to achieve emotion work as Hochschild argued is the case for individuals, social emotional work, I would suggest, relies on sensorial elements. These sensorial elements, such as movement and crowding, odours and flavours, sounds and music, are able to impact upon groups of people: they are shared experiences. Hochschild uses the example of being sad at funerals as a feeling rule (1983:63-8). But how is it that we know we should be sad at a funeral? At least partially it is by culturally accepted sensorial cues through particular styles of dress, of music, perhaps processions, and flowers. These sensorial elements evoke the emotions for both individuals and groups in a way that need not be consciously known. Events such as funerals or feasts do the emotion work sensorially for the groups of people who attend these social situations to ensure they comply with feeling rules.

Yet feeling rules should also not be seen as static and given. Clearly, the rules for social situations shift over time, and with the particularities of any given situation. So there are funerals which convey a more celebratory atmosphere than usual, or are more formal. Some deaths carry more weight of sadness than others. Shifts in feeling rules are marked by sensorial shifts in the social situations, and such sensorial shifts provide cues or evoke the appropriate feelings, as well as their intensity and duration. This can be seen in the case study in this chapter through the changes in women's right to openly express hostility.

Postscript

On my return to Lihir in 2011, I found that the Tutorme building at the small boat harbour had been condemned and abandoned. I knew that the Co-ordinator had left Lihir in 2005, and, as women had predicted and feared, Tutorme's continued existence was unsustainable without the driving force of the Chair of the Advisory Committee and the Co-ordinator. The industrial and domestic sewing machines, bought with LMC money, were stored in shipping containers in front of the building. While there was some talk of reinvigorating the Tutorme Sewing Centre, it seemed unlikely in the short term. While Lihirian women were unsuccessful in acting to gain control of Tutorme in 2002, their exclusion from knowledge and decision making clearly had longer-term consequences.

References

Bolyanatz, A.H. 2000. *Mortuary Feasting on New Ireland: The Activation of Matriliny among the Sursurunga*. Westport, CT: Bergin and Garvey.

Brouwer, E.C. 1980. 'A Malangan to cover the grave: Funerary ceremonies in Mandak'. PhD Thesis, University of Queensland, Queensland.

Davidson, J. and C. Milligan. 2004. 'Embodying emotion, sensing space: Introducing emotional geographies', *Social and Cultural Geography* 5(4): 523-532.

Ekman, P. and W.V. Friesen. 1975. *Unmasking the Face: A Guide to Recognizing Emotions from Facial Expressions*. Englewood Cliffs, NJ: Prentice Hall.

Eves, R. 1996. 'Remembrance of things passed: Memory, body and the politics of feasting in Papua New Guinea', *Oceania* 66: 266-277.

Feld, S. and K. Basso. 1996. *Senses of Place*. Santa Fe, NM: School of American Research Press.

Foster, R.J. 1995. *Social Reproduction and History in Melanesia: Mortuary Ritual, Gift Exchange, and Custom in the Tanga Islands*. Cambridge: Cambridge University Press.

Goffman, E. 1971. *The Presentation of Self in Everyday Life*. Harmondsworth, UK: Penguin.

Hastrup, K. 2011. 'Emotional topographies: The sense of place in the Far North'. In J. Davies and D. Spencer (Eds.), *Emotions in the Field: The Psychology and Anthropology of Fieldwork Experience* (pp. 191-211). Stanford: Stanford University Press.

Hemer, S.R. 2011. 'Local, regional and worldly interconnections: The Catholic and United Churches in Lihir, Papua New Guinea', *The Asia Pacific Journal of Anthropology* 12(1): 60-73.

Hemer, S.R. 2013. *Tracing the Melanesian Person: Emotions and Relationships in Lihir*. Adelaide: University of Adelaide Press.

Hemer, S.R. 2011. 'Gender and mining: Women's associations and women's status in Lihir, PNG', plenary paper presented at the *Mining and Mining Policy in the Pacific*, Noumea, New Caledonia, 22 November 2011.

Hochschild, A.R. 1979. 'Emotion work, feeling rules and social structure', *The American Journal of Sociology* 85(3): 551-575.

Hochschild, A.R. 1983. *The Managed Heart: Commercialization of Human Feeling*. Berkeley: University of California Press.

Macintyre, M. 2002. 'Women and mining projects in Papua New Guinea: Problems of consultation, representation, and women's rights as citizens'. In I. Macdonald and C. Rowland (Eds.), *Tunnel Vision: Women, Mining and Communities* (pp. 26-29). Fitzroy: Oxfam Community Aid Abroad.

Macintyre, M. 2003. 'Petztorme women: Responding to change in Lihir, Papua New Guinea', *Oceania* 74(1-2): 120-133.

Matsumoto, D. 1996. *Unmasking Japan: Myths and Realities about the Emotions of the Japanese*. Stanford: Stanford University Press.

Matthee, D.D. 2004. 'Towards an emotional geography of eating practices: An exploration of the food rituals of women of colour working on farms in the Western Cape', *Gender, Place and Culture* 11(3): 437-443.

Paterson, M. 2009. 'Haptic geographies: Ethnography, haptic knowledges and sensuous dispositions', *Progress in Human Geography* 33(6): 766-788.

Rodaway, P. 1994. *Sensuous Geographies: Body, Sense, Place*. London: Routledge.

Ross, F.C. 2004. 'Sense-scapes: Senses and emotions in the making of place', *Anthropology Southern Africa* 27(1 & 2): 35-42.

Tuan, Y-F. 1977. *Space and Place: The Perspective of Experience*. Minneapolis: University of Minnesota Press.

Wagner, R. 1986. *Asiwinarong: Ethos, Image and Social Power among the Usen Barok of New Ireland*. Princeton: Princeton University Press.

Wood, N. and S.J. Smith. 2004. 'Instrumental routes to emotional geographies', *Social and Cultural Geography* 5(4): 533-548.

7 Anxious Spaces:

The intersection of sexuality, the senses and emotion in fieldwork in Nepal

Sarah Homan

Abstract

This chapter argues that personal sensorial and emotional experiences in fieldwork can be important for the acquisition of anthropological knowledge. Conducting research on gendered subjectivities and discourses of honour and shame in remote Western Nepal as a first-time female fieldworker, I had a clear realisation of the intersection of senses, emotions and space. The Nepali lifestyle and lived spaces gave rise to a specific bodily praxis, in which corporeality, senses and emotions played an important role. In particular, being categorised as both woman and other attracted much unwanted sexual attention. As a result I 'felt' myself 'in' my body acutely, which at times gave rise to a high level of anxiety and awareness. My chapter will focus on this experience, which led me to feel and (re)act in certain ways. This relates to wider themes of gender, sexuality, comportment and honour in Nepali life, which are issues that Nepali women confront on a daily level. In the chapter, I explore the extent to which managing my visibility and 'dulling the senses' (see Desjarlais 1997) of sight and hearing as techniques of comportment and ease of movement during fieldwork had a significant impact on my understanding of how it 'feels' to be a woman in Nepal. This chapter will seek to explore the importance of such corporeal and emotional experiences of the intersection of senses, space and emotion in the acquisition of anthropological knowledge in 'the field'.

Introduction

To feel like a woman in Nepal and feel like a woman in Australia are different experiences. In Australia as a woman I feel more confident, respected and carefree. It's almost shameful to say, but I never thought about what it meant to be a woman in Australia, what it feels like from the inside looking out at the world. In Nepal it is a completely different and embodied experience. In Nepal I mentally prepare myself as I step out of the house, my own private space. I put up a shield to protect my sensitivities, as people are prone to laughter, sniggers and catcalls. Or not even so nasty as this; a simple 'Namaste!' still requires me to prepare and return the pleasantry in a language I am not accustomed to. The smile and hand prayer signal is a performance I am not familiar with. I feel my shoulders drop and my eyes cast downwards as I walk past large groups, especially men. I shut my mouth and listen more than I talk. I act demure and subordinate. I wear sunglasses not for the glare but for the shield it offers my face and eye contact. When I engage in a pleasant and wanted discussion with someone I take them off. When I don't want to do so, I put them straight back on, to act as a barrier between the unwanted and me. I feel entirely naked without them for they are, in a sense, a weapon of sorts. I wear loose 'Western' clothing or Nepali clothing to prevent the attention my body attracts to men. Pornography and alcohol[1] and lack of opportunity (education, too) are some major problems of young men in this district, presumably much of Nepal. Many people tell me young men gather, drink raksī and even watch pornography together, forming an objectified view of women, particularly foreign women. I am one of two young Western women in this town. The other is a good friend of mine and has lived here three years. We both share experiences of being addressed as though we were prostitutes and constantly asked, 'I fuck you?' with a dirty snigger from the Nepali boys. In Australia I would more likely talk back, feeling a little braver. Here you physically feel stopped by an unseen force. That force is a mixture of things I cannot place; language barrier, propriety, fear, culture, uselessness. They want photos of me all the time and I can't help but wonder, 'Why?' I feel so desperate to be invisible. They perceive me as a promiscuous Westerner from American film. That is the violence I experience and feel every day. (Excerpt from field diary, 2009)

This chapter will look at womanhood in Bhaktanagar, Nepal[2], and my experiences in my first field site, as I sought to study gendered subjectivities in relation to discourses of honour (*ijjat*) and shame (*lāj*). While I came across a variety of ethnographic information, reflexivity generated by personal experiences was, in many ways, very

---

1 The Nepali word for alcohol is *raksī*.
2 The name of this town is a pseudonym.

informative. Through my own experiences, I came to understand the central influence *ijjat* played in directing women's practices, understandings and experiences. That is, I shared 'similar processes of embodiment' (Unnithan-Kumar & De Neve 2006:8) with my informants. Reflexivity is useful as long as it contributes to the anthropologist's understandings and generates knowledge (see Bourdieu 2003). As a term it 'makes a problem out of what was once unproblematic: the figure of the fieldworker' (Strathern 1991:108). It dares the ethnographer to subject herself to the same scrutiny to which she subjects her informants and asks, 'What is the basis for my knowing?'

This chapter looks at a number of intersecting elements — namely, gendered subjectivity, sexuality, honour, comportment, senses, emotions, and space/place, and how the interaction of these led to the acquisition of a level of knowledge within me.

> By contextualising sexuality in the fieldwork experience, anthropologists may add elegant tools to their scientific and intellectual toolboxes. This involves working from the body, as well as from the mind. By funnelling data gathered in this way through the senses, fuelled by access to the full range of human emotions, it is possible to create texts which I contend will better enhance our understanding of other cultures (or groups within them) and of ourselves. (Altork 2007:93)

Altork's sexual experience in her field site was predominantly a positive one. Mine was a mixture of both negative and positive aspects. However, examining this dimension of fieldwork and the emotions that arose out of it — whether a positive engagement in a consensual relationship or the experience of sexual and verbal harassment — was an informative element of my project. To omit emotions in the pursuit of objectivity would obscure what I experienced and learnt in the field, which, at least in part, helped me to understand the situations and relationships of the unfamiliar social world I had entered. I do not argue that experiential knowledge is somehow 'denser', and therefore better, than other forms of knowledge. However, I do propose that it adds valuable insight and depth to the anthropologist's understanding and is, therefore, useful when carried out in conjunction with other ethnographic methodologies (see De Neve & Unnithan-Kumar 2006).

It was through analysing my emotions in the context of the unfamiliar that for the first time I actually 'felt' what it was like to be a woman — or, as Altork puts it, 'I became more aware of myself as a gendered being' (2007:107). I never really felt I understood the abstract data I was reading until I 'experienced' my gender, and was influenced by frameworks of honour and shame in ways similar to my informants. In this chapter, I will look at negative sexual experiences I encountered in the field, particularly verbal sexual harassment both from members of the community and as a by-product of the commencement of a new relationship. I will look at these as a context in which certain emotions were evoked, which in turn prompted me to engage with my senses and my body differently. Upon looking back on some of my diary entries, I realised that in an attempt to cope with the anxiety I felt from sexual harassment and maintaining my reputation, I was 'dulling my senses'. I also transformed my normal bodily comportment, which aided me in understanding the experiences of my informants, as I had become aware of similar occurrences through interviews with, and observations of, them.

Visibility, gendered performance and comportment in and between public and private spaces were of great importance to the women in my field site, because it was through these that they acquired and maintained honour and managed their reputations. As I engaged in a new relationship and experienced harassment, I also became aware of 'being seen' and tried to manage my visibility and comportment in ways that would make me seem honourable. The consequences of this were the production of tension and anxiety. Furthermore, it is noteworthy that both emotion and space were mutually constitutive. That is to say, the space elicited certain emotions; and in turn, my emotions — as constructive, complex and processual — altered my experience, and therefore the meanings, of the space.

Using the senses in ethnography: Experiencing and dulling the senses

> Come now, observe with all thy powers how each thing is clear, neither holding sight in greater trust compared with hearing, nor noisy hearing above what the tongue makes plain, nor withhold trust from any other limbs, by whatever way there is a channel to understanding, but grasp each thing in the way in which it is clear. (Empedocles, as cited in Guthrie 1962:139)

This statement from ancient Greek philosopher Empedocles (490-430 BC) displays the longevity of the debate between reason and sensorial intelligence. Throughout history, there has been a rivalry over the importance of using senses and emotion versus rationality and reason in the acquisition of knowledge. There has for some time been an acknowledgement of cultures consisting of 'contrasting ratios of sense' (see Carpenter & McLuhan 1960). However, despite its fundamentally subjective foundations, paying attention to the senses, particularly in anthropology, is relatively new and has influenced a number of anthropologists (Jackson 1983; 2010; Feld 1988; Stoller 1989; Classen 1990; 1997; Howes 1991c; 2003; Feld & Brenneis 2004; Desjarlais 2005; Pink 2006). Essentially, anthropology of the senses grows out of the interest in bodily modes of knowing and the place of the body in the mind (Howes 1991a:3). In an anthropology of the senses, we are directed to looking at 'the sensorium', defined as 'the entire sensory apparatus as an operational complex' (Ong, as cited in Howes 1991a:8). This is combinatory, for it is through the combination of the five senses that humans come to perceive and form understandings of the world (Howes 1991b:167). An anthropology of the senses is not only concerned with the patterning of sense experience from one cultural context to the next, but is also concerned with 'tracing the influence such variations have on forms of social organisation, conceptions of self and cosmos, the regulation of the emotions and other domains of cultural expression'

(1991a:3). Howes advocates that we do this in three ways: first, by reconvening our senses; second, by recognising cultures as 'ways of sensing the world'. Finally, we do this by learning how to use and combine our senses in accordance with the preferences of the cultures we study, 'so that we actually *make some sense* of them, instead of looking for a worldview where there may not be one ...' (1991a:8, italics in the original text).

I would add that it is necessary not only to learn to use our senses in accordance with other cultural paradigms, but also to pay attention to how we, as anthropologists, engage with our own senses, and to the effect this has on our anthropological projects. I did not seek to engage with the senses in approximate accordance with Nepali custom, but spontaneously doing so led me to certain understandings. Instead, over time, I recoiled from my senses, dulled them and made an effort *not* to engage with them as a form of protection from those elements of Nepali behaviour which were uncomfortable. However, in order to dull them, I had to be aware of them. Becoming so elicited valuable knowledge with regard to Nepali notions of womanhood and gendered experience.

> I am walking down a dusty, hot and littered street in Bhaktanagar and my cheeks are burning bright red. A group of young men of about eighteen years old have just gathered around almost blocking me as I walk past. Each of them has got out their 'camera phones' and are pointing them in my direction, smirks on their faces. One brave young teen yells out after some jeering from his friends, 'Eh! Kuireni! I fuck you?'[3] and he is met with a sea of laughter from his peers. I know there is nothing I can do or say. I rearrange my scarf as I round my shoulders, keep my sunglasses on, look down and keep walking. (Excerpt from field diary, 2009)

I became aware that my bodily comportment changed. This was almost instantaneous upon arriving in Kathmandu, and intensified later in Bhaktanagar. I went about changing my bodily movement and posture and cutting off the visual, olfactory, auricular and tactile senses in every way possible in an attempt to make myself less noticeable. I focused particularly on covering my body and blocking out sounds and avoiding eye contact, with the hope that doing so would, in turn, block out any unwanted, potential physical contact. I would not go outside without a broad cotton scarf, which I used to wrap my shoulders and blonde hair and cover my nose against unsavoury smells. I was always anxious when I left the house without my sunglasses or headphones. These tactics helped to quell my anxiety and to limit unsought interactions. They did not always work, though, as I found myself more than once reduced to tears from unwanted whistling, photography, profanity and, occasionally, the grabbing of my arms and breasts.

Desjarlais speaks of his informants 'dulling the senses', which he observed when conducting fieldwork amongst the 'homeless mentally ill' of downtown Boston (1997; 2005). What is of concern to him are certain 'subjective orientations to time, space,

---

3   The term *kuireni* means 'light eyes' and can be considered derogatory.

sound, otherness, meaning and distress that are commonly adopted by many during their stays in the shelter' (2005:369). He talks about seeing this in his informants. What is of interest to me here is seeing this manifest itself not only in my informants, for it often did, but also in me, the ethnographer. Desjarlais says:

> For many, the sensorium of the street involved a corporeal existence in which a person's senses and ability to make sense soon became dulled in response to excessive and brutal demands on those senses. Bodies sometimes became the most prominent instruments of engagement and awareness. (2005:372)

After being confronted with overt and covert sexual harassment by Nepali men, I noticed myself become more drained and weary. I called my headphones, scarf and sunglasses 'weapons' and dressed in Nepali clothing because the laughter and debasement of my person were 'brutal demands on my senses'. I became anxious because 'in short, considerable effort was required at times to act, think and move about in life' (Desjarlais 2005:374). I did not have to rationalise why I needed to protect myself through dulling the senses. I simply responded to the stimuli; the verbal abuse, sounds, smells, sights and touch, and the emotions they invoked — namely, anxiety, tension and shame. Thus I found myself dulling the modes of information acquisition, especially sight, sound and touch, as a matter of course. As Desjarlais says of those staying in the shelter, '[they] sought refuge from the world in certain ways' (374) — and so did I.

'Being seen' as a woman in Nepal

> 'Can you drop me on the back road please?' my Buddhist translator Priya says to me from behind me on my scooter.
>
> 'Sure, but isn't this road in the market place quicker?' I ask her, yelling back over my shoulder.
>
> 'Yes, but I don't want to go that way. I don't want people to see me in the market place twice in one day and I was already here this morning. I don't want them thinking, "What is she doing outside her home twice in one day?"' (Excerpt from field diary, February 2010)

Priya was the first woman to bring the issue of visibility to my attention, but once she had, I saw concern for it amongst most of my informants. Women felt they needed to calculate when, how and with whom they were seen outside the home because these things factored greatly into the ways they garnered and maintained honour and respect. It became very clear that for women generally it was important to 'be seen' — especially to 'be seen' to be 'good'. In Nepal, being a woman is particularly associated with the bodily comportment of passivity. There is the notion of an *asal mābila*, a 'good' or respectable woman, who acts and speaks in certain ways. With the exception of bad luck or bad morals, which by contrast makes a *kharāb mābila*, a 'bad' woman, it is presumed that a Hindu woman will follow a particular and socially accepted life path (Holland, Lachicotte Jr, Skinner & Cain 1998).

Socially, this concept is generally attached to many other non-Hindu Nepali women. However, the life-world of Nepal is complex and it is rare that anyone falls into one identity category. Instead, people activate certain elements of complex and multifaceted identities according to different contexts and relationships (see Holland et al. 1998). Priya's comment to me that day implied that being seen outside the home twice in one day would portray her as a *kharāb māhila*. It also displayed the extent to which women strategise in order to visibly maintain their reputations as *asal māhila*. Therefore, for women, it can be said that being *seen* to fall into the category of *asal māhila* is of the utmost importance.

Women and men often voiced notions of what it meant to be a 'good' woman, and these notions resonated with how women should be and act as set out in Hindu or Brahmanical texts (see Holland et al. 1998). The traditional view of women and their reputations is dichotomous in nature; in basic terms, they can be seen as belonging to one of two categories. In one, women are seen as *asal māhila*: ideal, ritualistically clean, pure and chaste. A woman should control her body, mind and speech, keeping them in line with the wishes of the respective male in her household at all times. In the other category, women are seen as *kharāb māhila*, who are dangerous, sexually potent and deviant (Bennett 1983). A woman is presumed to be linked to male relatives: her father before marriage, her husband during marriage and her son (presuming she has one) after the death of her husband. One informant, Jyoti, told me:

> So honour is always linked with male and family ... So there is no any honour of women ... If woman go late home then her honour is always linked with her husband, or with her father or with her son. Everyone says that, 'What type of woman is this? She's travelling around in midnight. Whose daughter is this? Whose wife is this? Whose mother is this?' (Interview with Jyoti, 11 August 2009)

The reason for women's reputation being so highly contested and visible is the Nepali notion of *ijjat*. Sociality in Nepal revolves around *ijjat*, which is defined as 'a learnt complex set of rules an Asian individual follows in order to protect the family honour and keep his or her position in the community' (Gilbert, Gilbert & Sanghera 2004:112). Both women and men 'have' *ijjat*; however, it is created, manifested and utilised in different ways. Honour in the Nepali context not only relates to an individual's personal sense of honour but is also explicitly linked to that of one's kin (Cameron 1998:136). In this sense, the responsibility to act honourably is not simply reflective of one person's positioning within society, but directly reflects on the social standing and honour of the family as a whole. However, as Cameron found in her field site in Far Western Nepal, while one is born into a caste, family and gender, one is not automatically ascribed honour; that must be earned (136). Women in this setting are afforded primary responsibility for a household's honour. Cameron states:

> It would not be an exaggeration to say that the honour of the collective depends on the honour of its women. A household's absence of honourable women (or abundance of dishonourable women) prevents a collective — be it a household, a patriline, or a caste unit — from claiming ijat. (137)

Simone de Beauvoir tells us, 'One is not born a woman, but rather becomes one' (1973:301). Butler (1999) reiterates this, saying there is always a 'doing' of one's identity. I argue that gender is 'done to' women through certain actions by others (see Quigley 2003). Thus, knowing that essentially everywhere, not just in Nepal, women both 'do' their gendered identity and have it 'done to' them, what does this say of gendered comportment for Nepali women? Dr Gita, a prominent woman's activist and founder of a woman's empowerment NGO in Kathmandu, asserted to me that women are controlled in three ways in Nepal — through their production, sexuality and comportment. She brought up an idea during one of our interviews.

> Like first time when I menstruated then I was kept in a small dark cowshed for twelve days. Ha! ... So what it means that is, 'Okay, you are growing, you need to be under control' ... This is control over sexuality ... I don't know; I actually hate this. [Holds up the shawl around her shoulders.] Because without knowing, our family say to us, 'Okay, you are a woman so you cannot walk like this'. [Sticks her chest out.] You know. It means you can't show your boobs! All the time, 'Don't do this, and wear this type of clothes and do this type of thing and then don't do this!' (Interview with Dr Gita, 5 August 2009)

Comportment is key to being a woman in Nepal. Young asserts that the category *feminine* is a set of 'normatively disciplined expectations imposed on female bodies by male-dominated society' (2005:5). Young grounds this notion, of what is essentially an example of docile bodies (see Foucault 1977), within the context in which bodies learn such behaviours (Young 2005:7). Young writes that 'the body as lived is always layered with social and historical meaning and is not some primitive matter prior to or underlying economic and political relations or cultural meanings' (7). My body was neither layered with, nor a product of, Nepali social and historical meanings. However, I felt and learned to react to those social meanings quickly. I changed my bodily praxis due to the objectification of my body by others and in order to attempt to 'fit in' in a world where I clearly did not. These changes were often in terms of my comportment — how I dressed, the way I moved, and my behavioural patterns. Young makes an essential point, to my way of thinking, which is that women's bodily comportment, spatiality and mobility do not find their origination in biology or some 'mysterious feminine essence' (42); rather, they find foundation in the 'particular situation of women as conditioned by their sexist oppression in contemporary society' (42).

As a first-time fieldworker, I found it unnerving to be stared at and scrutinised so consistently. In my field diary I wrote:

> I can't get used to people staring. Especially men! Why are they staring? Taking photos? Other than that I am different, there's a quality to staring that is unnerving. I think I might dye my hair (dark) so people would just stop staring! (Excerpt from field diary, March 2009)

Ackerman, having studied sensory modes, tells us that, 'Seventy percent of the body's sense receptors are in the eyes, and it is mainly through seeing the world that we appraise and understand it' (1990:230). Many anthropologists have argued that the other senses are also important ways of sensing the world (see Classen 1990; Howes 1991c). However, in light of the attention my body received, the question I posed in my field diary was: Why is it that the prolonged gaze has sexual connotations? Ackerman draws our attention to the fact that lovers close their eyes when they kiss in order to shut out visual distractions. Altork (2007:97) reasons that this is why intense encounters in the field can have a seductive quality, or, as in my other experiences with male Nepali strangers, a sexually predatory one. When we are met with offensive stimuli, it is offensive to our senses as the means by which we understand the world. Changing my comportment in the manner described, and choosing different modes of presenting myself, were strategies I intuitively employed in order to avoid unwanted attention.

I had arrived in Bhaktanagar full of anticipation. My senses were stimulated as I took in the colours of women's saris, the smells of the market mixed with petrol fumes, the sounds of goats bleating and Nepali chatter wafting through the air. Very quickly, however, the effect of unfamiliar interactions, sights, smells and sounds overwhelmed me to the point that I felt compelled to alter my comportment on a day-to-day basis. Daily, I would negotiate my practice to try to lessen my discomfort. I changed my dress and wore loose Nepali clothing. I often rounded my shoulders and set my gaze at the ground when walking past large groups, particularly of men. I also lied about my whereabouts and about my life history. By no means was this a malicious attempt to deceive my informants. However, I had been told that in order to be understood and to 'fit in', it was best for me to say that my 'husband' was home in Australia, and that he could not leave his work and was happy for me to pursue my education.

This was, in fact, not far from the truth. I had been with my Australian boyfriend for three and a half years, and we were happy, although the time I was taking to fulfil my studies meant that we were apart. We knew he would visit at some time and so it just seemed like the right thing to do by Nepali standards and expectations. I even wore a plain gold wedding ring. When he came and stayed, he got along with members of the community extremely well. When he left, they asked after him often. As the months wore on, we started to grow apart. I chose not to tell anyone in Bhaktanagar about this aspect of our relationship. I never imagined that this would put me in any kind of predicament.

'Come and meet my colleagues', my new Indian-Nepali friend had said. I thought this was a great improvement socially, as I was in my sixth month in Bhaktanagar. While work was satisfying it was also difficult and I was starting to feel socially bored and isolated from people I could relate to. I met this young man on a flight from Kathmandu. We became friends for a time and I rode over to his house, a crew camp where he and his colleagues lived communally. He met me at the T-junction, followed by three strangers, two other Nepalis and a fellow foreigner. 'Who is he?' I thought to myself, taking in the appearance of the foreigner.

'Hi, I'm Hemi', he said in a New Zealand accent. He smiled and our eyes locked. I felt my knees buckle as I tried to smile back. 'We're going to the market, but I'll see you when we get back', he said as he strolled away.

My eyes followed the attractive figure down the road. What I did not know then was my life in Bhaktanagar was about to become a whole lot more complicated and interesting. (Personal notes based on field diary, 2016)

Hemi and I became friends and before long we started a romantic relationship. Two things compounded the complexity of this relationship. First, there was the fact that I had had a relationship with someone in Australia; though this had ended, all members of my community who knew me thought he was still my husband. Second, our relationship attracted unwanted sexual harassment from Hemi's colleagues living in the crew camp. After it started, I was struck with an enormous sense of wanting to keep it a secret. This was driven by the horror of what people would think of me should they find out I was 'cheating on my husband'. However, more issues arose out of this relationship, all too familiar from my experiences with young male strangers on the street. Hemi's colleagues started to harass me and make me feel sexually objectified by crudely indicating their interest in engaging in a relationship with me.

I draw attention to this example not as an argument for or against having intimate relationships in the field (see Jarvie 1988:428) but rather in order to explore how my behaviour changed as a result. I started to lie about my whereabouts to my Nepali landlords. I would arrive at, and leave, Hemi's house at certain times of the day. Furthermore, I was experiencing a great deal of anxiety and was fearful of being caught out by community members. My feelings were starting to mirror some of those of my informants, in terms of my anxious consideration for reputation management. I became concerned for my own *ijjat*.

Being brave in the field: A new sense of space and place

> As place is sensed, senses are placed; as places make sense, senses make place. (Feld 1996:91)

Traditionally, 'place' has been conceived of as 'space' imbued with meaning (Vanclay 2008:3). However, I felt strongly that the 'space' of Bhaktanagar was imbued with much meaning, those of its inhabitants as well as mine, even before I had a sense of it as 'place'. 'Space' in Vanclay's definition (2008) implies that to begin with there is a vacant expanse that is meaningless. However, Casey contests the idea that space is somehow 'waiting' for cultural configurations to make it 'placeful' (1996:14). For me, even before I arrived, I had assigned it a meaning ('the field'). When I was there, its meaning, I realised, was dynamic. It evolved and was inextricably linked to my (and my perception of others') experiences within its borders. Being 'in place' evoked emotions, which in turn reproduced meaning of the place, which elicited further emotions, and so forth, in a neverending dialectic.

Casey (1996) tells us that emplacement has a close relationship with embodiment and connects issues of place with the anthropological problem of knowing 'local knowledge'. Place is not secondary to space, nor is it laid over it, but rather 'is the most fundamental form of embodied experience — the site of a powerful fusion of self, space and time' (Feld & Basso 1996:9; see also Casey 1996). If we are to take knowledge as being of the localities (and associated meanings) in which knowing subjects live, then local knowledge and lived experience can be seen as one. As Casey argues, 'to live is to live locally, and to know is first of all to know the places one is in' (1996:18). Therefore, to be in place is to know, because the sensing, and therefore knowing, lived body is always already in place.

In Bhaktanagar, with so few foreigners on site, let alone women who looked like me, I was a highly visible presence. As a result, I became more visible to myself as a woman. Having my gender reflected so consistently by those with whom I came into contact brought me ultimately to a point where I became more aware of myself as gendered. Furthermore, I came to know how powerful a force *ijjat* is in the lives of Nepalis, because it became a powerful force in mine. It was through this that I was finding resonance in the experiences of the women I worked with. One day, I remember that I was complaining about the sexually charged calls of the strange men on the street to my research assistant, Priya, and I asked her if it was only me this happened to. She replied, 'No! Sometimes they say bad things to us. If we're brave we tell them off. If not, we walk in the other direction and ignore them. But it doesn't feel nice so I try to feel courage'. This helped me to analyse the concept of feeling brave, especially with regards to honour. For Nepali women, being 'brave' enough to speak out generally meant going against the concept of being a 'good' woman (Bennett 1983:3; see also Skinner 1990). As was explained to me several times, to voice discomfort, even when catcalled by strangers on the street, often risks people talking about the woman's lack of decorum. This is changing, however; as Priya notes, the desire not to suffer the embarrassment of being sexually harassed is, on occasion, starting to outweigh a willingness to suffer in silence. Slowly, women are finding it honourable to raise their voices (see Kunreuther 2009).

De Neve and Unnithan-Kumar contest the idea that anthropologists construct knowledge. They argue that they 'slowly build upon the practical and theoretical reflections' of their informants (2006:6) — and, I would add, upon their experiences embedded in relationships and the field. For me, over time and with a follow-up field visit, while the physical space remained relatively the same, the meaning changed for me, and so did my behaviour and comportment. I learned the bravest retorts, such as '*Tero Āmalai ban?*' or '*Kāsto lāj-sharam nabhayeko?*', meaning respectively, 'Do you say that to your mother?' and 'Don't you feel ashamed?'. These phrases served to highlight the shame of the men doing the yelling. I found that when I had bravery, as suggested by Priya, I felt lighter and satisfied. I learned to laugh more and hold myself with confidence.

For example, I remember that one day, towards the end of my fieldwork, I was sitting in a local café, with my head down peering over my field notes, when all of a sudden a flash of light occurred. Shocked, I looked up to see a Nepali man with his camera pointing straight at me. I was outraged. 'Did you just take my picture?' I demanded in English, before thinking — forgetting both propriety and the need to speak in Nepali. The man cowered in fear. He stammered in simple Nepali, 'No, Sister, I didn't take your picture'. Furious, I stood up and walked over, as I did not believe him. By this time, the whole restaurant had stopped to watch the spectacle. He cowered down and fumbled with his camera, deleting, I believe, the photo he had just taken. '*Ma herna sākchu?*' — 'Can I see?' I demanded in Nepali. He passed his camera to me and I searched his pictures for my image. Then I handed it back, and resumed my seat without speaking, satisfied there was no photo of me. I would never have felt able to do this had this occurred at the beginning of my fieldwork.

> First was the question of reflexivity — or the reciprocal interplay of one's relationship with oneself and with others — or, as I phrased it at the time, the twofold movement that takes one out into the world of others and returns one, changed, to oneself. (Jackson 2010:36)

I do not wish to find myself straying into a narcissistic mode of inquiry, for that is not, in my view, at the heart of what anthropology is. However, for the purposes of *my* ethnography, I cannot ignore the fact that my experience, and the knowledge that arose from it, were pivotal in my knowledge of the people I was seeking to understand. By putting ourselves 'in place', we engage with embodied experiences, from which we can gain valuable knowledge. Where there has traditionally been a dominant view that to be emotional equates to a failure in the rational processing of information and therefore undermines the possibility for intelligent action and informed ethnography (Lutz 1986:291), there is now a shift in the weight given to emotions and senses in the acquisition of anthropological knowledge (see De Neve & Unnithan-Kumar 2006; Davies & Spencer 2010). The task is to uncover how the anthropologist's emotions and senses provide useful ways to understand the people, interactions and contexts that make up the life-worlds in which we immerse ourselves. The point is rather not to ignore them but to learn from them. Emotions and experience, when treated with the same intellectual rigour as empirical work, can support, more than inhibit, an anthropological project and can assist our understanding of the community in which we find ourselves (Davies 2010:1).

For me, paying attention to senses, emotions and space did at least two things. First, it engaged me directly with the themes of my study: namely, gendered subjectivity and honour, and how these influenced women's practice. Second, it forced me to think about how my experiences generated knowledge that might, in part, find resonance with someone else's experience, and therefore help me to understand their experience better. Through my experiences, I became aware of the multitude of ways which exist of feeling like a woman, as well as of how to use my body to acquire knowledge — which is, after all, the anthropologist's job. This was not the means by which I 'constructed knowledge'; it was one of the means by which I 'came to know'.

Upon reflection on my fieldwork, I have come to know that people's practices in, and understandings of, the world are crafted in the crucible of our everyday lives, which include a gamut of experiences, including our anxieties, senses and emotions. That we might, at least partially, share these experiences with others is no surprise. That they were unavoidable was, for me, argument enough for embracing anxiety and emotion in the field. If we deny that anxieties exist and fail to look at what we experience with and through our instrument (that is, our body), we fail to acknowledge the question posed at the beginning of this chapter: 'What is the basis for my knowing?' In not acknowledging that question, we disconnect ourselves from accessing valuable knowledge itself.

References

Ackerman, D. 1990. *A Natural History of the Senses.* New York: Vintage Books.

Allen, N.J. 1997. 'Hinduization: The experience of the Thulung Rai'. In D.N. Gellner, J. Pfaff-Czarnecka and J. Whelpton (Eds.), *Nationalism and Ethnicity in a Hindu Kingdom: The Politics of Culture In Contemporary Nepal* (pp. 303-323). Amsterdam: Harwood.

Altork, K. 2007. 'Walking the fire line: The erotic dimension of the fieldwork experience'. In A.C.G.M. Robben and J.A. Sluka (Eds.), *Ethnographic Fieldwork: An Anthropological Reader*, 1st edn (pp. 92-107). Oxford: Blackwell Publishing.

Bennett, L. 1983. *Dangerous Wives and Sacred Sisters: Social and Symbolic Roles of High-Caste Women in Nepal.* New York: Columbia University Press.

Bourdieu, P. 2003. 'Participant objectivation', *Journal for the Royal Anthropological Institute* 9: 281-294.

Butler, J. 1999. *Gender Trouble: Feminism and the Subversion of Identity.* 10th anniversary edn. London: Routledge.

Cameron, M.M. 1998. *On the Edge of the Auspicious: Gender and Caste in Nepal.* Urbana and Chicago: University of Illinois Press.

Carpenter, E. and M. McLuhan. 1960. *Explorations in Communication: An Anthology*. Boston: Beacon Press.

Casey, E.S. 1996. 'How to get from space to place'. In S. Feld and K.H. Basso (Eds.), *Senses of Place* (pp. 13-52). Seattle: School of American Research Press.

Classen, C. 1990. 'The taste of ethnographic things: The senses in anthropology', *American Ethnologist* 17(4): 800.

Classen, C. 1997. 'Foundations for an anthropoly of the senses', *International Social Science Journal* 49(153): 401-412.

Davies, J. 2010. 'Introduction: Emotions in the field'. In J. Davies and D. Spencer (Eds.), *Emotions in the Field: The Psychology and Anthropology of Fieldwork Experience* (pp. 1-33). Stanford: Stanford University Press.

Davies, J. and D. Spencer (Eds.). 2010. *Emotions in the Field: The Psychology and Anthropology of Fieldwork Experience*. Stanford: Stanford University Press.

De Beauvoir, S. 1973. *The Second Sex*. 38th edn. New York: Vintage.

De Neve, G. and M. Unnithan-Kumar (Eds.). 2006. *Critical Journeys: The Making of Anthropologists*. Hampshire, UK and Burlington, VT: Ashgate Publishing Limited.

Desjarlais, R. 1997. *Shelter Blues: Sanity and Selfhood among the Homeless*. Philadelphia: University of Pennsylvania Press.

Desjarlais, R. 2005. 'Movement, stillness: On the sensory world of a shelter for the "homeless mentally ill"'. In D. Howes (Ed.), *Empire of the Senses: The Sensual Cultural Reader* (pp. 369-379). New York: Berg.

Feld, S. 1988. 'Aesthetics as iconicity of style, or "lift-up-over sounding": Getting into the Kaluli groove', *Yearbook for Traditional Music* 20: 74-113.

Feld, S. 1996. 'Waterfalls of song: An acoustemology of place resounding in Bosavi, Papua New Guinea'. In S. Feld and K.H. Basso (Eds.), *Senses of Place* (pp. 91-135). Santa Fe, NM: School of American Research Press.

Feld, S. and K.H. Basso. 1996. 'Introduction'. In S. Feld and K.H. Basso (Eds.), *Senses of Place* (pp. 3-11). Santa Fe, NM: School of American Research Press.

Feld, S. and D. Brenneis. 2004. 'Doing anthropology in sound', *American Ethnologist* 31(4): 461-474.

Foucault, M. 1977. *Discipline and Punish: The Birth of the Prison*. London: Allen Lane.

Ghimire, D.J., W.G. Axinn, S.T. Yabiku and A. Thornton. 2006. 'Social change, premarital nonfamily experience, and spouse choice in an arranged marriage society', *American Journal of Sociology* 111(4): 1181-1218.

Gilbert, P., J. Gilbert and J. Sanghera. 2004. 'A focus group exploration of the impact of izzat, shame, subordination and entrapment on mental health and service use in South Asian women living in Derby', *Mental Health, Religion & Culture* 7(2): 109-130.

Guthrie, W.K.C. 1962. *A History of Greek Philosophy*, vol. 1. Cambridge: Cambridge University Press.

Hangen, S. 2007. *Creating a New Nepal: The Ethnic Dimension*. Washington: The East-West Center.

Holland, D., W. Lachicotte Jr, D. Skinner and C. Cain. 1998. *Identity and Agency in Cultural Worlds*. Cambridge, MA: Harvard University Press.

Howes, D. 1991a. 'Introduction: "To summon all the senses"'. In D. Howes (Ed.), *The Varieties of Sensory Experience: A Sourcebook in the Anthropology of the Senses* (pp. 3-24). Toronto: University of Toronto Press.

Howes, D. 1991b. 'Sensorial anthropology'. In D. Howes (Ed.), *The Varieties of Sensory Experience: A Sourcebook in the Anthropology of the Senses* (pp. 167-191). Toronto: University of Toronto Press.

Howes, D. (Ed.). 1991c. *The Varieties of Sensory Experiences: A Sourcebook in the Anthropology of the Senses*. Toronto: University of Toronto Press.

Howes, D. 2003. *Sensual Relations: Engaging the Senses in Culture and Social Theory*. Ann Arbor, MI: The University of Michigan Press.

Hsu, E. 2006. 'Participant experience: Learning to be an acupuncturist, and not becoming one'. In M. Unnithan-Kumar and G. De Neve (Eds.), *Critical Journeys: The Making of Anthropologists* (pp. 149-163). Hampshire, UK and Burlington, VT: Ashgate Publishing Limited.

Jackson, M. 1983. 'Knowledge of the body', *Man* 18(2): 327-345.

Jackson, M. 2010. 'From anxiety to method in anthropological fieldwork: An appraisal of George Devereux's enduring ideas'. In J. Davies and D. Spencer (Eds.), *Emotions in the Field: The Psychology and Anthropology of Fieldwork Experience* (pp. 35-54). Stanford: Stanford University Press.

Jarvie, I. 1988. 'Comment on Sangren's "rhetoric and the authority of ethnography"', *Current Anthropology* 29(3): 427-429.

Kunreuther, L. 2009. 'Between love and property: Voice, sentiment, and subjectivity in the reform of daughter's inheritance in Nepal', *American Ethnologist* 36(3): 545-562.

Liechty, M. 2010. 'Paying for modernity: Women and the discourse of freedom in Kathmandu'. In M. Liechty (Ed.), *Out Here in Kathmandu: Modernity on the Global Periphery*, vol. 1 (pp. 307-342). Kathmandu: Martin Chautari Press.

Lutz, C. 1986. 'Emotion, thought and estrangement: Emotion as a cultural category', *Cultural Anthropology* 1(3): 287-309.

Manandhar, L.K. and K.B. Bhattachan. 2001. *Gender and Democracy in Nepal*. Kathmandu: Central Department of Home Science — Women's Studies Program.

McHugh, E. 2001. *Love and Honor in the Himalayas: Coming to Know Another Culture*. Philadelphia: University of Pennsylvania Press.

National Planning Commission Secretariat, Central Bureau of Statistics. 2012. *National Population and Housing Census 2011 (National Report)*. Kathmandu: Government of Nepal.

Pink, S. 2006. *The Future of Visual Anthropology: Engaging the Senses*. Oxford: Routledge.

Quigley, D. 2003. 'Is a theory of caste still possible?'. In M.S. Chatterjee and U.M. Sharma (Eds.), *Contextualising Caste: Post-Dumontian Approaches* (pp. 25-48). Jaipur: Rawat Publications.

Skinner, D. 1990. 'Nepalese children's understanding of self and the social world: A study of a Hindu mixed caste community'. PhD thesis, The University of North Carolina.

Stoller, P. 1989. *The Taste of Ethnographic Things*. Philadelphia: University of Pennsylvania Press.

Strathern, M. 1991. *Partial Connections*. Savage, MD: Rowman and Littlefield.

Tamang, S, 2009. 'The politics of conflict and difference or the difference of conflict in politics: The women's movement in Nepal', *Feminist Review* 91: 61-80.

Unnithan-Kumar, M. and G. De Neve. 2006. 'Introduction: Producing fields, selves and anthropology'. In G. De Neve and M. Unnithan-Kumar (Eds.), *Critical Journeys: The Making of Anthropologists* (pp. 1-16). Hampshire, UK and Burlington, VT: Ashgate.

Vanclay, F. 2008. 'Place matters'. In F. Vanclay, M. Higgins and A. Blackshaw (Eds.), *Making Sense of Place: Exploring Concepts and Expressions of Place through Different Senses and Lenses* (pp. 3-11). Canberra: National Museum of Australia Press.

Young, I.M. 2005. *On Female Body Experience: 'Throwing Like a Girl' and Other Essays*. New York: Oxford University Press.

8

Interrupted research:
Emotions, senses and social space in (and out of) the field

Anthony Heathcote

Abstract[1]

This chapter reflexively explores the emotions, senses and social spaces that are shared between researcher and informants. I examine the ways in which an interruption to my ethnographic fieldwork on online memorialisation in Vietnam transformed the experience of research, as well as the ways I was positioned in relation to informants. Drawing on reflexive material, I demonstrate how the experience of returning home to my critically ill mother transformed my social space as a researcher when returning to Vietnam. Through the heightened emotional experience of coming home and being with my mother, amplified by the dulling of senses within the hospital walls and the monotony of illness, I underwent experiences which could be usefully applied to my relationship with informants. Consequently, when I returned to

---

1 The material for this chapter primarily appears, with slight alterations, in Chapter 2 of Heathcote 2015: 41-63. The author would like to acknowledge The University of Adelaide, which supported the work with a postgraduate scholarship. Thanks also to the editors of this volume, and in particular to Dr Susan R. Hemer and Dr Sal Humphreys, who helped immensely in the shaping and completion of my doctoral studies (this chapter included).

Vietnam, an altered social space opened up where I could empathise more readily with the emotions associated with having a family member close to death, and was accepted in a new way by informants.

Introduction

> The detachment of the scientific observer … by itself can never be sufficient; there has to be a way of providing for readers imaginative access to the emotional significance of events as felt by the informants … One has to become inward with a culture, and one possible avenue here is by a confrontation of one's own emotional responses with those of the people with whom one lives. (Watson 1999:144)

In 2012 I undertook twelve months of ethnographic research within the three major cities of Vietnam: Hanoi, Da Nang and Ho Chi Minh City. The research was concerned with remembering the dead in Vietnam via new mediated forms of communication such as the internet, and the various connections and tensions this created with the dominant forms of ancestral worship[2] in the country. Such research was largely undertaken in the online memorial website *Nghĩa Trang Online*[3] [NTO], and also through offline encounters with members of the site. In this I was immersed in the experiences of those who had lost loved ones, sometimes in 'good deaths', such as the passing of a grandparent in their home, and often through 'bad deaths', such as by abortion, motorcycle accidents and death through warfare. The fieldwork was underscored by an emotional intensity I was unfamiliar with, and it was one which at times was profoundly difficult for me. As an anthropology student who had recently completed an undergraduate degree, I had researched funeral, burial and commemoration practices in Vietnam extensively, but I was entering a community with little emotional experience of the subject I was studying.

Four months into the research, my mother was diagnosed and became critically ill with leukaemia, and I immediately returned home. I was uprooted from the field site and was brought into contact with a reality absolutely personal and not at all 'academic'. I was home in Australia for two months, spending extensive time at the

---

2 Ancestor worship is the central relationship Vietnamese have with the dead. The Vietnamese believe that in death the ancestors continue with an existence in the other world. It is an expectation that the living take care of the deceased and remember them through offerings of food, drink and other goods (often in the form of paper votive objects). Offerings are primarily placed on the ancestor altar, and are thus deemed to be transmuted to the other world for use by the ancestors (see Jellema 2007; Phan 1993). In return for care and remembrance, ancestors bring good luck and guidance to the living, or punish them for lack of respect and filial piety (see Endres & Lauser 2011:124-5; Kwon 2007:91-3).

3 The site is referred to as both *Nghĩa Trang Online* (Cemetery Online) and *Nhớ Mãi* (Remember Forever). It can be accessed at www.nhomai.vn.

hospital with Mum. It was a time of heightened emotions — stress, anxiety, anger, sadness, guilt, isolation — wherein my senses were dulled by the primary environment of the hospital, and the familiarity of home after the sensorial undertaking that had been Vietnam.

This chapter concerns an interruption to the primary research I was undertaking, and reflexively explores the emotions, senses and social space that are shared between researcher and informants. Through the heightened emotional experience of coming home and being with my mother, who I thought might die, amplified by the dulling of senses within the hospital walls and the monotony of illness, I underwent experiences which were similar to some of my informants and which I could share with them. Consequently, when I returned to Vietnam, a new social space opened up where I could empathise with the emotions associated with having a family member close to death, and I was accepted in a new way by informants. The interruption to my research transformed it. Additionally, this new emotional understanding meant I could experience the multitudinous sensations of online and offline memorial research, and the meanings they held in the lives of informants, in a way which was more personal and closer to my own experiences than before. Researchers need not have mirroring experiences, but when the subject material is sensitive and despairing, an acceptance of both researcher and informants as beings with emotional experiences is required.

The initial section of this chapter will demonstrate how reflexivity is a key way of thinking through relationships in the field, our positionality and the emotional experiences we encounter. Moving on, this chapter will introduce the research project, the field site and my social space within the field. The chapter will then bring the reader into the emotional and sensorial world I inhabited when returning home to my seriously ill mother. The vibrant senses of travelling to a new country and, in turn, coming home to the physical dullness of a hospital setting created a juxtaposition which this chapter then explores. From there, the chapter will examine the ways in which my experiences at home enabled a social space in the field previously unavailable to me. By reflexively engaging with these experiences, exploring emotion, senses and space, this chapter contributes to a growing body of research concerned with encounters in (and out of) the field, and the simultaneity of researcher and informant experiences.

A turning inwards: Reflexivity and emotions

It is not long after talking with fellow anthropologists arriving home from the field that the emotional experiences — otherwise often left out — become apparent. After a presentation one morning by a fellow researcher, a presentation they had woven 'to take out all the messiness', we discussed the reality. Far from the serene gaze of the anthropologist looking out over some tropical island lagoon, my colleague stated, 'Yeah, we don't talk about it, but it really was just terrible at times'. It was much besides, but a reflexive understanding can strengthen the research material and help illuminate important anthropological insights.

Reflexivity, as defined by Davies (1999:4) is 'a turning back on oneself, a process of self-reference'. In this way

> [t]he relationships between ethnographer and informants in the field, which form the bases of subsequent theorizing and conclusions, are expressed through social interaction in which the ethnographer participates; thus ethnographers help to construct the observations that become their data ... In its most transparent guise, reflexivity expresses researchers' awareness of their necessary connection to the research situation and hence their effects upon it. (5-7)

Such an awareness of our positionality in the field has at times been unwelcome within anthropology, as these experiences and relationships have been understood as a contaminating influence that is outside of an objective scientific worldview (Clifford 2013 [1988]:483; Rabinow 1977:5-7). However, in the last thirty years there has been a broadening of reflexive anthropological work, with many anthropologists concurring that by being reflexive about our positionality, experiences, relationships and emotions in the field, we can gain insight into our own relationships with the material and the research findings themselves (Davies 2010; Rosaldo 2004 [1989]; Watson 1999).

Researching material closely aligned with death and dying can be an emotionally heightened experience. As noted by Davies (2005:x), death is a subject matter in which our interest is 'unlike the interest we possess in other subjects. This one is infused with emotion, whether that of the experience of bereavement or of its anticipation, or of the thought of our own mortality'. Researchers are reflexively engaging with the themes of death and dying, whether they research the experience of patients in palliative care and residential aging homes (Hockey 2007; Lawton 2000:vi-viii), cemeteries in England (Woodthorpe 2007; 2009), organ transfer research (Shaw 2011), or Holocaust photography (Liss 1998:v-vii). This list is not exhaustive, with a growing body of research now interrogating the researcher's personal contact with death and dying, and the deeply unsettling experiences and emotions relating to it (see also Johnson 2009; Valentine 2007).

Woodthorpe (2007:3), in her doctoral fieldwork among cemeteries in England, notes that the subject matter was difficult for her to research, making her at times feel 'so exhausted, lonely, fed up'. Her research was a 'highly charged activity' (3) which had an influence on her motivation and state of mind, as it was 'emotionally draining and physically exhausting' (4). She argues that social researchers should remember that they are working among emotionally sentient beings: 'Emotion cannot be left out of the ethnographic picture. It informs the way we negotiate, interpret and communicate our reality'; and consequently a reflexive stance can 'enable emotions to be incorporated and identified as a key analytical strength in our interpretation of the social world' (8). Throughout my research, I engaged with my own emotional encounters in relation to the research, as both an outsider looking in and as an active participant trying to better appreciate and understand online memorialisation in Vietnam.

The initial months of fieldwork and social space

My primary field site was the Vietnamese online memorial *Nghĩa Trang Online* [NTO], which contains a vast spectrum of remembering: Buddhists, Catholics, revolutionary war martyrs, children, babies and fetuses, among others, all have their own sections. Site members create a 'grave' for their loved ones where they write to them, upload online offerings (food, beer, clothes, mobile phones and so on), 'light' candles, and interact with other members. The NTO members who participated in my research also regularly interacted offline, whether at NTO-specific catch-ups such as death days and charity events, or in non-related social interactions such as tennis outings and coffee gatherings. I met offline with informants at many of these events.

The research had a particular focus on disenfranchised grief (Doka 2002) — grief not socially sanctioned and difficult to express in society — and the stories related to me by informants included deaths through motorcycle accidents, abortion, suicide and warfare; these were deaths not easy to reconcile with forms of ancestor veneration and wider religious, social and political issues in the country. They were at times profoundly difficult and problematic to express for some Vietnamese (see Heathcote 2014; 2015).

With informants or alone, I visited cemeteries, pagodas, war museums and what Tumarkin (2005:12) calls 'traumascapes', which she defines as 'places across the world marked by traumatic legacies of violence, suffering and loss'. I also spent countless hours on NTO, reading through the comments written for the deceased and other members. Such comments were painful at times, and deeply unsettling. Reading and listening to the experiences of NTO members occasionally left me feeling physically unwell: there were moments when I questioned if I could continue the research project. Re-examining field notes now takes me back into a world where I describe feeling at times numbed by the subject matter, and at other moments anxious and depressed. After one interview I noted: 'Perhaps I am the wrong person for the job':

> I am finding field notes difficult to write. Today when meeting with Ha[4], she stated that her brother was killed during a war with Cambodia and had his throat cut. She made the sign with her hand. And as for her cousins, she would never create an online memorial for them because it was too awful, it was worse than that. She went silent after telling me this and the conversation did not continue easily. I felt like an imposter, prying into a subject matter so sensitive. The whole experience was draining, awful. Perhaps I am the wrong person for the job. (Field notes)

---

4 Throughout this chapter I have used pseudonyms for those connected to the research. I have also altered minor details concerning informants, members and those memorialised in order to preserve their anonymity.

Another field note entry, after I had talked with a Vietnamese woman about her experiences of abortion, described similar feelings of disconnection and anxiety:

> After meeting with Phuong I had difficulty keeping myself together. She became visibly distressed towards the end of our discussion and I had to end it early. This is a very intense situation and it made me wonder why I thought I could even deal with this. These are people's lives now, this is real to them. Who am I? (Field notes)

At times of particular intensity, I would neglect to write field notes at all after key events, which led to anxiety about completion of the research.

Anxiety was compounded by feeling I was removed from the *social space* I was studying. Rabinow (1977:79), in his seminal reflexive work in Morocco, writes that 'however much one moves in the direction of participation, it is always the case that one is still both an outsider and an observer'. I was particularly aware that my personal experiences fell completely outside the experiences of those whom I was studying. Who was I to delve into the emotional experience of losing a loved one, especially with deaths so deeply painful and disenfranchised? I had trouble relating to these experiences. For the purposes of this chapter, I define *empathy* as the ability to reflect and imagine another's point of view. While this can certainly be achieved in part without similar experiences, I argue that my own experiences helped forge a better empathetic understanding of my informants. The process of empathy can never be entirely unbiased, and, as Hollan (2008:476) notes, such a process is ongoing and dynamic: 'The empathizer can try to keep up with fluctuations in the other's emotional states, but can never claim to know or capture them once and for all' (see also Hollan & Throop 2008).

During the initial stages of the research project, I became familiar with Linh, who helped me gain early access to NTO members. Linh, a key informant of the site, had memorialised her father on *Nghĩa Trang Online* and also used the site to inform members about the health of her niece Thuc, who was seriously ill and in hospital. A page on NTO was created by Linh so that members could light an online candle for the sick child and leave comments, such as: 'I hope she gets better soon', and: 'I am thinking of you'. Linh related how she was feeling about her own poor health and about the sickness of Thuc. She spoke of long days sitting next to her niece in hospital, and the things she had done to brighten up the room for her. She also spoke of the emotional turmoil this brought about in her family, as members had to find ways around their usual work and studying routines, at the same time as being concerned for their sick child. While I was concerned about the health of Thuc, the experience of having a family member ill in hospital was one I was unfamiliar with. I was interested in how Linh used NTO to communicate, but there was an emotional disconnection, as I had difficulty empathising with her. Four months into the fieldwork, I received a message which had a profound impact on my own relations and connections in the field.

Returning home

My four months in Vietnam had been a sensorial avalanche. Travelling the country, I found each meal a new flavour and texture, from take-away *phở* (Vietnamese noodle soup) in a plastic bag for breakfast, to sidewalk beer *hoi* and the chanting of *một, hai, ba, vô!* ('1, 2, 3, cheers!') whilst hoisting beer or *bia* before each drink. There was the initially overpowering coffee: the strength in flavour, the sweetness of the milk. There was also the traffic, its intoxicating cacophony, along with the smell of burning votive paper offerings wafting down the street. So many senses were virtually replicated in my studies also, as online candles were 'lit' and online food, beer, clothing, utensils, accessories and money were 'sent' to deceased loved ones on *Nghĩa Trang Online*. The days of being emotionally daunted by the subject matter took place in this new and exciting environment. Online and offline, physically and intellectually, Vietnam was incredibly stimulating, and it was all to end just as I felt it was beginning.

Hi Anthony, please contact Ben, Dad or myself ASAP, it's important, ASAP it's very important. These words from my sister appeared on a chat screen on my laptop while I was sitting down for breakfast. The lack of context, the brevity and the repetition could not be the usual negotiation of a Skype session with family at home. That my mother was not mentioned as someone to contact did not occur to me at the time. Half an hour later, I was sitting in a phone booth in the local post office and heard the words 'It's not good mate. Mum is sick'. And by 'sick', my brother stated, she was very sick: leukaemia. It was getting worse and in the doctor's opinion, I should return home quickly. My brother did not say it but the message was clear: she could die. Everything afterwards was a whirlwind of booking flights, the emptying and cleaning of a newly leased apartment, confused goodbyes to new and very kind neighbours, and being unable to sleep on the long flight. I did not know what would await me.

Back home, I encountered the white sterility of my mother's hospital room, the regulated beeping of machines. While I had undergone an onslaught of experience in Vietnam, nothing had changed at home except for the overwhelming fact of her illness; it was all my family talked about. Her white blood cell count was so precarious that she was confined to a tiny hospital room, which had to be kept sterile. She was to be there for nearly one month. Vietnam's colour, noise and tastes juxtaposed against Adelaide (my home town in Australia) made it seem as though the sterility had bled beyond that hospital room, blanching my surroundings: the orderliness of the traffic, the mindless flicking through TV channels. While Mum ate her carefully weighed hospital food, we would eat only for utility at home. There was even an absence of touch, as I was too fearful to hug her lest I infect her, or create more of the blue-black bruises that covered her body. The emotions and senses converged and pretty much everything induced anxiety: the smell of disinfectant, the sound of footsteps in the corridor and not knowing if it was a doctor bringing bad news, the near-constant ambulance sirens outside.

Where Vietnam had been all senses, and a disconnection of emotions from those I was in contact with, returning home was a blunting of the senses with an amplification of emotions: the stress and worry; the difficult emotion of seeing my mother in severe pain and not knowing if it would end or get worse. Life settled into a routine that revolved around hospital visits and, when she was home, the provision of a litany of drugs several times a day.

The response from NTO members was almost instantaneous, and I received messages via Facebook, NTO and email in the days after I had left Vietnam:

> Hello Anthony. Is your mom's health getting well? I hope it'll end soon. Best regards for you and your mom. Hiep. (Personal communication)

> How are you? I've just heard about your mother's health. Your mẹ![5] I'm very sorry to hear … I hope that she will be treated well and have progress soon. Please give her my words. Best wishes! Phuong. (Personal communication)

NTO is an example of a community, a group of online kin who articulate their fears, anxieties and grief relating to the loss of a loved one, and some members effortlessly drew me into their community of reciprocation of feelings. On my birthday, a particularly exhausting day, Linh emailed me:

> How is your birthday today? I hope you have been enjoying a great time of birthday though I know it must be hard today. I think about you much, especially on this day. It is a difficult time. I have been busy recently for my working and studying. We hope to see you soon and your mother well again. Regards. Linh. (Personal communication)

Linh, whose niece was seriously ill in hospital, was empathising with my own situation of caring for a loved one, knowing all too well how long an hour spent in hospital lasts. Though our emotional responses were deeply shaped by the culture we lived in, it was reassuring to have support from an informant who herself was undergoing a similar experience. It was the beginning of a transformation that would continue when returning to the field.

Back to the field

I returned to Vietnam two months after the diagnosis of my mother's illness. I was emotionally exhausted and felt guilty returning to Vietnam while she was stable but still very ill. I was back and stimulated when just taking a walk down the street, or chatting to a waiter when ordering a meal. In comparison, my mother needed to be removed from the senses, avoiding interactions with people for fear of infection to her low immune system, forcing herself to eat food that either tasted metallic to her or that she could not taste at all. After spending several hours on NTO one particular day, I came across a memorial of someone else's mother and was hit with an emotional

---

5   Translation: mother.

intensity which was different from any that I had experienced before. As I noted in the field notes:

> Today I stumbled across an online memorial for a mother, similar in age to my own. I look at her face and the comments below. She looks so young, so youthful, just like my own mother. It is too difficult as I wrench myself away from the computer, looking for anything, fresh air, something, anything but this. (Field notes)

Another day, I interviewed a moderator of the site, who asked about the health of my mother, and my field notes reveal anxiety about *being* in Vietnam at all.

> Thinking about Mum again. It is hard being a world away. Skype is good but it cannot start to bridge the barrier of not seeing her. Mum, how are you doing? What a wretched thing to have. No one deserves this. (Field notes)

Without my being aware of it at the time, a shift had occurred in the research I was conducting: I was undergoing experiences that could be usefully shared with informants. I am not suggesting here that I was experiencing the same emotions as informants, but that my experiences were an entrance to further dialogue and understanding in the field. Sometimes these experiences were similar, at other times profoundly removed, but it was an invitation to new conversations nonetheless. Without knowing it, my social space with informants had changed. Hastrup writes:

> The difference between 'knowing' and 'understanding' … amounts to a difference between an intimate and implicit 'native' knowledge, and an external and explicit 'expert' understanding. The point of doing anthropology is to bridge the two. *The key factor is the sharing of experience* and the making of ethnography. This making implies both an implicit knowing and an explicit understanding of the other world. We 'know' the social space as participants and we 'understand' it as detached analysts. The important thing is to note that this is not a linear process, but a simultaneity. And the scope of our comprehending others remains dual: anthropology is about the discovery of a definitional reality. (1993:175, italics added)

The social space I came to 'know' was that of the emotional experience of nearly losing someone, and being aware of death. Before, our relationship was one-sided, and I felt little connection with such emotions and experiences. Now, I could bring this new empathy to the field, which transformed my relationship with many informants.

When I was talking with Huong, whose father had passed away, she would ask about my mother and relate how she felt when her father died. The act of my going home demonstrated to Huong that we were alike in that I, too, cared deeply for my parents and perceived NTO — where many parents who had passed away were memorialised — as a valid area of research. Huong was visibly moved as we discussed our parents, and I spoke of how challenging it was being away from home at that time. I showed her a photo of my mother, which had been emailed to me. In the picture, my mother is standing outside in the Mount Lofty Botanic Gardens in the Adelaide Hills region, with a beanie on to keep her warm, since she had lost her hair. Huong showed me pictures of herself with her father and invited me to light a candle for her father in the future. This sharing of photos took place alongside my research questions about NTO and Vietnamese memorialisation more generally, but there was no solid demarcation between our talking about our parents, or the website; there was a natural movement back and forth.

With my enhanced emotional understanding, I believe I engaged more comprehensively with the primary research. The digital reflections of offline memorialisation seemed to resonate more with me, whereas before I may have been simply gathering data. Tens of thousands of online candles are lit for the deceased on NTO, and an uncountable array of items are uploaded: money, food, beer, clothing, cars. By uploading these items, members understand that they are 'sent' to the other world to help the deceased. This reflects the offline act of burning votive paper items, where the smoke 'sends' the item to the other world. After returning to Vietnam, I could more readily feel these two-dimensional replications, and see them as extensions of individuals going through pain, or sadly remembering a loved one. I could appreciate the comfort that simulated smoke and offerings would give.

This new understanding of online memorialisation, and the site's sensorial landscape, was brought about by both my empathy and my ongoing research into how members interacted with each other in the face of loss. From the beginning of this research, informants noted that the online portal was one where they could remember and recall the deceased. In remembering the dead, members wrote of being fond of, attached to, and carrying much love in their heart for those now gone. Informants spoke of the intense pain that could be written about to the departed and other members, described by some as a deep pain and mourning, an immense and excruciating pain, and profound sadness. For some members it was a feeling that was physically and spiritually painful, and one which left them feeling empty, restless and tired when thinking about the future.

In experiencing loss, members noted that confiding (*tâm sự*) in others and speaking of their grief was central to their time on the online memorial.[6] As noted by a young woman supporting her friend, whose child died in infancy, 'empathy and sorrow together are the most important things' (translation). For her, *tâm sự* was to release her inner feelings and to express what was in her heart with another person. Within NTO an affinity was created, an inner conviction that remembering and empathy could be forged together. It became 'a very significant web site' for this member, even though at times she could not bear to read some of the difficult narratives.

---

6   That individuals use online memorials to express emotion is a key finding in the scholarly literature. For recent contributions concerning the expression of emotion online, see Christensen and Gotved 2014; Graham, Gibbs and Aceti 2013; Haverinen 2014; Moreman and Lewis 2014; Sofka, Cupit and Gilbert 2012.

During the research, I came to know Hanh, whose father had passed away several years beforehand. Her experiences of this were deeply painful and unsettling. There were many times she felt lonely even with the support of family and friends. And so Hanh entered into the NTO community: 'After my father died I joined NTO to create a grave ... to remember my father and to show my loss. When my father died, I was sad and devastated'. The expression *chia buồn* is one which resonated with her: 'It is where I meet people with the same pain. We have a similar situation, the pain should be shared with other members so as to overcome the loss' (personal communication). Taking care of someone in their sadness and grief, and consoling and sympathising with them, was to informants in my research regarded as *chia buồn*. This is a well-known expression in the Vietnamese idiom, which translates to 'sharing/dividing the grief/sadness'. As Hanh noted: 'People in our country have many ways of sharing the sadness with other people by action, by speaking to help the other pass away the pain. This is *chia buồn*, it is the action of expressing your consideration for her/his sadness'.

The expression of *chia buồn* resonated with my own experiences after news of my mother's illness. It highlighted the responses from NTO members to my own pain back in Australia, and also mirrored the language they used specifically within the online memorial site. While it was an expression culturally relevant to the Vietnamese I was encountering, it connected to my own experiences both in and out of the field. Returning to the field, I was also able to comprehend in a new way the participation of informants during death day anniversaries.

Undertaken yearly to commemorate the death of an individual, the death day anniversary is a time of family reunion where family, friends and neighbours feast with the dead and each other, remembering them and also, importantly, including them in the celebration. Those death days for parents or grandparents who had died at an older age, in their home and surrounded by family, are 'good' deaths, compared to 'bad' deaths, where the body of the deceased may be missing or the circumstances of the death are tragic, such as the death of a young person (see Kwon 2006:12-16; Malarney 2002:179; 2003). One 'good' death day I attended for a grandparent of an informant felt more like a celebration. There were quiet, sombre moments praying upstairs at the family altar, but, for the most part, the day was loud and festive: female family members had been preparing the bounty of food since early morning; friends and neighbours walked in with slabs of beer. After eating, some went to another room to play the card game *Tiến lên*, and gamble. Some went outside to burn votive paper. The senses came alive and, upon reflection, this added a sensory dimension to the online memorial I was researching. Though I had experienced the senses of online and offline memorialisation before returning home for my mother's illness, the addition of both my empathy and my feeling more secure in the social space allowed for a more thorough engagement after returning.

A death day towards the end of my fieldwork was for a young woman killed in a motorcycle accident. It was her second death day, sombre and, at times, heartbreaking. Sitting around the table lined with food, I reflected on how I would react to the loss of my own mother. Would I create an online memorial for her? Would my grief be difficult to express? Who would be the people I could confide in, and who would demonstrate *chia buồn*? In essence, how would I express grief within my own society, and would anyone be there to listen? Just as my previous understanding of cancer was that it happened 'to other people', so, too, the mother of the daughter at this death day said that such accidents 'happened to other people, not our daughter'. It was through NTO that I was connected to this mother, and though our experiences were literally and figuratively a world apart, we had forged an emotional connection and shared a social space.

Conclusion

It has been several years since my mother was diagnosed with leukaemia and the heavy medications and intrusive procedures have come to an end: she is now in remission. Writing this chapter in itself has been an emotional act: my memories both of Vietnam the country and of my PhD are tied to her illness. I have had life-altering experiences since — the birth of my daughter Eleanor, and of my son Morrissey — and when I contact informants, they now ask about my children, and the health of my mother, as I ask about their families and online kin from NTO.

I went to Vietnam with a great deal of academic knowledge but little personal insight into loss and grief. The reality of death and the emotionality of remembering were things I was unprepared for. My research proposal, written for The University of Adelaide before I travelled overseas, was encapsulated on thirty pieces of paper: complete, thorough. Then I was suddenly in the bustling country of Vietnam, a whole sensorial world away from those papers which seemed so safe and succinct, and in an emotional world on *Nghĩa Trang Online* that I could not connect to.

My research was interrupted by my mother's illness but, after returning to it, I was positioned within a new social space. The sensorial extravaganza of fieldwork — online via NTO, offline in the streets of Ho Chi Minh City, death day anniversaries and so on — gave me solid ethnographic research. However, my experiential understanding profoundly enhanced these sensations thereafter. My experiences, when discussed with informants, in turn allowed them to share more with me; we shared a similar social space through simultaneity of emotions and senses.

References

Christensen, D.R. and S. Gotved. 2014. 'Online memorial culture: An introduction', *New Review of Hypermedia and Multimedia* 21(1-2): 1-9.

Clifford, J. 2013 [1988]. 'On ethnographic authority'. In H.L. Moore and T. Sanders (Eds.), *Anthropology in Theory: Issues in Epistemology* (pp. 476-492). Oxford: Blackwell Publishing.

Davies, C.A. 1999. *Reflexive Ethnography: A Guide to Researching Others and Selves*. New York: Routledge.

Davies, D.J. 2005. *A Brief History of Death*. Oxford: Blackwell Publishing.

Davies, D. 2010. 'Introduction: Emotions in the field'. In J. Davies and D. Spencer (Eds.), *Emotions in the Field: The Psychology and Anthropology of Fieldwork Experience* (pp. 1-34). Stanford: Stanford University Press.

Doka, K.J. (Ed.) 2002. *Disenfranchised Grief: New Directions, Challenges and Strategies for Practice*. Champaign, IL: Research Press.

Endres, K.W. and A. Lauser. 2011. 'Contests of commemoration: Virgin revolutionary martyrs, state memorials, and the invocation of the spirit world in contemporary Vietnam'. In K. Endres and A. Lauser (Eds.), *Engaging the Spirit World in Modern Southeast Asia* (pp. 121-143). Oxford: Berghahn.

Graham, C., M. Gibbs and L. Aceti. 2013. 'Introduction to the special issue on the death, afterlife, and immortality of bodies and data', *The Information Society: An International Journal* 29(3): 133-141.

Hastrup, K. 1993. 'The native voice — And the anthropological vision', *Social Anthropology* 1(2): 173-186.

Haverinen, A. 2014. 'Editorial — The digitalisation of death culture(s)', *Thanatos* 3(1): 5-8.

Heathcote, A. 2014. 'A grief that cannot be shared: Continuing relationships with aborted fetuses in contemporary Vietnam', *Thanatos* 3(1): 29-45.

Heathcote, A. 2015. 'Remember forever: Relationships with the living and the dead in a Vietnamese online memorial site'. PhD Thesis, University of Adelaide, Adelaide.

Hockey, J, 2007. 'Closing in on death? Reflections on research and researchers in the field of death and dying', *Health Sociology Reviews* 16: 436-446.

Hollan, D. 2008. 'Being there: On the imaginative aspects of understanding others and being understood', *Ethos* 36(4): 475-489.

Hollan, D. and C.J. Throop. 2008. 'Whatever happened to empathy?: Introduction', *Ethos* 36(4): 385-401.

Jellema, K. 2007. 'Everywhere incense burning: Remembering ancestors in Doi Moi Vietnam', *Journal of Southeast Asian Studies* 38(3): 467-492.

Johnson, N. 2009. 'The role of self and emotion within qualitative sensitive research: A reflective account', *Enquire* 4: 23-50.

Kwon, H. 2006. *After the Massacre: Commemoration and Consolation in Ha My and My Lai*. Berkeley: University of California Press.

Kwon, H. 2007. 'The dollarization of Vietnamese ghost money', *Journal of the Royal Anthropological Institute* 13(1): 73-90.

Lawton, J. 2000. *The Dying Process: Patients' Experiences of Palliative Care*. London: Routledge.

Liss, A. 1998. *Trespassing through Shadows: Memory, Photography and the Holocaust.* London: University of Minnesota Press.

Malarney, S.K. 2002. *Culture, Ritual and Revolution in Vietnam.* Richmond Surry: Routledge Curzon.

Malarney, S.K. 2003. 'Weddings and funerals in contemporary Vietnam'. In N.V. Huy and L. Kendall (Eds.), *Vietnam: Journeys of Body, Mind and Spirit* (pp. 172-195). Berkeley: University of California Press.

Moreman, C. and D. Lewis (Eds.). 2014. *Digital Death: Mortality and Beyond in the Online Age.* Santa Barbara: ABC-CLIO.

Phan, C.C. 1993. 'The Vietnamese concept of the human souls and the rituals of birth and death', *Southeast Asian Journal of Social Science* 21(2): 159-198.

Rabinow, P. 1977. *Reflections of Fieldwork in Morocco.* Berkeley: University of California Press.

Rosaldo, R. 2004 [1989]. 'Grief and a headhunter's rage'. In A.C.G. Robben (Ed.), *Death, Mourning and Burial: A Cross-Cultural Reader* (pp. 167-178). Oxford: Blackwell Publishing.

Shaw, R. 2011. 'The ethical risks of curtailing emotion in social science research: The case of organ transfer', *Health Sociology Review* 20(1): 58-69.

Sofka, C., I.N. Cupit and K.R. Gilbert (Eds.). 2012. *Dying, Death and Grief in an Online Universe: For Counsellors and Educators.* New York: Springer Publishing Company.

Tumarkin, M.M. 2005. *Traumascapes: The Power and Fate of Places Transformed by Tragedy.* Melbourne: Melbourne University Publishing.

Valentine, C. 2007. 'Methodological reflections: The role of the researcher in the production of bereavement narratives', *Qualitative Social Work* 6(2): 159-176.

Watson, C.W. 1999. 'A diminishment: A death in the field (Kerinci, Indonesia)'. In C.W. Watson (Ed.), *Being There: Fieldwork in Anthropology* (pp. 141-164). London: Pluto.

Woodthorpe, K. 2007. 'My life after death: Connecting the field, the findings and the feelings', *Anthropology Matters* 9(1): 1-10.

Woodthorpe, K. 2009. 'Reflecting on death: The emotionality of the research encounter', *Mortality* 14(1): 70-86.

9 | Voices in the park:
The composition of sacred space and public place

Judith Haines

Abstract

City parks and gardens are environments established to enhance, complement and offset the economic and residential conditions of urban living. Composed of life forms attributed to the 'natural world' for human pleasure and wellbeing, these 'green spaces' are socially inscribed with liminal potentialities. As ontological islands in geographic space, urban parks and gardens exist in, and generate tensions between, orderings of reality in modern societies. An Adelaide group of environmentalists and their friends meet regularly in the Adelaide Park Lands to practise Reiki spiritual healing. In their group healing sessions, they bring a cultural discourse of health and harmony associated with green and natural places to the social foreground in their use of spontaneous, ambient vocalisation. Drawing on understandings of healing energy derived from notions of ultimate truth as a universal, animated energy of love, the members of the Reiki group give voice to their spiritual experience of communal healing. As a feature of improvisation, the emotional spiritual tone of vocalisation is not a formal component of Reiki healing technique, and it challenges the social constraints of conduct in public place as rational space. This chapter explores how ambient vocal sound produced as spiritual emotion takes up conceptual gaps in social ambivalence about 'natural' and 'unnatural' space, composing public space as cosmic spiritual space.

Introduction

> Just begin making a sound, then it becomes comfortable. Next, explore ... the sound, directing it to the person; then become immersed, absorbed in the energy of the sound and there's no ... space between oneself and the sound for ... thought, a dissolving of barriers, preconceptions, self-consciousness of whatever is between you and the other person. (Interview with Tom, 1 April 2011)

In the long, late summer grass, the Reiki healing session was now well underway. Tom lay flat and straight on his back with his eyes closed, surrounded by six others who were conveying healing energy to him from the palms of their hands, laying them softly on his shoulders, stomach, knees, ankles and feet. At irregular intervals, individuals lifted their hands, held them at a short distance from Tom's body, moved them backward and forward or in circular motions, or made broader sweeps of his body to ascertain where to apply healing next. A nimbus or aura was now gathering around the group, a sentient, energetic field of union and communion of the focus of loving care for Tom and for the whole group.

Overhead and around us, the trees stood in their own grace, part of the group in their enduring presence, part of this place called Rymill Park, and part of a wider parkland on the edge of Adelaide, South Australia. Around us, at an uncertain distance from the healing group, the hum and bustle of late-peak-hour traffic was audible. Within this layered and seemingly incoherent soundscape, Mira began to softly vocalise in a lilting, simple melody an 'Ah' sound, which rose and fell in gentle undulations similar to forms of humming that people engage in while they are relaxed and content carrying out another activity. However, Mira's sound was not a composition of mundane expression. A delicate and knowing tone of voice and a melodic structure of predominantly sharp and flat notes in trailing and circular movements expressed a spiritual process and response within her Reiki healing practice. This sound did not resonate as an accompaniment to Mira's healing activity but as belonging within it, as part of her practice. The form of Mira's vocalising with an absence of markers and direction for melodic resolution began to take the form of an ambient chant within a short space of time.

Soon after, Arien began to hum softly, loosely joining Mira's chant. Arien later explained that her humming was in fact her sounding of 'Om' in a conflation of a separate practice of chanting the mantra in Buddhist meditation. Adding to these soundings, Lisa began to repeat the name 'Gaia' clearly but not loudly in a near monotone, with slight variance of the two notes in alternate upwards and downwards movements for each syllable of what, for her, is a deity name for Planet Earth. These three voices, each with their own sonic quality, meaning and musical representation, continued and merged to form an ambient unity within the energy field of group Reiki healing as spiritual practice. Weaving through and around this ambient chanting, another layer of humming started, only just audible, from Rada. Lisa broadened her chant to: 'Gratitude to Gaia, we give thanks to Gaia' in a tone of deepening devotion. At this time, Kim joined in, chanting, 'Gaia, with thanks to Gaia', and Mira began to chant, 'Kahli', in a clear but soft tone in slightly varying, sustained notes for each of the two syllables of the Indian Hindu deity name.

The Reiki group broke with traditional and orthodox styles of group singing by vocalising together for a unified purpose of healing. It has been argued that, as a musical instrument, the human voice has unique capacities for expressing emotion, basic needs and power (Bruscia 1987). The singing voice provides force in expressing emotions in social contexts such as collective singing (Bodner & Gilboa 2006). In the same way, emotional engagement in groups and social movements shape collective actions and play a key role in their success or failure (Bensimon 2012:242). Schutz (1971:177, 174-5) describes social relationships as entered into in different dimensions of time, lived through simultaneously by group members who become '"tuned-in" to one another … living together through the same flux of musical process'. Within the Reiki group, multiplicities of sound and meaning, duration, starting and ending points, and chanting of deity names established a 'flux of musical process'. Deification of the environment as Planet Earth in the name of Gaia recast relationality as inclusively biospheric and 'tuning in' as biotic. According to Schutz (77), the musical event unfolds in inner time in which each vocalist forms sounds that connect with those hearing them, while 'making music together' occurs in outer time, in direct relationship, in 'a community of space'. This dimension unifies the movements of inner time toward synchronisation in a vivid present. In the Reiki group, the vivid present occurred in a flow of multifarious openings that drew people, places and sacredness together.

During healing and vocalising, the group predominantly had their eyes closed, opening them occasionally when preparing to change healing location and sometimes when interpreting or encountering specific aspects of energy or body temperature in the person being healed. At these times, individuals usually continued their vocalisations and could appear to be in trance-like states. However, trance was only discussed by group members as playing a minor role, and was not a sought-after experience on its own.

In this Reiki healing session, ambient vocalisation and chanting retained a quiet, reflective tone. Throughout Tom's healing, the group continued to apply Reiki healing as before. When Tom's healing time ended, Lisa took her turn moving into the centre of the group and lying down to receive healing. Healing time for each person usually extended for a duration of roughly ten minutes regardless of the numbers present in each session. During Lisa's healing, Mira again vocalised 'Ah' in a form similar to her ambient chant during Tom's healing. Kim and Arien hummed quietly and periodically for several minutes, then began tapering off. As an artefact of Reiki group practice, vocalisation also existed as an entity with meaning independent of the inner worlds of its creators. Throughout the eight months that the Reiki healing group met in Rymill Park, vocalisation was a consistent feature of the group's healing practice, taking an organic, spontaneous form which according to group members reflected the mood, ambience and energy of particular sessions.

The texturing and layering of vocalisation throughout the Reiki sessions varied from one person, often Mira chanting or singing quietly, to two or three members chanting and humming, to stronger (though never loud) vocalisation, when the group engaged in more projected sounds, words and chanting of deity names. Occasionally, the same names, words or phrases were used in unison, but more often there was a weaving of different deity names through and around each other. On occasions, Mira chanted traditional Indian chants or chants popular in contemporary alternative Western spiritual culture. Some vocalisation combined a subdued sense of play with reverence. Shamdasani (1994:xix) notes the popularity of musical artefacts, including chants and mantras borrowed from ancient and Eastern cultures, which often illustrate efforts to seek spiritual knowledge beyond 'Western' paradigms of religiosity.

Vocal sound produced as chanting, magical words, emotional songs, ambient sound and sound vibrations can also act as a portal for movement from mundane reality to transcendence. Hume (2007:45-6) has asserted that sound and its emotional characteristics can make the singer/listener/musician receptive to transcendent experience by altering states of consciousness; it can also induce trance states. Since the Renaissance, magical power has been attributed to music, and earlier European beliefs held that vibration is produced in the existence and unfolding of reality itself, composing a universal harmony. Sonic emissions were believed to accompany vibrations with an attunement of resonances reverberating in affinity with the first sound (43). Drawing from classical texts, beliefs circulated throughout the Renaissance that music held potential for curing disease by the benefit it brings from celestial attunement and 'the invocation of the gods' (43). Many belief systems demonstrate notions of spiritual or religious music having powers of enchantment and attunement with other realities and practices of harnessing their resonance for human benefit.

Alterations of consciousness produced in vocalisation in the Reiki group overturned notions of space and place as fixed, replacing them with conceptions of cosmic fluidity. Feld (1996:94) has observed that considerations of sound and place have been largely underrepresented in the European dominance of visualism rooted in the aesthetics of landscape painting and scientific epistemology. Carpenter and McLuhan (1960) sought to address this imbalance with the notion of 'acoustic space' in their exploration of oral and literary history in the context of twentieth-century electronic communications. At this time, the term 'auditory space' emerged, when the notion of music as an experience of tone and time exclusively was contested. Within musical philosophy in this era, space was detailed as 'audibly fused with time in the progression and motion of tones' (Feld 1996:95).

Meeting weekly in the Adelaide Park Lands for the purpose of spiritual healing, the Reiki group disrupted dominant orderings of reality with their ambient vocalisation in conflating and overturning social norms of place, space, time, embodiment and meaning. While, historically, musical vocalisation in the form of protest songs has been widely used for 'conveying political messages' about the need for change (Bensimon 2012:246), the Reiki group's expression of spiritual healing practice brought about change through transgressive behaviour in public spaces. In this sense of lifestyle choices lived publicly, the Reiki group gave voice to transformation.

In this chapter, I explore how a reorientation to self, community and locality amongst a group of young environmental activists and their friends eroded and displaced the nature-culture dichotomy. Focusing on one group and network with ecospiritual beliefs and practices, I explore what Maffesoli (1996:43) has described as an organic dynamic of the sharing of spiritual passion for social vitality and survival, set into action by a pervasive rationalism of late modernity. The broader social context for practices of vocalisation that include expressions of spiritual emotion is charted in the group's networks in a meditation group named The Seed Meditations and in social gatherings in Sound Circles. The Reiki group and its formation within wider networks of environmentalism, spiritual seeking and alternative lifestyles can be understood as a contemporary formation arising from a saturation of modern rationalist principles, of overarching ideological, economic and value structures precipitating a turn away from atomised individualism, and abstract social structure. The Reiki group is also concerned with perceived environmental threats.

According to Maffesoli (1996:95, 6), this turn towards affinal groupings is oriented to the local, to present time and shared feelings in sociality. Maffesoli presents this paradigm as closed in a 'mass-tribe dialect', an endless, undefined movement of form without centre and border in increasing 'massification and the development of micro-groups'. This chapter diverges from Maffesoli's paradigm in charting how the Reiki group, in their practice of vocalisation, created and explored openings in the understanding and experience of the lived world which ontologically served to reposition humans within the context of environmental connectivity and cosmological relationship. Within conventional frames of social ordering, the Reiki healing group was out of place, out of time (Douglas 1966:36) and outside modern rational constructs of personhood in its public displays of effervescence. It was ambient vocal sound generated as spiritual emotion in group Reiki healing practice which projected this displacement into the social foreground in Rymill Park.

Rymill Park, East Adelaide Park Lands

The parklands that surround the city of Adelaide on all sides are a predominant feature in its status as a 'garden city', a feature of the city's original plans, which sought harmony and balance between the urban environment and the natural world. While the parklands are widely enjoyed for leisure and recreational activities, on weekdays during peak hours they become green, alternative thoroughfares for commuters walking to and from work or study. At these times, the parks provide respite and shelter from the intensity of noise and fumes and the material features of vehicles congesting traffic grids along concrete and asphalt roadways. While it was not uncommon to see individuals resting in parks at this time, organised gatherings for expressive spiritual purposes were outside the modern ordering of social reality. As havens for relaxation and leisure or as thoroughfares for commuters, urban parks are ontologically constructed by the societies that establish them.

According to Descola and Palsson (1996:2), a blurring of the nature-culture opposition in contemporary science has initiated a revaluation 'of traditional Western cosmological and ontological categories'. While traditionally nature was seen to shape culture, with culture then imposing meaning on nature, there is presently 'opposition between dualist and monist approaches in human ecology' (3). The dualist approach is considered insufficient for approaching issues of sustainability, while a monistic approach is believed by some to be a sound premise for contextualising traditional and pre-industrial societies (3).

The Reiki group and many in their environmental and spiritual networks have taken up monistic ideas and practices in their desires to reconnect with and protect the environment. Vocalisation in Reiki sessions in Rymill Park situated this group and its spiritual practice in an open public setting. Each week, the Reiki group met at the edge of Rymill Park near the corner of East Terrace and Rundle Street on the edge of the city. Mira chose this location because she liked the area's centrality and convenience. She believed that the potential for healing was increased in places of nature and that the healing energy of the Reiki sessions would also contribute healing energy to the city. When asked about her orientation to notions of nature within the context of human-made parks, Mira replied that a tree is still a tree; it still has its own life and energy. Mira considered parks to be

> both nature and ambiguous, tampered with and interfered with by human design, but at the same time there are trees, sky and grass which is better for the health of the biological body than metal and concrete. (Interview with Mira, 10 April 2011)

Rymill Park is situated within the wider parkland area surrounding the city of Adelaide on the southern side of East Terrace. Allocation for parklands that fringe the city of Adelaide was made in the original plans for the city (Jones 2005a:73). Ecologically, Adelaide is situated on a floodplain that is the traditional land of the

Kaurna Indigenous people, whose cosmology binds their cultural conceptions of land with corresponding features of sky such as stars and planets. With European settlement, almost all of the woodland of the area was cleared and the Kaurna people were driven away and retreated from the European settlement site. In 1899, German horticulturalist August Pelzer was appointed to design and oversee the development of the Adelaide Park Lands and he created much of the parkland landscape in existence today (Jones 2005b:357).

Alongside an extensive planting program, Pelzer's vision for the parklands introduced curvilinear lines, pedestrian avenues and the establishment of gardens and playgrounds, with clusters of trees around the edges of each parkland block. Pelzer is considered to have exerted one of the strongest influences in establishing the parklands fringe for Adelaide and as having been instrumental in achieving Adelaide's status as a 'garden city'. The *Park Lands Management Strategy* of 1999 (Bedford 1999:43-4) charted a planting agenda that favours natives and, particularly, indigenous species that have environmental relevance and that fulfil low-maintenance and low-risk objectives. The strategy outlines a trend in planting towards natives that will not conflict with the parklands' cultural heritage (Jones 2005b:370).

Hirsch and O'Hanlon (1995:4) have argued that it is difficult to isolate *landscape* as a distinct analytical concept and cultural idea from other related concepts such as *space* and *place*, *inside* and *outside*, and *representation* and *image*. As a conventional Western notion, landscape has a significance and presence that has been submerged in anthropological accounts, where it has been deployed for framing a study and informing a view or objective position such as a 'recognisable' landscape of a particular people (1). Landscape has also served as a reference to the meaning that local people impute within their physical and cultural surroundings in practice and in appearance (1-2). The word *landscape* was introduced into the English language as a technical term used by painters in the late sixteenth century. The meaning of the word was originally tied to an experience of the physical world that reminded the viewer of European landscape paintings (2). Rural scenery was called landscape because it looked *picturesque*, in the sense of appearing similar to a painting. This introduced an idealised, imagined world which became desirable in the physical world as a way to improve it (2). The development in the late nineteenth century of the garden city is a case in which urban planning aimed to marry town and country. Such aspirations demonstrated desires to unite the social and economic opportunities provided by towns with possibilities for idyllic, Arcadian notions of existence associated with the countryside.

Within a relationship between the ordinary workaday life and an imagined ideal existence, notions of landscape entail 'a relationship between the "foreground" and "background" of social life' (Hirsch & O'Hanlon 1995:3). The foreground can roughly be understood as corresponding to the formal context of everyday experience, while the background refers to perceived potentiality. Historically, the purest form of potentiality is emptiness itself, with sacred sites and places sometimes being physically empty or mostly uninhabited and situated at a distance from populations for which they hold significance (4). Landscape can be understood as the relationship between foreground and background 'in any cultural context' and is therefore a cultural process producing 'cultural landscape' (4). Landscape cannot be entirely objectified, though, as an element of intrinsic subjectivity prevails. '[T]here remains an aspect of meaning in landscape which lies "beyond science", the understanding of which cannot be reduced to formal processes' (Cosgrove 1984:17). This marks a tension in the relationship between place as subject position and space as non-subject position in understandings of landscape as an analytic concept. A tension between romantic depictions of landscape and more scientific ethnological accounts has established the 'typical landscape' as a representation eliciting a 'sense of people and place characteristic of' a particular area (Smith, as cited in Hirsch & O'Hanlon 1995:11).

An ambivalence is built into parks and green spaces, animating uncertainties in modern societies about both what is 'natural' and 'unnatural' and the social valuing of these spheres. The foreground of ontological meaning in these green spaces is that of the modern rational worldview of atomised individuals (Foucault 1977), which informs personal orientation and social conduct in public space and place. Veiling the unstable ground of ambivalence about notions of 'nature' and its relation to culture is the ontological composition of public parks and gardens as rational space delineated by constraints of political organisation. Vocalisation practised by the Reiki group in their healing sessions served as an artefact and sensory vehicle for connecting background with foreground in bringing the emotional tone of spiritual devotion into public place and space. While it is not uncommon for individuals and groups to practise alternative modalities such as Tai Chi, yoga and meditation in parks and gardens, these do not express emotional tone within a 'rational' public place. Emotional expression, assigned to the private, personal and domestic sphere, is out of place here, as are many forms of expressive physical contact. Rather than adhering to abstract modern notions of nature and culture, and notions of public and private, the Reiki group ontologically constructed connections between the materiality and spirit of the parklands in a cosmological wholeness.

Maffesoli (1966:130) asserts that time and space are easily discerned within place, legitimising the corporeality of being together. The 'valuing of space, through image, the body and territory is both cause and effect of the submerging of the individual in a vast whole' (138-9). According to Maffesoli (132), a 'religion of the soil' is central to renewed engagement in neighbourhoods, 'urban villages' and communities that emphasise affinity, shared sentiment and intersubjectivity. Constituting a spiritual materialism, the bond between space and collective sentiment expresses a unifying logic. A link between the 'genius of place' and 'community of destiny' generates the social body and ensures stability (133). This is an organic orientation to the world which articulates the ancestral drive for safety in an increasingly rational and mechanical world (133). An understanding of the 'self' as social contests individualist ideologies, and favours stability in the awareness of common responsibilities (134).

According to Maffesoli (136), such spaces make up a territory that crystallises an aura of place built on the sedimentation and laying-down of pathways. A close relationship exists between collective memory and territory; groups 'trace their shapes in the earth and connect with their collective memories' (Halbwachs 1992:166). Associated with the revaluing of community, networks and groups is the revaluing of space. The sentiment of the collective marks out a space, which in turn influences sentiment. This space expresses an immanent transcendence that surpasses individual atomisation, becoming a symbol for the social cohesion of the group (Maffesoli 1996:130). In much New Age and contemporary spiritual belief, the notion of holism rests on understandings of space as bound to the social and the natural (131).

Reiki in the parklands

As well as providing a meeting place for the Reiki group, Rymill Park and the neighbouring Botanical Gardens served as general meeting places for the group and their broader social networks: for picnics and celebrations, yoga classes, Qi Gong sessions, meetings for spiritual discussions and as a thoroughfare to nearby activities such as fire-twirling and ritual in Botanic Park. The northeast Adelaide Park Lands became a social locality for these networks, with familiar pathways and sites of significance. Although comprising public places, the particular areas these groups frequent have established an aura based on the beliefs, practices and meanings invested in them. Layerings of liminality have been added to that of urban parklands at the city's edge, as these groups inhabit orthodox places in unorthodox ways. Frequenting of the parklands by these networks over time has created a type of sovereignty of place as relational. The groups and individuals belonging to these networks seem as much claimed by these places as they have come to claim them.

For these networks, this is a secret land for imagining and practising realities not acknowledged in orthodoxy. These imaginings and practices infuse notions of locality with a globalised timelessness in discourses of environmental connectivity, and with the cosmic in monistic spiritual and religious beliefs. Engaged by the poles of space in the parks and gardens at the northeastern corner of the city, and by the symbol of the Earth as sacred, the Reiki group and their social networks appear as ghetto-like in a contemporary urban expression of 'the tribal'.

Reiki is a modality that draws on perceived external and internal energy activated for the purpose of healing the self and others. Founded in Japan in 1922 by Dr Mikao Usui, Reiki is promoted as being capable of healing physical disease as well as conditions such as anxiety, nervousness and poor constitution (Sweeney 2002:38, 92). The name

Reiki derives from the combining of the two words *Rei* and *Ki*. *Rei* has a meaning similar to the English word *universal*, referring to an energy that is universal and in all places at once. The word *Rei* is associated with, and includes, soul, spirit and ghost, and can refer to ethereal or supernatural power (38). Contemporary understandings and definitions of this energy include concepts such as the 'highest spiritual consciousness', associated with a quality of love in 'ultimate truth'. Experience of this form of love is likened to feelings of God-consciousness, to going Home, or to 'being in a heavenly place' (155). Sweeney describes this as feeling 'the love of your creator' (155). Reiki healing is advocated by its proponents as providing opportunities to channel and share this love (155). Reiki energy is believed to be life-giving, and practitioners strive to channel it for healing purposes. This mode of healing is defined by practitioners as spiritual healing (39).

The word *Ki* refers to energies that are non-physical but that animate living things; it corresponds to the Chinese notion of *chi*, the Indian word *prana*, and Hawaiian *mana*. *Ki* means the exertion of force on a physical object affecting movement, such as moving a cup on a table. Chinese references to *Ki* date back over 4000 years, with the notion widely embraced in practices of martial arts and acupuncture (39). *Ki* is conceived of as life-force energies that surround and permeate all living things. Good health is associated with high levels of *Ki* energy. *Ki* is not perceived as containing *Rei* or spiritual energy, and is believed to generate at a lower frequency than *Rei* energy (39). Being a more immediate and direct energy, *Ki* healing is considered capable of restoring healthy balance in living things faster than Rei energy. Reiki practitioners believe that they can channel these low-frequency, *Ki* energies to promote physical, mental and emotional balance.

These monistic and holistic principles present a point of coherence between this Japanese healing system and the New Age and alternative spiritualities that are the orienting principles of environmentalists with spiritual conceptions of the earth. The political significance of accessibility of this healing method is also important among these networks, as Kim highlighted in his description of Reiki at the first session I attended, stating that everyone can practise Reiki healing. The connection of notions of spirituality, healing and power reflects the importance given to egalitarian principles that span most of the environment movement and many New Age modalities.

Reiki is essentially a touch method of healing, drawing on a synthesis of perceived wideranging spiritual energy with specific, localised energies permeating and surrounding living forms. If a non-touch method is requested, the hands are held very close to the body of the 'healee'. Although spirit is believed to radiate from the practitioner's whole body, Rei spiritual energy is conceived of as travelling in through the top of the practitioner's head, downwards into the arms and hands, and out through the palms of the hands into the healee (346). Traditionally, Reiki healing is directed over the body and head, as these were considered to have the most need of healing (347). However, practitioners in the Adelaide Reiki group did not view the limbs as secondary in significance to other parts of the body.

The Reiki healing group was initiated by Mira in September 2005, meeting at Rymill Park at 5.30 pm on Mondays. Sessions usually got underway between 6 pm and 6.30 pm. Mira sent out an email among her social networks inviting them to participate in the Reiki healing group. Drawing from the historical traditions of her Greek family members and ancestors, Mira identified herself as a healer. Her paternal grandmother and great-grandmother were village healers in Greece with widespread reputations among local communities, and her maternal grandmother possessed clairvoyant and clairaudient abilities. Mira believed that she could access knowledge from the beliefs and practices of her ancestors, that this knowledge was 'encoded within her' and that she could access it from a 'cellular, biological level' (interview with Mira, 28 October 2005). In Mira's view, simultaneous healing by a group of people could increase the benefits of healing (28 October 2005). Another motivation for initiating the Reiki group was Mira's desire for social activity with a spiritual focus rather than traditional norms of socialising organised around sharing food and conversation (interview with Mira, 18 December 2005).

According to Maffesoli (1996:77), the saturation of the abstract, theoretical and the purely rational is producing culture in the broad sense made up from participation and the tactile. A return to sensation and image marks a 'logic of touch' (77). For the Reiki group and their networks, 'touch' was coherent with beliefs about connectivity as holistic and spiritual. Walking, bushwalking and cycling were valued activities, and touching and embracing each other produced personal and social bonds. Attendance in the group did not require formal membership and over a two-year period, three to four core groups evolved, with Mira and Tom as core members. The fluidity and flexibility of the group meant that weekly sessions could be made up from between three to a dozen people.

Vocalisations and their meanings

Vocalisation in Reiki healing practice in Rymill Park held multifarious meanings and purposes for group members. The open-endedness of its articulation and meanings gave it a position of emergence rather than of tradition, and in this context vocalisation communicated publicly emerging threads of belief and practice. Schutz (1971:169) has claimed that social references within music can be hidden and that musical knowledge is 'socially derived', bearing the 'prestige of authenticity and authority' of social influences (168). According to Bensimon (2012:249), shared vocal sounds, as well as chanting and songs, 'can contribute to the construction of a collective memory which can later be recalled at other times and places'.

Mira initiated the practice of vocalising in the Reiki group because other Reiki practitioners had suggested that it can be beneficial for healing to chant the names of Reiki symbols. The combination of healing modalities and ambient vocalisation is also present in alternative spiritual cultures that engage holistic notions of healing with contemporary expressions of primal and spiritual music genres. Both spheres are concerned with alternative notions of embodiment, space and ultimate truth. Arien and Rada often hummed and chanted 'Om', with these sounds holding a rich diversity of meanings that could be layered or singular at different times in and between different Reiki sessions. For Rada, these sounds had connection with vibration as an aspect of healing, while at the same time ' … giving voice to the visual side of what was happening' (interview with Rada, 28 March 2011). For Arien, chanting 'Om' was partly about the group experience and partly a personal experience that for her could not be fully explained or described. '"Om" helps me get back to my true nature … [I]t resonates with my true nature' (interview with Arien, 30 March 2011). Describing a broader context for this chant, Arien explained that 'Om' was a chant commonly used in social-spiritual settings, that many people and groups she came into contact with chanted this mantra. From this broader, social context, 'Om' could have an externalised, social meaning across time, connecting people rather than engaging with internal processes.

Mira's 'Ah' sound was influenced by her reading about different realms of reality and, in particular, heavenly realms. Some individuals she encountered in social circles and networks had told her they 'sensed an energy of a heavenly realm about [her] and [she] too felt an influence of having experience of a "Christian realm of angels singing God's praise"' (interview with Mira, 10 April 2011). Singing the praise of God is a devotional practice and expression of spiritual love for deity. Mira's vocalising 'Ah' was also an expression of imaginative, creative process for her, of ' … finding something in myself' (10 April 2011). Disclosure and revelation of hidden or inaccessible aspects of self, as well as existential mysteries, were as significant for Reiki group members as communing with life forces that are unnameable. Within these multiple, simultaneous positionings of meanings and access, bounded selves of modernity became ontologically reconstituted as porous and permeable. According to Flournoy (1994:162-4), the imaginative, lyric linguistic style precedes prose, reason and the didactic, drawing closer the echo of a past, 'primitive state of mind', 'common to all human beings … at the root of all language'. Within their practice of vocalisation, group members sought to bypass dominance of the mundane, rational world and its orderings of reality in order to achieve connection with a broader reality.

A name chanted by Mira, Lisa and Kim in the Reiki healing sessions was 'Gaia', the Greek deity name made popular in environmental consciousness by James Lovelock (2000). Bensimon (2012:253) asserts that chanting of deity names holds potential for experiencing spiritual transcendence in feelings of fusion with the group as a whole and with the numinous. Chanting the name 'Gaia' in Reiki healing sessions in Rymill Park brought an awareness of the environment into the sphere of human healing, reinforcing beliefs in the group of imbalances in environmental wellbeing and perceptions of these problems as linked to human health. Within the context of Reiki healing, the deity name 'Gaia' served in large part as a symbol for a holistic worldview underpinning Reiki technique and philosophy, notions of environmental connectivity, and contemporary beliefs of the sacred as immanent. Vocalising 'Gaia' was the sounding of an opening to immanent transcendence.

Mira liked the deity name 'Gaia' because it is a representation of the Earth as a feminine deity and because it connected her to her Greek ancestry and to the ancient Greeks. Chanting 'Gaia' held spiritual-political significance for Mira, who claimed that Pagans continued to be persecuted in Greece. She stated that her extended family in Greece continued to dance traditional circle dance (interview with Mira, 10 April 2011). Mira also liked the sound of the name 'Gaia'. The global use of the deity name 'Gaia' in environmental and popular discourse has strengthened global awareness of environmental conditions and of the human relationship with the environment, and has disseminated contemporary notions of ultimacy as immanent in the world.

A potential within this naming was the ability to translate environmental concern into emotional tone. The range of emotional tone in vocalisation practice was given devotional dimensions by Gaia's position with the gods. Earth conceived of as deified facilitates reviewing and repositioning of the human place in the world and universe. Maffesoli (1996:128) asserts that a restoration of holistic connection 'between the spatial, the global', the intuitive and the emotional is in process and that communal types of behaviour emerge from an emphasis on nature and relationship with the global and the environment. Several of those who attended Reiki sessions vocalised and chanted 'Gaia', underlining the group's environmental allegiance within spiritual contexts. As such, the deity name 'Gaia' can be analysed as what Bensimon (2012:249, 253) has articulated as an 'emotional key word', both containing a dynamic of devotion and unification within the group and providing a context for the expression of sadness and mourning for environmental damage.

Chanting the Hindu Goddess name 'Khali' originated in part from Mira's desire to gain spiritual enlightenment as quickly as possible. Mira learned at a retreat that surrendering one's attachments gained Khali's mercy and liberation from them, thus making the path to enlightenment quicker. Mira found this potential benefit intoxicating, as she wished to attain the highest level of enlightenment possible and felt that the usual path would take a long time. Khali is a deity ascribed to the darker, shadow or negative aspects of human experience. As a slayer of demons, her powers are understood by devotees to be wrought against human forces such as anger and fear rather than against mythical or mystical beings (interview with Mira, 10 April 2011). Drawing from ancient deity names constitutes what Schutz (1971:169) has described as a 'thematic kernel' of mystical wisdom of the ages. The taking-up of archaic deities that are representations of the Earth and natural processes served the added purpose for members of the Reiki group of spiritual alignment with the Earth and cosmos across time.

For members of the Reiki group, vocalisation during healing sessions was spiritual practice in itself and within the context of spiritual healing. Vocalising added to the spiritual tone of sessions for individual members, for the cohesion of the group and for the process of spiritual healing. Rada experienced vocalisation as spiritual and as adding a meditative dimension that lent a holistic sense to the healing sessions. For Rada, vocalising was an inclusive and spiritual experience engaging a vibrational aspect of healing. 'Reiki is a very physical spiritual healing. Vocalising is a lot to do with the vibration of healing, so it added to that aspect of the physical healing' (interview with Rada, 28 March 2011). Vocalising also served to strengthen Rada's ability to focus during the sessions, countering mental distractions by adding a meditative dimension and making the sessions a more holistic experience.

Arien was experienced in chanting Eastern and Buddhist mantras, had chanted and sung in Pagan groups and settings, and had sung in a choir. Her 'stock' (Schutz 1971:168) of experiences shaped her particular knowledge of spiritual musicality within the Reiki group's practice of vocalisation. While she did not perceive herself as participating greatly in producing sound, preferring to focus on Reiki healing energy, she felt that she still participated in the sounds of vocalisation. Arien's perception of vocalisation dissolves the boundaries of compartmentalisation of sensory experience.

> Vocalisation is bound up with energy so you're still contributing to the vocalising sound. It's not an isolated sound ... like at a concert, the audience is contributing to the sound. Reiki healing energy and vocal energy are combined. Vocalising is an expression of the energy that's there anyway [and] helps to focus it. (Interview with Arien, 30 March 2011)

For Arien, chanting, humming and other ambient sound contributed another dimension to the sessions, facilitating the accessing of healing energy and the sacredness of that energy. In Arien's understanding, sound, healing and place existed within a unified whole. 'The vocalising is part of the energy happening in Reiki, it was about creating the space ... [T]hey were inseparable ... [T]hey arise from the same place' (30 March 2011).

Before his participation in the Reiki group, Tom had practised Hindu and Buddhist chants in his personal spiritual practice and in groups, as well as chanting and vocalising in the Seed Meditations and Sound Circles (discussed below). In the Reiki healing sessions, he sometimes chanted the sounds or names of the Reiki healing symbols such as 'Chocuray'. He likened this form of vocalising to Japanese toning and believed that chanting these names opened up and activated their energies. Like Arien, Tom held the view that the energetic influence of vibration from sound was effective for healing, and that the meaning and intention of sound produced in this context could make it beneficial to others. The sounds he produced in the healing session were not, in his words 'any old sound', but an expression of 'an inner source of love, inner truth and beauty' (interview with Tom, 1 April 2011).

Within the Reiki group, the healing energy of love had an inclusive, holistic meaning in a continuum in which human and divine love were not distinct from each other. Norager (2011:50) asserts that notions of love, like religion, are ideological and that 'love cannot be organised because its place of worship is in the hearts of those involved'. In modernity, according to Norager (150), a secularisation of religion and love has facilitated a 'culture of authenticity' alongside 'a certain divinisation of human love', so that love has become a primary purpose of life throughout the Western world. Ideas of God as holding personal agency and absolute power have 'been replaced with the notion of God as the power of love' (51). These notions of ultimacy were coherent with alternative and New Age beliefs held by the members of the Reiki group and their networks. A spiritual focus on love held political nuances in negotiating personal responsibility in the lived world and as an antidote to rationalism. In these contexts, love mediates moral pathways and grants personal freedoms.

Mira believed that vocalising in healing practice 'connects baser energies with a transcendental source' (interview with Mira, 10 April 2011). Mira associated sound with creation itself.

> I believe that sound is the origin of the universe … is a well-wisher to all beings and therefore … must have their best interests at heart. Therefore the sound of the universe … is by nature a healing source and force. (10 April 2011)

Sound, music and vocalisation held a focal position in Mira's spiritual practice, with song comprising her favourite form of meditation. For Mira, sound and chanting were an expression of the Reiki healing energy. 'I would get into … position and connect with the energy and wait for a tune to come into my mind and then I would voice' (10 April 2011).

Ambient vocalisation, as chanting, humming, singing and soundings of non-formal linguistic representations, found its way into expression in the Reiki healing group along the alternative cultural pathways of spirituality, environmental concern and activism, and through communication technologies in social and environmental networks. As a salient feature, ambient vocalisation was present in the earliest formation of this social network in organised meditation gatherings with a focus of directing human energy to plant seeds in order to facilitate their germination and growth. The 'Seed Meditations', as they were named, was a project initiated by Lisa as an adjunct to her honours course in biological science. Lisa held Pagan, Buddhist and New Age beliefs that for her were entwined with her appreciation, awareness and concern for living things and for the environment inclusively. In Lisa's personal reading on these subjects, she found reports of studies in the popular New Age book *The Celestine Prophecy* (Redfield 1993) in which plants responded to qualities and tones of thought and sound in ways that impacted their vitality and growth rate. When Lisa set up the Seed Meditations, she encouraged those attending to direct sound as well as meditative focus towards the seeds. It was common for those attending the Seed Meditations to describe their practice as 'sending Love to the seeds'. Out of this focus group, strong social bonds and friendships developed, along with confidence and trust in sharing and developing activities including spiritual practices together.

Maffesoli (1996:161) asserts that an organic orientation prefers collective, tactile, emotional and conjunctive characteristics. Small groups structurally restore symbolic power in building a mystical network and an increase in social life. The mystical is defined by Maffesoli (156) as 'that which tries to understand how things stay together, even if in a contradictory way'; the astonishment at the 'good at work in all things'. Groups hold a 'source of life' which generates heat, reanimating hearts and opening them to sympathy. Durkheim predicted that emotion would play a significant role in the 'associations of the future' (as cited in Maffesoli 1996:87). Such a sociality is at work in the re-enchantment of the world (83). A mystical sociality generates flux, mobility, experience and emotional life. In this, postmodern sociality is restoring archaic values of community in which everyday life offers valid everyday knowledge (148).

Shared valuing and concern for the environment with notions of the Earth as sacred comprised a specific group ethic that functioned within the Seed Meditations group and its wider networks. Human beings gathering to meditate on seeds for the purpose of facilitating their growth marked an organic way of thinking and holistic values in which intuition and commonly felt experience both belong with living knowledge and search for new knowledge in experimental practices. These concerns shaped the life ways of this network, articulating its sociality as mystical. Mira was one of those drawn to the Seed Meditations, and she formed strong friendships with Lisa and Tom, and enduring friendships and social connections with most in the group. Mira shared Lisa's interest in healing and in the positive uses of focused and directed sentient energy. When the Seed Meditations ended, Mira took three consecutive courses in Reiki healing and followed her desire to work in healing practice as spiritual vocation.

Sound Circles

One social expression of affinal connection shared within the group was the practice of 'Sound Circles' as spontaneous social communion. These occurred at parties, dinner parties, rituals and conferences as well as publicly, in the form of busking and public spiritual practice; thus the group maintained its style and preference for ambient sound free of structuring and orchestration, with each person following 'authentic' vocal expressions. In Sound Circles anyone was free to participate, including being simply present and not producing sound. Sound Circles were unbounded, the significance of which was highlighted by the complete absence of comment on attendance or non-attendance of individuals at these gatherings. The translation of terminology, and specifically religious terminology, from Latin and ancient languages bears traces of the ideology and positions of those translating. The style of circle formation practised in Sound Circles, Seed Meditations, Reiki sessions and others was closer to Starhawk's (1989) translation of *religare*, to 'relink'. Starhawk is an ecofeminist activist and proponent of witchcraft, whose writings are widely known among environmental and New Age practitioners. Notions of linking and relinking in contemporary social practice carry inferences of flexibility and impermanence. Sound Circles and other circles participated in by these networks played an important role in creating and strengthening social-spiritual-activist connections, while at the same time ensuring space for personal, group and ideological experimentation. This space, which is itself ideological, was a feature of circle gatherings, making the composition of these formations porous.

At one Sound Circle, which took place at a large dinner party at Mira's home, almost all the members of the former Seed Meditation group, some of whom now comprised the core of the Reiki group, were present, and other dinner guests joined in as well. These guests included environmental activists, volunteers and paid workers, and others whose connections to Mira and the Reiki group were spiritual and/or social. Throughout this group, notions of environment and spirituality were not clearly delineated from each other. A richness, intimacy and complexity of sound and social ambience produced via almost an hour of uninterrupted vocalising, drumming and other percussive sound was a revelation within the context of the norms of day-to-day rational, social conduct.

Mira was a focal presence throughout the first half of the Sound Circle, although not leading or dominating the group. She simply seemed in fine voice with much to express and apparently touched by her muse on this occasion. Some of her prominence in this Sound Circle may have derived from her role as host of the dinner party and her obvious sense of pleasure and comfort in gathering a large group of friends in her home. While most of those participating in this Sound Circle produced non-linguistic ambient sound that progressively deepened in emotional tone, Mira at times sang parts of popular songs that she is fond of but with modified melodies; at other times, she moved into another practice, peculiar to her, of long dialogues based on spiritual subjects that she was exploring at the time. During these dialogues, there sometimes seemed to be an invisible other with whom she engaged in intense and animated conversation, with a dynamic of conversation being conveyed by the occasional nodding of her head forward, as if addressing someone. At other times, her dialogues were addressed in such a way as to imply that the conversation was with herself or with the numinous.

This linguistic practice of Mira's resembled glossolalia in utterances sometimes incoherent, sometimes ecstatic and including occasional emotional exclamations. Her vocalisation did not have the tone of 'purely intellectual calculation', comprising a more 'aesthetic order' (Flournoy 1994:123, 155). During these vocalisations, Mira's upper body sometimes swayed and, rather than nodding in a forward direction, her head moved slightly from side to side, sometimes staying upright and sometimes dropping forward slightly. Throughout this Sound Circle, most of those participating vocalised with their eyes closed, sitting upright on the floor with legs crossed; others sat in armchairs. About three-quarters of those participating played drums or music sticks or other instruments they had fashioned from found objects for that occasion, such as empty juice bottles and sticks.

Without a focus on seeds or human healing, this Sound Circle engaged with the social and the personal mediated with richly layered, complex ambient sound. A 'sonic bonding' (Turino 2008) was created by the group vocalising together. The commitment of time, focus and creative and emotional communion in the course of this Sound Circle led to altered states of consciousness for me, the researcher. I experienced time, space and personal boundary collapse throughout this session, along with the experience of overcoming awkwardness in what was for me an unfamiliar situation; at the same time, I was also attending to the modulations of sound and physical presence of the group as a whole and of the individuals comprising it.

Epiphany in a vivid presence, according to Schutz (1971), is achieved in syntony, the 'mutual tuning in relationships'. Two flows of inner time take place in this communal vocalisation: one is 'the stream of consciousness of the composer', and the other is 'the stream of consciousness of the beholder' (Schutz 1971:173). These streams of consciousness are experienced simultaneously in the flux of musical process. Sharing the flux of others' inner time creates a mutual vivid present (173). Vocalising in the Sound Circle opened into multiplicities of streams of consciousness and flows of inner time being lived through, both in the numbers of participants producing individual authentic sound, with some not vocalising, and in the flux of individuals entering and leaving the circle within its duration. The vividness of present time in the epiphany that I experienced held dynamics of time as shifting, moving and slipping: oceanic and falling away at the same time. Within the context of this Sound Circle, syntony was an experience of a vivid presence carrying its knowledge of non-presence, an organic glimpse of life and death constantly composed of each other.

The emotional tone that emerged from this Sound Circle was, first, that of joy and pleasure in communing in this manner with each other and together as a single organism. At times, awareness presented itself of individuals singing and sounding themselves into being and simultaneously the group sounding itself into a strength and coherence of union. The physicality of bodily organic engagement in projecting authentic sound into a smallish room holding up to fifteen people became woven with a mystical ambience with traces and representations of the inner landscapes being traversed and negotiated in this social ritual. At the same time, a physicality of an organic group body was being made and its inner emotional and psychical landscape being felt, discovered and produced. Within the fluid dynamics of these interrelationships, an emotional tone of love was predominant.

The spontaneous dynamic of Sound Circles constituted them as simultaneously explorative, experimental, personal, social, emotional and abstract. The social context for establishing such richness was made possible by the foundations of love, friendship, support and comradery produced and reproduced from shared values and commitments of care, healing and celebration of self, group and the environment. An encompassing emotional tone as 'loving' was engaged within Sound Circles as ontologically holistic, an orientation congruent with notions of love constructed in Reiki healing practice and the Seed Meditations. These practices of 'tuning in' in environmental consciousness construct a vivid presence in which 'We' (Schutz 1971:161) becomes biospherically inclusive. In this context 'Love' is ontologically moved from private, individual experience and exchange to a way of perceiving and engaging with the lived world. Bensimon (2012:243) asserts that '[a] shared music culture allows people to intimately feel part of a community'. The communal activity of Sound Circles played a significant role in the bonding and coherence underpinning the achievements of environmental goals in Adelaide at this time.

Maffesoli (1996:66) suggests that 'the "effervescent" community can signify both the loss of the individual and the reappropriation of the person', reflecting what Bensimon (2012:250) has described as 'the wish to transform reality'. A density and intention of sociality achieves an alternative space-time of fluidity and non-contemporaneity. This density is always in existence as multidimensional experience, the lived concreteness of life, feelings and passion, and constitutes an essential ingredient of social aggregations (Maffesoli 1996:36). With increased rigidity in social institutions, a separation or break occurs and this density becomes 'exiled to another space-time' and to a potentiality for new forms of expression (36). Rather than non-rational as irrational, affinity groups establish a logic other than that of modernity. The affectual and the symbolic can contain a broader and more generous rationality of their own (144).

More than reappropriation of the person from individualism, practices of intersubjectivity in Sound Circles as well as Seed Meditations and the Reiki healing group ontologically reinstated the person in biospheric connectivity. The agency of the individual was retained in a political reclamation of personal will. These groups and networks took up more than the affectual and the symbolic. Rather than wishing to transform reality, they sought to enter biospheric reality, with its mystical qualities. Within these practices, lines of logic established in biological sciences were taken up and explored further in desires for biospheric relationality. Such practices cannot be scientifically reduced to irrational evaluation; instead, they broadened the range of existential possibilities. The density of fluidity and non-contemporaneity of these groups and networks, while gathered at spacial distances of sociality, did not entirely break with social institutions. Instead, they actively permeated their rigidity in practices of biospheric awareness, activism and the insertion of multiplicities of life ways into public space.

Several of those present in the Sound Circle were musicians and artists of considerable ability, and all participating were either artistic or creatively capable. A mix of confidence and creative dexterity with affinal trust articulated sculptural shapes and textures of sound that were at times as playful as they were reverential, interspersed with emotional richness and occasional flickerings of pure absurdity, with all these nuances received as valid and holding equal sway within an affinal soundscape. A distinctive constant in the practice of ambient vocalisation within this group was an absence of apparent self-conscious shaping or directing of sound by individuals for themselves and in contributing within the group. The mode of participation was the sharing and production of sound as authentic, and shaped by shared values and beliefs of personhood and sociality.

Conclusion

An 'Easternisation' of the world has been in process since the late nineteenth century, from which the culturisation of nature has begun a move towards a naturalisation of culture. This process is expressed in alternative lifestyles and taste in music, art and dress and in ways of occupying the body and space. These include increasing variety in alternative medicines and group therapies. The integration of these practices into social spheres is overturning their marginal status, supported by syncretist ideologies that are introducing a variety of life ways, and the blurring of body-soul separation. A significant quality of this naturalisation of culture is a revaluation and reordering of the relationship of time and space. While the near and effectual are emphasised in uniting persons and groups to place, this ontological unity simultaneously occurs as contextualised within biosphere and cosmos.

Parks composed of natural forms are social representations of nature and the natural: nature-culture, irrational-rational. Parks offer islands of nature and the natural to urban dwellers, creating a traditional distinction between human-built environments as 'unnatural' and trees, plants, grass, stones, earth and water as 'natural'. As symbols of nature and naturalness, parks and gardens confer on cities an inference of naturalness and of belonging within modern orderings of reality. They also represent an awareness of human reliance on, and identification with, nature. This relationship, though, is based on tensions precariously contained and negotiated in the ambivalence about these spaces. This ambivalence is managed by the institution of rational principles and values of modern society on these places, so that public place is conceived of as rational space, and personal and social conduct is prescribed accordingly. But this process of rationalisation is far from seamless, with gaps of logic and slippage between layers of incongruous ontological orders. The problems inscribed within these ontological tensions rest in the social category of meaning. The Reiki group both contested and utilised modern constructions of meaning in overturning and conflating modern categories of public, private, rational, irrational and self so that these categories were no longer individual or atomised.

The Reiki healing group demonstrated a response to the increased distance between, and decline of, institutional structures in their development of 'grass roots' community, nourished by an immediate, lived reality of soil, nature and locality, which rests in holistic ideas of ultimacy. This form of sociality conflated distances inherent in rationalist thinking in relating to the world as a natural, cosmic environment. Ambient vocalisation in Reiki healing in Rymill Park symbolically voiced growing detachment from the abstraction of the public sphere in an ontological vitalism. Within this vitalism, an empathic sociality replaced a rationalised 'social'. The shared collective feeling of ambient vocalisation in the Reiki group contained a mystical sensibility, marking desire for communion and for continuity. Love expressed as spiritual emotion gave rise to Reiki healing energy, present and accessible throughout the environment even though it is perceived as vulnerable. Ambient vocalisation by the Adelaide Reiki group in Rymill Park engaged an ontological reconfiguration of social relationships in an opening-out towards ecological relationality, which sought to renegotiate public, local place as personal, and which transformed space as sacred.

References

Bedford, J. 1999. *Park Lands Management Strategy Report: Directions for Adelaide's Park Lands 2000-2037*. Adelaide: City of Adelaide.

Bensimon, M. 2012. 'The social role of collective singing during intense moments of protest: The disengagement from the Gaza Strip', *Sociology* 46(2): 241-257.

Bodner, E. and A. Gilboa. 2006. 'Emotional communicablility on music therapy: Different instruments for different emotions?', *Nordic Journal of Music Therapy* 15: 3-16.

Bruscia, K.E. 1987. *Improvisational Models of Music Therapy*. Springfield, IL: Charles C Thomas.

Carpenter, E. and M. McLuhan (Eds.). 1960. *Explorations in Communication: An Anthology*. Boston: Beacon Press.

Cosgrove, D. 1984. *Social Formation and Symbolic Landscape*. London: Croom Helm.

Douglas, M. 1966. *Purity and Danger*. London: Routledge and Keegan Paul.

Descola, P. and G. Palsson. 1996. *Nature and Society: Anthropological Perspectives*. London: Routledge.

Feld, S. 1996. 'Waterfalls of song: An acoustemology of place resounding in Bosavia, Papua New Guinea'. In S. Feld and K. Basso (Eds.), *Senses of Place* (pp. 91-135). Santa Fe, NM: School of American Research Press.

Flournoy, T. 1994. *From India to the Planet Mars: A Case of Multiple Personality with Imaginary Languages*. New Jersey: Princeton University Press.

Foucault, M. 1977. *Discipline and Punish: The Birth of the Prison*. Trans. A. Sheridan. London: Allen Lane.

Halbwachs, M. 1992. *On Collective Memory*. Ed. and trans. L.A. Coser. Chicago: The University of Chicago Press.

Hirsch, E. and M. O'Hanlon (Eds.). 1995. *An Anthropology of Landscape: Perspectives on Place and Space*. Oxford: Clarendon Press.

Hume, L. 2007. *Portals: Opening Doorways to Other Realities through the Senses*. Oxford and New York: Berg.

Jones, D.S. 2005a. 'The ecological history of Adelaide 3: The historical evolution of the present landscape'. In C. Daniels and C. Tait (Eds.), *Adelaide, Nature of a City: The Ecology of a Dynamic City from 1836 to 2036* (pp. 68-86). Adelaide: Biocity, Centre for Urban Habitats.

Jones, D.S. 2005b. 'The urban forest 1: Redesigning the Adelaide Plains landscape'. In C. Daniels and C. Tait (Eds.), *Adelaide, Nature of a City: The Ecology of a Dynamic City from 1836 to 2036* (pp. 349-374). Adelaide: Biocity, Centre for Urban Habitats.

Lovelock, J. 2000. *Gaia: A New Look at Life on Earth*. Oxford: Oxford University Press.

Maffesoli, M. 1996. *Time of the Tribes: The Decline of Individualism in Mass Society*. Trans. D. Smith. London and Thousand Oaks, CA: Sage.

Norager, T. 2011. 'Difficult but necessary: Conditions of a contemporary theology of love', *Dialogue: A Journal of Theology* 50(1, Spring): 47-52.

Redfield, J. 1993. *The Celestine Prophecy*. London: Bantam Books.

Schutz, A. 1971. 'Making music together: A study of human relationship'. In A. Schutz, *Collected Papers*, vol. 2: *Studies in Social Theory* (pp. 159-178). The Hague: Martinus Nijhoff.

Shamdasani, S. 1994. 'Introduction'. In T. Flournoy, *From India to the Planet Mars: A Case of Multiple Personality with Imaginary Languages* (pp. xi-li). New Jersey: Princeton University Press.

Starhawk. 1989. *The Spiral Dance: A Rebirth of the Ancient Religion of the Great Goddess*. New York: Harper-Collins Publishers.

Sweeney, A. 2002. *Reiki Manual*. London: Mastership Pathway UK Ltd.

Turino, T. 2008. *Music as Social Life*. Chicago: The University of Chicago Press.

10

Ngadha being-in-common:
Emotional attachment to people and place in Flores, Indonesia

Jayne Curnow

Abstract

For the Ngadha people of Central Flores, Indonesia, residential clan land, nua, *is imbued with emotional connections as the locus of Ancestors, ceremony and the key symbols of clan unity, the Ngadhu post and Bhaga miniature house. Prominently located in the centre of the* nua, *the Ngadhu and Bhaga are grounding symbols, constant reminders of interdependence between clan members and their Ancestors. This spiritual commons (McWilliam 2009) anchors emotional connections not just to place but also to fellow clan members, living and deceased. To articulate the emotional ties that bind clan members to one another, I draw on Nancy's concept of 'being singular plural' to illustrate that to be Ngadha is to have a keen sense of being implicated in the existence of others. Being with others is a human concern, as people cannot exist in the singular. For Ngadha people, this is particularly explicit, so that individual independence is not a coveted state of being; rather, being singular plural is the principal mode of existence. In this context, the* nua *is the central heartland for the spatial and material expression of clan unity, although the emotions of being singular plural transcend time and space.*

Introduction

For the Ngadha people of Central Flores, Indonesia, residential clan land, *nua*, is imbued with emotional connections as the locus of Ancestors, ceremony and the key symbols of clan unity, the Ngadhu sacrificial post and Bhaga model house. Prominently located in the centre of the *nua*, the Ngadhu and Bhaga are grounding symbols, constant reminders of interdependence between living and deceased clan members. Bomolo *nua*, located on the outskirts of the town of Bajawa, exemplifies Ngadha configurations of material symbols, intangible associations and emotional connections.[1] Bajawa has a population of approximately 15 000 and a small grid-pattern of streets dotted with shops and government offices surrounded by private homes. Following a string road out of town, privately held residential blocks end abruptly at the edge of the corporately owned land of Bomolo.[2] Entering Bomolo, the Ngadhu and Bhaga are striking features in the large *nua* square, which is bordered on all sides by houses facing into the square.

The Ngadhu and Bhaga symbolise the strong bonds that tie the Ngadha people of Bomolo to each other and to the *nua*. These symbols and bonds are intimately linked to a community economy that strives to cater to the physical, mental and spiritual wellbeing of all.[3] Ngadha practices of interdependence are reflected in this community economy, which privileges Ancestor worship, community cohesion and group distribution of resources above the needs and desires of the individual. This chapter will focus on an aspect of this interdependence, Ngadha people's emotional connection to *nua* and other clan members, as an expression of what the philosopher Jean-Luc Nancy has termed 'being singular plural', or in other words, the being-with-others which is a common condition of our shared existence (2000).

Interdependence is a dominant feature of everyday Ngadha life and organisation. Ngadha people's views of their own society involve a sense of self that questions the conceptual separation of the self from others. Frequently, people alerted me to the ways in which everyone and everything is connected. To analyse Ngadha society from an emic perspective requires mindful acknowledgement of the implication of the self in the existence of others. To this end, I employ the work of Nancy to explore the essential plurality of human existence. Nancy's concept of 'being singular plural'

---

1 Bomolo and all personal names are pseudonyms.

2 I resided in Bomolo with a family of subsistence farmers from 2004-05 while conducting ethnographic fieldwork for my doctoral dissertation — see also footnote 5.

3 *Community* is a term liberally used in development circles and anthropology (Walker 2001). It can refer to a geographical area, an administrative unit or a 'target population': farmers, the poor or women. Community is usually contested, is rarely egalitarian and can also be negative, constraining or oppressing for its members. Community may also include absent members such as migrant workers, or temporary members such as development workers or anthropologists. I use the term *community economy* to highlight these aspects, and the interdependence and sociality of the economy (see Gibson-Graham 2006, Chapter 4).

opens an intellectual space to discuss a way of being in the world that differs from the philosophical notion of the singular, separate individual. In Nancy's (2000:30) own words:

> Being singular plural means the essence of Being is only as co-essence ... [C]oessentiality signifies the essential sharing of essentiality, sharing in the guise of assembling, as it were. This could also be put in the following way: if Being is being-with, then it is, in its being-with, the 'with' that constitutes Being; the 'with' is not simply an addition. This operates in the same way as a collective power: power is neither exterior to the members of the collective nor interior to each one of them, but rather consists in the collectively as such. Therefore, it is not the case that the 'with' is an addition to some prior Being; instead the 'with' is at the heart of Being ... [I]t is absolutely necessary to reverse the order of philosophical exposition.

For anthropology, working from *being singular plural* provides an opportunity to explore the *being-with* of human existence. This I propose as a segue to a discussion of emotional connection between Ngadha people, and between Ngadha people and place. This is a different approach to much of the anthropological literature on emotions, comprehensively reviewed by Lutz and White, who identify a dearth of material on the 'phenomenological and communicative aspect of emotion' (1986:429). More recently, attention has been drawn to the *cognitive-evaluative* view of emotions. Emotions in this view are 'forms of evaluative judgement that ascribe to certain things and persons outside a person's own control great importance for that person's own flourishing' (Nussbaum 2001:22). In other words, people need each other, and my contribution is to examine how Ngadha people express their needs through emotional connections to each other, including Ancestors, and to their clan land centred on the *nua* through daily and ceremonial practice. These expressions of emotional connection may at times be muted, amplified, or ignored; however, cognitive-evaluative emotional connection and being-with fellow clan members and clan land are ubiquitous in Ngadha cosmology.

Conceptualising Ngadha interdependence as 'being-with'

Five generations have now inhabited Bomolo *nua* since its establishment by the founding Ancestors. Being-with is established in moral and ethical norms guided by *adat*[4], which is grounded in the Ngadhu, Bhaga and *nua* earth, and interpreted and administered by resident *adat* experts. Intra-*nua* politics and disputes rarely require recourse to government agencies. Ngadha *adat* also ensures continuity and a culturally prescribed level of subsistence for all members of the Bomolo community. Food, wood for cooking fires and construction, and medicine are sourced in the fields and surrounding land. In many spheres, the Bomolo community is self-sufficient. Many productive tasks are carried out co-operatively, such as harvesting crops or repairing a

---

4   *Adat* refers to customary manners and practices which extend to the legal, moral and ethical aspects of life.

house, but production is not simply for production's sake. Labouring in accordance with *adat* is of great concern and guides work practices. Emphasis is placed on the way people work together, the being-with-others of the occasion, rather than the banal expediency of the task at hand. While this labour does not attract cash remuneration, it can be argued that it is compensated for by providing other rewards such as love, protection, emotional support and companionship (Gibson-Graham 2006:62). A sense of identity and emotional connection emerges, as to share the workload is seen as an intrinsically Ngadha characteristic. Ngadha people's sense of identity and emotional connection is also strongly linked to Ancestor worship and Catholicism, both of which are predominantly enacted within the Bomolo milieu, with only a small proportion of residents regularly attending Catholic services or engaging in pastoral activities outside the *nua*.

Bomolo residents are, however, increasingly orienting themselves to services and economic opportunities in Bajawa. Water is now piped to the *nua* from the town supply and all homes have access to electricity. Economically, people may now look to the town as a source of waged employment and to its central market as a site of trading. They must also pay taxes and are subject to the laws of the Indonesian government. Children attend school and when ill can attend the local health clinic. While this may appear to be quite an extensive range of goods and services accessed outside Bomolo, on a day-to-day basis these are secondary to the relationships, religiosity and resources that sustain the Bomolo community. In Bomolo, as throughout eastern Indonesia, state and market influences 'can lead as often as not to strengthened ritual expression of house or community solidarity and adaptive transformations of tradition rather than fragmentation' (McWilliam 2009:167).

The complexity of practices of economic interdependence and engagement with the market economy first presented as an issue during my residence in Bomolo while I was conducting ethnographic fieldwork on economic development in the district. I drew on diverse economy theory (see Curnow 2008) to augment my ethnographic study of the local economy.[5] My research drew attention to the Ngadha community economy, which is grounded in interdependence and practices of group surplus distribution (2008). This finding was significant, as it revealed a fundamental clash with development initiatives in Bajawa based on capitalist economic principles predicated on an assumption of individual surplus accumulation. The focus on the individual,

---

5   This research was undertaken as part of my work with a team of academics exploring a new approach to local economic development through an action research project titled 'Negotiating alternative economic strategies for regional development in Indonesia and the Philippines'. This project was jointly funded by the Australian Research Council [ARC], the Australian National University [ANU] and the Australian Government Agency for International Development [AusAID]. I would like to acknowledge the stimulating input of the project research team at ANU: Amanda Cahill, Katherine Gibson, Ann Hill, Deirdre Mackay, Andrew McWilliam, Kathryn Robinson and Catarina Williams.

which remains unarticulated yet is so influential in development policy formulations and programs, presupposes a suppression of our connectedness to others in order to maintain a façade of impersonal economic transactions. The 'with' of 'being-with' is quashed to enable unfettered profit maximisation and capitalist growth.

In Bomolo, this connectedness is highly valued and is not so easily relegated to the margins. Personal transactions facilitate interdependence or being-with, as it is enshrined in Ngadha *adat* and is constitutive of identity. To be Ngadha is to be interdependent to varying degrees with family, clan, neighbours, Ancestors and God. In Bomolo, *adat* is the central tenet around which the economy is negotiated and enacted. The economy in Bomolo is not a space of action or thought separate from other aspects of life. Economic action is intrinsic to Ngadha cosmology, exemplified by exchange with Ancestors (as I will discuss below). In Bomolo, as among Lio people who live to the east of Bajawa, society includes living and deceased members; this belief system 'takes the [exchange] process out of the realm of inter-personal or inter-group relationships to the socio-cosmological domain in which individuals are less important than the whole' (Howell 1989:422). This speaks to emotional connections that extend being-with into an esoteric domain beyond the material world.

Human society frequently prioritises group wellbeing, and the assumption of individuality is critiqued by Nancy (2000), who raises the possibility that our shared humanity belies conceptualisations of the individual self as singular, individuated and *against* others. Understandings of what constitutes the individual vary, and a lack of conceptual clarity around the use of 'self', individual'and 'person' in anthropology has been identified by Spiro (1993), who takes up the issue specifically in relation to Geertz's discussion of the Western conception of the person. Geertz typified the Western person as 'organised into a distinctive whole and set contrastively *against* other such wholes and *against* its social and natural background' to highlight different cultural manifestations of selfhood (1984:126, italics in the original text).

In this chapter, I want to take Geertz's notion of the Western individual being *against* other individuals and *against* society and nature as a point of departure to argue that rather than being *against* others, all people are *with* others. Nancy (2000) has argued that the very being of our existence involves being *with* others.[6] While the extent to which any person or group cosmologically conceives and articulates being-with may vary, the point that Nancy makes is important for anthropology, as 'there is no meaning if meaning is not shared … because meaning is itself the sharing

---

6   I introduce the work of Nancy here, as his philosophical point is particularly insightful for sociocultural analysis. In a different register, anthropological examination of the individual or personhood has been taken up by scholars such as Geertz (1973) on the depersonalised concept of personhood in Bali; Leenhardt (1979); Strathern (1988); Strathern and Stewart (1998), writing on relational personhood in Melanesia; and Dumont (1986) on the 'dividual' versus the individual on India.

of Being' (2). I conceptualise the sharing of meaning as a connection, and specifically as an emotional connection, through which we sense those with whom we co-exist and those who we are being-with.

Gibson-Graham highlight the importance of the epistemology of being-with: of how we are to be one amongst many, or in other words how individuals can be a community. They draw our attention to the 'inessential commonality of negotiating our own implication in the existence of others' (2006:88), advancing the philosophy of Nancy to envisage 'the foundational relationship between being-in-common and Being ... refus[ing] to suppress the togetherness implied in any singularity, any identity or concept of Being' (Gibson-Graham 2006:82). Obscuring the primordial commonness of being is particular to Western philosophy. This vision denies the 'proper plural singular co-essence' of being (Nancy, as cited in Gibson-Graham 2006:82). Gibson-Graham find that, by privileging the individual as the basic unit of being, Western thought has problematised being-with rather than taking this position as a point of departure for thought or action. In contrast, Ngadha cosmology does take being-with as a point of departure. In the Ngadha milieu, individual independence is not a coveted state of being; rather, being-with is understood to be the principal mode of existence. In the following section, I discuss how Ngadha being-with coalesces in the physical space of the Bomolo *nua* and the ceremonies held there, thus creating links to other realms and activating practical and emotional connection to this specific place.

Nua: The emotional heartland

Dewa zeta, Nitu zale: God above, Ancestors below. This short, simple phrase encapsulates Ngadha cosmology. For Ngadha, there are three planes of existence — that of the divine (God), the material world (human beings) and the exact inverse of the material world (Ancestors). God above and Ancestors below exert control in the material world of human beings. Put succinctly by a senior Bomolo woman, ' ... people are in the middle dancing'. These three planes have spatial associations: the invisible world of the Ancestors, who live in objects in the *nua*, in the field and below the earth; the sky, which is associated with God; and the physical world of human beings in the village and the fields (as cited in Molnar 1994:242). In this respect, Ancestors are tied to place and are proximate, sharing the *nua* and fields with the living. The term *heartland* is an interpretation of the Ngadha term *nua dada*, which literally means 'village heart'. Ngadha people I met who were elsewhere and not residing in their village of birth, *nua dada*, would invariably speak with great emotion of their people and place of origin. For those that had been away for an extended period, talk of their village would prompt wistful descriptions of the bonhomie among family and clan, the taste of food and specifically the *moke* (mildly alcoholic palm wine) and corn so closely associated with Ngadha identity and articulated in the following oft-recited ditty:

Orang Flores makan jagung goreng,	Flores people eat roasted corn and
minum dengan moke,	drink palm wine,
Satu kali masih baik,	One time is fine,
Dua kali sudah mulai,	Two times it's already begun
Tiga kali berkelahi!	Three times and there's fighting!
	(Author's translation)

At all ceremonies and lifecycle events, people sit together and drink *moke* and, when it is in season, eat corn. Babies are given a taste of *moke* and young children will also have a small drink. Consuming palm wine together is constitutive of being Ngadha, as it was in the past, enacted in the present and taught to children to continue in the future. For those absent from their village, the sense of longing is also mixed with feelings of guilt if the absence has been for an extended period, particularly if they are missing the annual Reba ceremony during their absence (discussed below). Further, the connection is more than visceral and emotional, as the spiritual connections to Ancestors on clan lands is immutable.

Ngadha clan land is corporately owned by clan members and is a residential location, a symbol of interdependence, clan unity and social relations, a primary site of being-with activity. As Hastrup suggests, 'space affects intersubjectivity deeply, because intersubjectivity is embedded in place ... [which] is not simply a matter of relationships between persons but involves relations between people and places and ideas about places' (2010:203). This intersubjectivity is the medium for emotional connections, inextricably linking people to place and to each other through place: 'We are, in short, placelings' (Escobar 2003:163). The interplay of emotions between people, and between people and place, is clearly evident among those who temporarily or permanently leave the *nua*. Out-going migrants describe a sense of longing associated with an unbreakable bond with the *nua*, and with people of the *nua*.

Bomolo *nua* is an emotional heartland for members of two different clans, Paru and Dala. Clan Paru has the greatest presence, occupying thirteen houses in Bomolo with clan Dala members living in five houses. All houses face into the central courtyard, forming a clear and discrete spatial unit of co-residence. Kitchens are typically at the back of the house and are imbued with the strong smell of firewood used for cooking. Although cooking is done primarily by women, men also frequent the kitchen, adding a miasma of thick clove cigarette smoke. When going to one another's houses, members of the Bomolo community call out and detour directly to the kitchen back door, thus expressing the intimacy and closeness within the Bomolo community, in contrast to acquaintances or visitors, who always approach via the front door. *Nua* land is for the use of all clan members and their guests, and is to be held in remembrance of Ancestors who, until prohibition by state health regulations, were buried in the central courtyard of the *nua*. Recently, a few Ngadha clans in other locations have agreed to divide *nua* land for individual government certification, but most clans are resisting this, as it paves the way for the sale of *nua* land without clan approval (Ngani & Djawanai 2004:87). Individual sale of parcels of clan land challenges current interpretations of *adat*, which includes the understanding that *nua* is held in trust for clan members yet to be born, and thus alienation of land may result in Ancestral sanctions.

Ngadha cosmology incorporates the volition of Ancestors acting in the material plane of human existence. Coining the term 'spiritual commons', McWilliam (2009:164) indicates that ' ... belief in spirit agency acting in the world, and the possibility that humanity can engage this realm, arguably provides some of the more powerful motivations and rationale for social practice and collective endeavour'. Clan membership is matrilineal, descending from a shared female and male Ancestor, which locates the Ngadha individual within complex relationships of interdependence with Ancestors as well as living kin and clan members. All of these relationships have widespread repercussions, with *adat* guiding practices of interdependence which inculcate the individual with a sense of their 'implication in the existence of others' (Gibson-Graham 2006:88). To maintain the spiritual commons, *adat* directs people to protect themselves from the wrath of Ancestors, which manifests in the form of poor harvests, infertility, ill health, bad luck or catastrophe.

All ceremonies are focused on the *nua* and at some stage offer food in exchange for the benevolent attention of the Ancestors to the fertility of people and land.[7] As Howell found amongst the Lio people who live to the east of Ngada district[8], exchange was not just between people but also between the living and the dead (1989:434). This exchange *par excellence* is the sacrifice of chickens, pigs and buffalo. The atmosphere is electrified as ritual leaders call out to Ancestors before the chorus of pigs squealing and buffaloes lowing and snorting erupts with the chop of machetes. Animal sacrifice is one type of exchange that ' ... expresses the moral order of a society and should be seen as a life-giving process — not a reciprocal, time specific act in which two things are exchanged between two individuals' (434). Although the smallest of the sacrificial beasts, chickens are a medium through which the deceased communicate with the living. Ritual experts interpret the configuration of the sacrificed chicken's entrails for messages and signs from the Ancestors. Bomolo residents being-with Ancestors guides earthly actions and maintains cosmic order.

In the realm of the living, houses on *nua* land are primarily bequeathed through matrilineal inheritance. It is common nowadays for young couples to co-habit once the

---

7 A notable exception is during the first phase of Reba when, after an initial address to the *nua* Bhaga, a ceremony attended by a small congregation is held at a miniature ritual altar in a field adjacent to the *nua* before moving back to the *nua* for the remainder of the ceremony.

8 'Ngadha' spelt with an 'h' refers to an ethno-linguistic group of people; 'Ngada' without an 'h' refers to the district, a political-geographic area of land.

woman is noticeably pregnant, or more traditionally once they are married — which can mean an *adat* marriage and/or a Catholic Church wedding. Once a woman's family accepts the man into their home, he becomes a part of the economic and social life of the family while retaining secondary rights and responsibilities in his home and clan of origin. Emotional links for the spouse marrying into the *nua* are forged on an interpersonal basis and through their children's clan identity and status, which follow the mother. More rarely, a woman can move to the home of her husband once the man's family have agreed to pay bridewealth (*belis*) to the woman's family. The woman and their children then derive their clan identity and status from the house of the man. Thus the 'with' of 'being-with' is not static. The collectively manifest state of being-with described by Nancy is in every moment contingent on the others that a person is being-with.

Practical and emotional connections to the *nua* are exemplified by Dhone, who is twenty-eight years old and married with two children (field notes, n.d.). While Dhone lives on family land purchased on the other side of Bajawa, she still frequents her family home in Bomolo *nua* on a weekly basis. As far as the government administration is concerned, Dhone is still a resident of Bomolo *nua*. This is where she is enrolled to vote and she participates in formal administration, too, such as being a member of the committee organising the ballot for the presidential election in 2004. She has also kept her registration at the health post (*puskemas*) closest to the *nua* and visits or stays over if she or her daughters are ill.

Even if Dhone had notified the government of her change of residence, she, her husband and her children would still be inextricably linked to Bomolo *nua* as members of clan Paru. As the oldest daughter she stands to inherit the family home, land and *adat* objects.[9] Although her young family no longer resides in Bomolo, she is still an integral part of the household economy. Maria, Dhone's mother, will care for the children if Dhone has casual work or is busy with other responsibilities. Dhone and her daughters often stay in the *nua* for days at a time before and during an important ceremony such as Reba and Neku (discussed below). She injects significant contributions to the household on these occasions in the form of labour and food stuffs. Her labour is in constant demand from others in Bomolo during these periods. These demands for labour are a significant aspect of interdependence, and the emotional connection clan members feel for each other is discussed in both positive and negative terms, which speak to an emotional connection that may be based on either a feeling of joy or of burden borne out of a sense of duty. The sharing of mundane practical tasks constantly brings people into each other's company, where this corporal being-with creates and

---

9   *Adat* objects are an important part of lineage inheritance and can include gold jewellery, cloth, swords, the spirit ladder, and the *mataraga* altar rack.

maintains the basis for political, social and emotional support reinforced with ritual and ceremony.

Ngadhu and Bhaga: Symbols of emotional connection

Ngadha clan relationships are of the utmost importance and are primary factors in social, political and economic dealings. 'Clan membership is often defined in terms of rights and obligations: the right to inherit land and heirlooms correlates with [other] obligations ... ' (Molnar 1994:219). Clan membership is grounded in the two core symbols that are a striking physical presence in the *nua*: the sacrificial post, Ngadhu, and model house, Bhaga. The Ngadhu and Bhaga are seen as the material embodiment of Ancestors crucial to the continuity of the clan '... [which] is dependent on the correct construction and maintenance of these material embodiments ... as well as the proper performance of rituals and rites' (241). On the upward-sloping side of the central courtyard in Bomolo is the sacrificial Ngadhu post. This is a tall, intricately carved wooden post covered with a pointed, thatched roof resembling a half-closed umbrella. On the side of the courtyard that slopes downwards is the Bhaga model house. Houses are arranged in a rectangle around the central courtyard in which the Ngadhu and Bhaga lie opposite each other, becoming the visual centrepiece of the *nua*.

The symbolism of the Ngadhu and Bhaga was explored by Molnar, who found that the Ngadhu post is associated with the masculine, is named after the founding male clan Ancestor or his first-born son, and is representative of this Ancestor and the clan (219). During Reba and Neku ceremonies, buffalo are tethered to the post and trussed pigs are organised in an arc of 180 degrees on the downward-sloping side of the post before being ceremonially sacrificed (see below). The model house, Bhaga, is a representation of a traditional single-room wooden house. The Bhaga is compared to a womb, and is named after the female founding Ancestor. In this respect, the female founding Ancestor gives birth to all members of the clan and so stands for the undivided whole of the clan (232). Initially, the Bhaga must be constructed before the Ngadhu as a marker of the primacy of wholeness over differentiation. The female Bhaga and male Ngadhu are seen as husband and wife and are symbols of clan organisation and identity. These objects are also seen as the material embodiment of the Ancestors, who are crucial to the continuity of the clan. Ancestral blessing is dependent on the correct construction and maintenance of these material embodiments of the Ancestors.

The Ngadhu and Bhaga in the Bomolo courtyard are owned by clan Paru, who are a sub-clan of the original Paru clan located on the other side of Bajawa town. Dala clan's primary Ngadhu/Bhaga complex is elsewhere, but members are also connected to the Bomolo Ngadhu/Bhaga through *nua* affiliation. Both Paru and Dala clans are internally divided into two sub-groups, *saka pu'u* and *saka lobo*. As with the clan, sub-group membership is determined by marriage arrangements. *Saka pu'u* (trunk riders) members and their associated main house are directly connected to the female Bhaga. *Saka lobo* (tip riders) are directly connected to the male Ngadhu post. The terms *trunk riders* and *tip riders* refer to the position of people on top of the Ngadhu post when it first enters the village. *Saka pu'u*, the trunk riders who sit near the roots of the tree, are the base or foundation of the clan and must be autochthonous clan members. *Saka lobo*, the tip riders, sit nearer the top of the tree trunk and may be clan members or may have married into the clan. *Saka pu'u* are considered the older siblings, *saka lobo* the younger siblings.

Each Ngadhu/Bhaga complex has an associated main house for both the *saka pu'u* and *saka lobo* groups within the clan. The main *saka pu'u* house is signified by a miniature house (*anah yea*) on the roof above the *adat* room. The main house of the *saka lobo* is identified by the upper trunk, arms and head of a person (*ata*) holding a spear and a sword. These main houses represent direct lineages to those who established that particular Ngadhu/Bhaga complex and are symbolic and ritual foci. All other houses either within or outside the *nua* are termed *sao dhoro* (descendant houses). A sense of belonging and connection to clan and Ancestors are thus associated with both the symbols and structure of residential houses on *nua* land. *Sao dhoro* rights and ancestral affiliations continue to be traced through the Ngadhu/Bhaga complex and main trunk or tip house. *Sao dhoro* houses must be smaller than the main house with which they are associated. Houses that are 'branches' and home to descendants of these main houses have three spiked prongs at both ends of the elongated, rectangular-shaped apex of the roof.

Although there is a primordial connection to one or the other, all people are connected to both the Bhaga and Ngadhu — they form a single indivisible unit. In the same vein, *saka pu'u* and *saka lobo* are also inseparable and one group cannot exist without the other. In discussing the clan divisions, Teresia, a Bomolo resident, explained that if you are alone you cannot do anything: you must work with others, and this includes co-operation between *saka pu'u* and *saka lobo* (field notes, n.d.). This is literally translated into daily life, where community members must consult and work together with each other, setting the stage for a close-knit community where interdependence is prioritised and celebrated.

Being Ngadha: Reba and Neku ceremonies

The clearest indication of 'being Ngadha' is participation in the yearly Reba ceremony (Schroeter 2005:319). The ceremony is enacted in the central space of the *nua* and extends to the spiritual realm, and thus participation is important for the maintenance of Ngadha identity. The annual Reba ceremony maintains the spiritual commons and is held primarily to give thanks to Ancestors and God for the results of hard work and harvests through the year. It is also described as a New Year party, a family celebration, a time to make peace, and an opportunity for flirting with the opposite sex (Djawamaku 2000:22). With hundreds of people in attendance, it also intensifies interdependence in the collective planning, preparation and celebration, a macro-expression of the day-to-day interdependence between kin and clan.

Reba brings together people from seven *nua* to articulate their shared existence; it is held in each of the seven *nua* on a rotating basis. The people of Bomolo classify themselves specifically as Bajawa Ngadha, a sub-group who trace their origins back to Magdha, on the east coast of India. This oral history is based on a narrative of the arrival of an Indian man, Djawa Meze, at what is now the small town of Aimere on the south coast, about an hour's travel from Bajawa via a steep, winding road. Local people still talk of a site recognised as the place where Djawa Meze lived in Aimere, but I was informed that it is not visited or maintained in any way. Djawa Meze reportedly had fourteen children — seven girls and seven boys. The seven boys went to Java while the seven girls stayed in Aimere. With the exception of those who have married in, members of the clans in the seven-village alliance trace their origins to one of Djawa Meze's seven daughters.

An image that is still important to Ngadha people is that they are tied together — they are of the same blood (Daeng 1985:294). Reba is an annual display of these emotional ties, which are both an expression of being-with and a reaffirmation of intra- and inter-clan alliances. Another ceremony, Neku, is held to honour specific deceased relatives at a time when their descendants can muster the resources required to successfully hold the event. I was fortunate enough to be living in Bomolo when a Neku was held. The following description, taken from my field notes of the time, teases out some of the sensorial aspects of the ceremony.

In preparation for Neku, six sturdy bamboo posts with supporting crossbeams were dug into the ground in front of the Ngadhu post to tether the six buffalo to be sacrificed. On the day, approximately 1000 people were gathered in the *nua* and the place was a bustling hive of activity. As the throng jostled for a good view, the first buffalo was roped around the neck, the rope then threaded through the fork of the Ngadhu post and secured to the Peo, a single rock partially buried directly behind the Ngadhu post. The buffalo's nose was tied to another rope attached with a slipknot to a forked bamboo pole. Pulling both ropes taut, two groups of young men struggled to hold the animal still. The eldest living man from the celebrating lineages, still sporting a smear of chicken blood down the length of his nose from a preliminary ceremony at home, stepped up and symbolically cut the buffalo's throat. Another man then stepped up and with one great hack to the lower throat killed the beast. Young men rushed in with bamboo containers to catch the blood spurting from a major artery. Blood was smeared first on the Ngadhu and Peo, to which the buffalo was tied, and then also applied to all the other adjacent Ngadhu posts (linked to other clans) to feed the Ancestors. Once severed, the buffalo's head was placed at the base of the Ngadhu post.

The buffalo carcass was cut up into separate sections, including each of the ribs, which later were placed in the fork of the post to feed the Ancestors.

Following the first buffalo sacrifice, deliberations about the correct *adat* procedure followed with senior men, led by Willi and Yusef, furiously yelling, consulting and arguing with each other. The buffalo on the left had to be killed first, progressing through to the last one on the right, so there was debate about which way was the correct left to right direction, facing to or away from the Ngadhu post. Yusef marched up and angrily untied the second rope holding the buffalo from the bamboo pole and threw it to the ground. The set-up was then changed in order for the buffalo that was to be killed first to be tethered at the other extreme of the bamboo posts.

Willi killed the first buffalo, and in one clear blow to the throat the buffalo fell quickly to its knees with blood spurting out, as young men rushed in with bamboo containers to catch the blood. Later, Willi told me that, in the minutes he stood ready to make the sacrifice, he was in communication with an Ancestor who had entered the buffalo. The Ancestor told him when the buffalo was ready to be sacrificed. Willi explained that he has the power and knowledge to communicate in this way, which is why he can make such a clean kill in one blow — a skill much admired and appreciated by all. One by one, the buffalo were sacrificed, each by different Bomolo men, and then they were dragged away by groups of younger men for butchering. Yusef, Willi's main political opponent in the *nua*, killed one of the buffalo, taking a number of blows to fell the beast. This is significant to the tension in the relationship between these two senior men, Willi's prestige and *adat* authority being further enhanced by comparison to the less sophisticated kill by Yusef.

Having dispensed with the buffalo, beasts of the highest and most prestigious order, it was time to kill the many pigs that had been tethered to bamboo stakes driven into the ground around the *nua* courtyard. Small groups of boys and men converged around each pig and trussed its legs. The screaming of approximately seventy pigs was deafening. Each man who was to kill a pig stood astride the trussed animal ready to deliver the fatal blow — a single chop from a sharp machete (*parang*) brought with a great swing of the arms between the ears and eyes of the pig. Using a microphone, a senior man addressed the Ancestors and threw uncooked rice on the head of the first pig. When he finished speaking, this pig was killed, signalling all others to do likewise. Men and pigs were screaming in unison as the pigs were slaughtered — some in a single clean blow, others needing a number of attempts to render the pigs immobile. Men barked instructions to boys on how to hold the pigs and where to place the bowls or bucket they held to catch the draining blood and brains (to be used in cooking). The pig was held on an angle by a number of men so that the blood could drain from the skull, and brain matter was scraped out with the sharp end of the machete or a stick. As the cacophony of the killing subsided to a dull roar, Bomolo residents and neighbours drifted into the *nua* houses, calling and inviting guests to join them for more food and socialising. Others swung into action to butcher and cook the buffalo and pig meat, along with rice and a spicy chilli condiment.

As part of the spiritual commons, performing Neku attracts benevolent attention from Ancestors and is a preventative against possible misfortune wrought by ancestral displeasure. Both Reba and Neku bring interdependence to the fore, as people provision and labour to make these large-scale, multiple-day events a success.

Conclusion

This chapter has focused on emotional connection between people and place as an aspect of Ngadha cosmology, based on a keen sense of 'being-with' rather than 'being-against' others. The culture and *adat* of Ngadha people foreground their implication in the existence of others. This interdependence is evident in numerous practical livelihood strategies and is frequently celebrated in ceremony. In Bomolo, I found a vibrant complex of interdependent practices of labour co-operation and food sharing. The spiritual commons includes Ancestor worship and Catholicism, which are valued in concert with the material commons of land and resources. The spiritual and material commons come together in the form of the Ngadhu sacrificial post and Bhaga offering house, positioned in the centre of the corporately owned Bomolo *nua* land. The Ngadhu and Bhaga are material symbols of clan unity and emotional connections to place, kin and clan.

The Reba and Neku ceremonies are crucial for the maintenance of clan and *nua*, and are collective expressions of Ngadha interdependence which, enacted on a daily basis, are significant in constituting what it means to be Ngadha. Moving away from the language of reciprocity and interdependence in terms of material sustenance and shelter, I have focused on a more abstract aspect of Bomolo interdependence in order to argue that the Bomolo community is founded on a keen sense of being-with: of being implicated in the existence of others. Bound tightly in a web of interdependence, being-with is both the grounds for action and the wellspring of emotional connections. The significance of practical interdependence and the shared understandings of symbols and cosmological order come together in a mutual sense of being Ngadha. 'There is no meaning if meaning is not shared and not because there would be an ultimate or first signification that all beings have in common, but because meaning is itself the sharing of Being' (Nancy 2000:2). Being-with and the sharing of Being are acknowledged and celebrated as definitive of Ngadha identity.

Moving beyond the ethnographic example of Bomolo, I think there is great promise in investigating the emotional currents that run between other groups of people based on the notion of 'being singular plural' — a concept which, for example, can transcend language and culture to include emotions such as mutual attraction or hatred. Whether they unite or divide, emotions are between people; being-with is therefore expressed and recognised through emotional connection to others and place. At the very least, this connection is evident in a shared sense of humanity and comprehension of meaning. This has been an admittedly preliminary foray into the application of Nancy's philosophical notion of 'being singular plural' to ethnographic data in order to articulate the concepts of interdependent being-with and emotional connection. While I have drawn predominantly on primary data of Ngadha people in Indonesia, I propose that being-with is common to the human condition, and there is therefore scope for further analysis in this and other contexts.

References

Curnow, J. 2008. 'Ngadha webs of interdependence: A community economy in Flores, Indonesia'. PhD thesis, Research School of Pacific and Asian Studies, ANU, Canberra.

Daeng, H.J. 1985. 'Pesta, persaingan dan konsep harga diri di Flores', *Peranan Kebudayaan Tradisional Indonesia* (pp. 287-311). M. Dove, unpublished manuscript, Jakarta, Yayasan Obor Indonesia.

Djawamaku, A. 2000. 'Pesta adat reba dan berberapa implikasi praktis sebuah perspektif pemberdayaan budaya', *Bajawa, Disajikan dalam Seminar makna Reba*, unpublished manuscript, 7 February.

Dumont, L. 1986. *Essays on Individualism: Modern Ideology in Anthropological Perspective*. Chicago: University of Chicago Press.

Escobar, A. 2003. 'Displacement, development and modernity in the Columbian Pacific', *International Social Science Journal* 55(175): 157-167.

Geertz, C. 1973. *The Interpretation of Cultures*. New York: Basic Books.

Geertz, C. 1984. 'From the native's point of view: On the nature of anthropological understanding'. In R. Shweder and R. Levine, *Culture Theory: Essays on Mind, Self, and Emotion* (pp. 123-136). Cambridge: Cambridge University Press.

Gibson-Graham, J.K. 2006. *A Postcapitalist Politics*. Minnesota: University of Minnesota Press.

Hastrup, K. 2010. 'Emotional topographies: The sense of place in the Far North'. In J. Davies and D. Spencer, *Emotions in the Field: The Psychology and Anthropology of Fieldwork Experience* (pp. 191-211). Stanford: Stanford University Press.

Howell, S. 1989. 'Of persons and things: Exchange and valuables among the Lio of Eastern Indonesia', *Man* 24(3): 419-438.

Leenhardt, M. 1979. *Do Kamo: Person and Myth in the Melanesian World*. Chicago: University of Chicago Press.

Lutz, C. and G. White. 1986. 'The anthropology of emotions', *Annual Review of Anthropology* 15: 405-436.

McWilliam, A. 2009. 'Spiritual commons: Some immaterial aspects of community economies in Eastern Indonesia', *The Australian Journal of Anthropology* 20: 163-177.

Molnar, A. 1994. 'The grandchildren of the Ga'e ancestors: The Hoga Sara of Ngada in west-central Flores'. PhD Thesis, Research School of Pacific and Asian Studies, ANU, Canberra.

Molnar, A. 1998. 'Consideration of consequences of rapid agricutural modernisation among two Ngada communities', *Antropologi Indonesia* 56: 47-58.

Nancy, J-L. 2000. *Being Singular Plural.* Stanford: Stanford University Press.

Ngani, N. and S. Djawanai. 2004. 'Hukum petanahan di kabupaten Ngada'. Unpublished report, Bajawa, Flores.

Nussbaum, M. 2001. *Upheavals of Thought: The Intelligence of Emotions.* Cambridge: University of Cambridge Press.

Schroeter, S. 2005. 'Red cocks and black hens: Gendered symbolism, kinship and social practice in the Ngada highlands', *KITLV* 161(2/3): 318-349.

Spiro, M. 1993. 'Is the Western conception of the self "peculiar" within the context of the world cultures?', *Ethos* 21(2): 107-153.

Strathern, A. and P. Stewart. 1998. 'Seeking personhood: Anthropological accounts and local concepts in Mount Hagen, Papua New Guinea', *Oceania* 68(3):170-188.

Strathern, M. 1988. *The Gender of the Gift.* Berkeley: University of California Press.

Walker, A. 2001. 'Introduction: Simplification and the ambivalence of community', *TAPJA* 2(2): 1-20.

11

Trust your senses:
Growing wine and making place in McLaren Vale

William Skinner

Abstract

This chapter argues that the tasks and processes of wine production undertaken by small-scale producers not only serve to bring forth or unlock a 'sense of place' in the wine but can also be seen to continuously produce place itself. In the skilled performance of these tasks, winegrowers engage intimately with the world around them at a sensorial level: including touching the soil and the vines, feeling the sun, wind and rain in the vineyard, smelling and feeling the warmth of the fermenting grapes, and tasting the wine at different stages of its production. For many, such physical interaction (hands-on doing) is extremely desirable in wine production, as wine's 'authenticity' is often considered to relate to the close interaction of people and place working in concert. It is this sort of deep and attentive sensorial engagement of people with their worlds, over time, that provides not only practical and intellectual 'knowledge' but also a rich topography of feelings and emotions attached to places and landscapes. I argue that the production of this sort of emotional space, via the hands-on tasks and activities of small-scale wine production, is a crucial element in the development among many such winegrowers of a relational or animic perspective, through which they see themselves, their vines, wines and other aspects of their worlds as fundamentally intertwined and interrelated. Wines, vines and wine places are thus invested with 'meanings' and 'emotions' — social products which are nevertheless linked inextricably to the sensuous materiality of production and consumption.

Introduction

> Too many people sit in air conditioned cabins in their tractors, with a charcoal filter so they can't smell anything and a CD player so they can't hear anything, driving up and down the [vine] rows, and they're not connecting to the land ... As a farmer, I think that you need to be really sensitive to the land: to feel the soil, touch the plants, take care and do things by hand. That's why we use basket presses as well. You could do it just as well with mechanised techniques but to actually do it by hand, to feel the grapes and work with them gently, you learn a lot more about what you're doing. (Peter, 17 April 2012)[1]

> If you're going to be a vigneron, growing those grapes and using them yourself to make wine, I think it's really important to do things by hand. You have a sense of achievement, but also that you are a part of the vineyard, that living being out there ... I am definitely a part of this place, and it's a part of who I am. (Mark, 25 June 2014)

The region of McLaren Vale, lying about forty kilometres south of Adelaide, South Australia, is home to around a hundred different wineries. These operate at very different scales of production, from tiny one- or two-person operations to large winery and vineyard concerns owned by corporate agglomerations. This diversity of scale is matched by a diversity in the techniques and attitudes towards winegrowing, from the high-tech, highly mechanised industrial production of large wineries to the avowedly rustic, low-tech, 'craft' or 'artisanal' approach taken by many small producers like Peter and Mark.[2] Such producers opt to manually prune and maintain their vines and harvest their grapes, and utilise non-mechanised processing techniques in the winery, stirring ferments by hand and pressing the grape must in wooden slatted basket-presses. Important winemaking decisions are, for these artisanal producers, often guided by senses of smell and taste rather than by laboratory analysis.

In this chapter, based on fieldwork conducted in McLaren Vale from 2012 to 2014, I examine the way the sensorial, bodily engagement of such winegrowers with

---

1   The names used in this chapter are pseudonyms.
2   'Winegrowing' is an umbrella term used to encompass the processes of grape growing (viticulture) and 'winemaking' (viniculture), particularly with reference to small-scale, hands on (so-called 'artisanal') production. Many of my interlocutors, who are directly involved with all aspects of wine production — from grape growing to harvesting, fermentation, and bottling — consider themselves 'winegrowers' or 'vignerons'; others are engaged with work primarily or solely in the vineyard or in the winery. Where necessary I will specify.

the land, the vines, grapes and wines in their day-to-day tasks and activities forges and reinforces powerful relational bonds between people, place and product. Outlining the ways in which sensorial experiences may be linked to emotional attachments to places and things, I show how the 'artisanal' production techniques employed by some McLaren Vale winegrowers serve to invest certain places of wine production — and the wine itself — with deep meanings and emotions. These connections allow us to view wines, the places of their production and the people involved in their manufacture as sharing a mutual essence born of their dynamic interrelationship.

Wine and the love of place

According to Ingold, the rhythmically interwoven activities of people working and dwelling 'in the world' inhere in what he sees as a continuously becoming landscape or 'taskscape' (Ingold 1993). In this chapter, I hope to show that dynamic landscapes may also be seen to be teeming with complex currents and knots of *emotion* generated through the ongoing sensorial interaction of people with the world. It is through the sensing body's direct, lived experience of the world that spaces and places can become imbued with specific feelings and emotional attachments and thus granted meaning: 'After all, our first and foremost, most immediate and intimately *felt* geography is the body, the site of emotional experience and expression *par excellence*' (Davidson & Milligan 2004:523, italics in the original text).

Heath and Meneley note that '[w]hat we eat and drink, and how we do so, indexes both the corporeality of our habitus and the processes of distinction that embody relations of power/knowledge' (2008:593). Wine is inescapably a cultural artefact, mired (in the modern, Western-inspired tradition, at least) in a world of complex symbolic meanings, social and religious traditions, notions of cultural competency, hierarchies of knowledge and class distinctions (see, for example, Bourdieu 2010). This symbolic, cultural significance is not *immaterial*, however, and the sensually perceived materiality of wine — its substance — is not to be overlooked. It is in the diverse sensorial properties of wine upon consumption that much value is thought to be held: the depth, complexity and deliciousness of aromas and flavours, viscosity, ability to refresh or quench thirst, brightness of colour, and the ability to alter mood and mind.[3] Wine thus appears to be an ideal location for an examination of interrelations between the sensing body, emotions, and feelings of space and place. Wine critics, writers and marketers are well aware of such circuits of connection, and popular wine discourse is replete with language that, explicitly or implicitly, draws upon these associations. Anthropomorphic metaphor is ubiquitous in wine description, with terms like 'body', 'backbone', 'flabby', and 'sinewy' pointing to an anatomical schema, and others, like 'brooding', 'sexy', 'boisterous', 'shy' and so on used to draw attention to the 'personality'

---

3   Here, wine not only is perceived sensually but itself also affects sensory perceptions.

of the wine (Suárez Toste 2007:58-59). This is certainly the case in McLaren Vale, where different personified characteristics are often attributed to particular wine varietals — Grenache wines are 'rounded' and 'feminine', Shiraz 'brawny' and 'masculine', Cabernet Sauvignon 'noble' and 'upstanding'.

Wine writer Andrew Jefford argues that wine lends itself well to a perception of anthropomorphism. In his view,

> wine is quietly unique in human experience: a creation in which human beings and the natural world have almost equal roles; a creation which is experienced sensually, intellectually and emotionally, and at its best has a spiritual force, too. (2012)

Wine is neither fully a 'natural' nor a 'cultural' product, but bridges this abyss. It is inextricably both, possessing temporalities and rhythms that render it familiar to the mortal human experience and help us to conceive of it and relate to it in human terms: it is born in fermentation, comes to maturity in the barrel, ages in the bottle and finally dies. 'Part of the affection we feel for wine', according to Jefford (2012), 'is that it mimics our own trajectory towards non-being'. As a living entity, affective upon, and expressive of, human emotions and personalities, wine also embodies the substance of the person. This is a connection frequently made in myth, where wine is taken to correspond to blood and thus to life, light, fecundity and cyclical renewal. It is symbolic of 'hidden life and triumphant, mysterious youth … Blood re-created by the wine-press is a sign of great victory over the anaemic flight of time' (Durand 1999:252). Wine, like blood (or as blood), is felt to be a powerful conduit of energies, emotions and memories, and drinking is thus an act of *communion* with the life-paths of others.

Places and landscapes are animated not only by movement and physical activity but also by the meanings and memories that they come to embody. As Jones states, '[l]ife is inherently spatial, and inherently emotional' (2007:205). As loci of belonging, peace, loss, anxiety, love, and so on, we may see such places and landscapes as features of what have been termed *emotional geographies* (Davidson & Milligan 2004; Davidson, Smith & Bondi 2007). The emotional attachment to place that is borne from sensory experience is neatly summed up by Tuan (1990) as *topophilia*, literally, the 'love of place' — 'the affective bond between people and place or setting' (4). Topophilia is used to describe a very broad category of emotion, from simple tactile and sensory pleasures and aesthetic responses to far deeper connections: 'More permanent and less easy to express are feelings that one has toward a place because it is home, the locus of memories, and the means of gaining a livelihood' (93). In particular, Tuan holds that there is a special sense of attachment felt by a farmer to their land, which relates directly to the physicality of their work and the interweaving of their own life's trajectory with that of their land, animals and crops: 'The farmer's topophilia is compounded of this physical intimacy, of material dependence and the fact that the land is a repository of memory and sustains hope' (97).

Such emotive, affective links not only position people and geographical places in relation to one another, but may also encompass a broad range of animal, vegetable, or other non-human entities. *Things* may be said to have a social life, engaging with people and other things along relational networks of movement, trade and so on (Appadurai 1988; Gell 1998), but they are also animated by emotions. Things, then, may come to manifest deeply felt emotions in the same way that certain places do. In his discussion of sheep farming in the Scottish Borders, Gray (1999; 2014) highlights the powerful ways that the interwoven activities of farmers and their flocks in the harsh outbye landscapes of the Borders serve to bind people, sheep and family farms together in such a way that the three may be seen as *consubstantial*, as refractions of one another. The 'hefting' of flocks onto the land is a mutual act of emplacement; 'it is an intertwining of lives that transforms the very being of sheep and people so that attachment to the land is "in the blood" or as the people of Teviothead say, "bred into you"' (2014:2).

In the sensorial/emotional interrelationship of winegrowers in McLaren Vale with their worlds, we can see a similar consubstantiation at work. People, land, vines and wines are felt to partake of the same 'essence of place' through the mutuality of their interrelation and involvement in the cycles and processes of production. Examining the significance of microbial communities to artisanal cheesemaking, Paxson and Helmreich (2014) point out that even the 'wildest', most apparently natural and autochthonous elements of such production — the yeasts, bacteria and micro-organisms that combine to add complexity to flavours — are inseparable from human cultivation. 'In constituting the particular materiality of a cheese, nature and culture are fully implicated in one another; neither may be said to ground the other' (184). In McLaren Vale, grapevines, soil and rocks, and the various animal, vegetable and microbial life forms of the vineyard similarly exist within a sphere of relational influence, with people, place and product being both materially and emotionally enmeshed.

Hands-on wine production

Intense sensory-emotional bonds become forged in the physical tasks of winegrowing in McLaren Vale: from the planting and maintenance of vineyards, to the harvest of grapes, to their fermentation and maturation as wine. This close engagement of winegrowers with the 'material world' — and particularly those engaged in small-scale, hands-on production — is a crucial element in their development of a *sense of place* and *terroir*, concepts which hold great currency in contemporary wine discourse. For many, such physical interaction with the vine, grapes and wine (hands-on *doing*) is crucial to the production of 'authentic' wine, where authenticity is said to relate to a close and concerted interaction and working together of people and place (Goode & Harrop 2011). In this view, authentic wines and wine places are products of a sensuous, physical engagement of winegrowers with the material world in production, as it is through this engaged relationship that places and products become imbued with emotional depth and meaning beyond the objectively material.

While there are in McLaren Vale a number of small-scale winegrowers who use 'hands-on' techniques in the vineyard and who perform all the tasks of the winery themselves, the vast amount of wine is made in larger production facilities where this is not the case. Nearly all of my informants acknowledged that it is economically necessary for larger wineries seeking to manufacture large quantities of wine of consistent quality to embrace more impersonal and high-tech production techniques.[4] Most, however — including many of those employed in such large-scale 'industrial' winemaking — considered wine made at a small scale using manual production techniques to be more real or authentic than that made by teams of workers at big, impersonal wineries. This view aligns broadly with discourses of terroir, which value local specificities over what is seen as the homogenising tendency of modern, mass-produced winemaking. Frequently, my interlocutors bemoaned the fact that most modern wine was made 'to a recipe'. They often made a distinction between 'authentic' winemaking undertaken by small producers and the industrial 'beverage manufacture' of many larger wineries. Key to this distinction was the close, hands-on engagement with land, vines and wines across various phases of production, which the small-scale winegrower was able to maintain:

> Being hands-on is really important, and I think it's something that is being lost … My wine is grown in that vineyard, and made right here in this shed. I planted the vineyard with my father-in-law, and do the whole works myself — picking, crushing, fermenting, bottling. I know I'm lucky to be able to do that. I couldn't work for a big corporation just making wine as a product, as a beverage, according to a recipe — that goes against everything that I love about wine. You have to do it properly, have a feel for it and an awareness of what you're doing. (Mark, 22 August 2012)

For the small winegrowers of McLaren Vale, the vineyards and wineries which are formed by, and which frame, the quotidian activities of wine production — places of deep sensual engagement with the world — are indeed important repositories of memory and emotion, as I will discuss below. They are crucial features of McLaren Vale's emotional geography as places of physical work and material interdependence encompassing individual and socially shared memories and senses of belonging, often tied to lines of descent across generations. In short, they are powerful centres of human dwelling.

---

4   Common practices include the mechanisation of vineyard tasks like spraying, pruning and harvesting; the measurement and chemical analysis of various properties of grapes and wine throughout the processes of production; automated temperature control; and the addition of cultured yeast strains, acids, tannins and other agents to the wine.

Knowing the vineyard

Among winegrowers, the assertion is frequently made that 'good wine is made in the vineyard'. If the grapes grown are of high quality, it is thought, the job of the vintner in the winery becomes not to *manufacture* the wine through clever manipulation, but rather to *guide* the wine through the processes of fermentation and maturation with a light touch. As such, vineyard work becomes of crucial importance. In the words of Ed, a contract viticulturist and consultant with a special interest in biodynamic winegrowing[5]:

> A good farmer pays attention to what's going on in the vineyard, and has an awareness of the big picture, how something might have an effect on something else. It's about being flexible and responsive to everything that's happening. That includes the bugs, funguses, the weeds that are sprouting up — it's all connected in one way or another; nothing happens in isolation and you need to have an awareness of the signs that the vineyard is giving you. (Ed, 2 August 2012)

Winegrowers come to *know* their vineyards emotionally as well as intellectually, as they, the vines, the land, and the other plants, animals and micro-organisms become relationally intertwined and interdependent. The interaction between person and vineyard becomes one not of mastery but of dialogue, of the grower 'working together' with the land across the changing seasons and annual vintage cycles in order for the grapes that are produced to be of optimal quality.[6]

> The seasons changing, winter and spring rains … Every vintage is different. That sort of variation is crucial. I'm not about trying to bring grapes up to a particular 'standard'; I rely on nature and therefore keeping the diversity of vintage is really important. It's all about the flavour. (Dennis, 15 August 2012)

Many producers harvest grapes according to a carefully measured balance of sugar ripeness and acidity confirmed by chemical testing; others prefer to trust their own palates and determine the time of harvest by taste: 'When the grape is sweet, but the seeds are still crunchy and taste nutty, biscuity — that's when we'll pick' (Karen, 2 March 2014). The sense of smell is also important in the vineyard: as one vine pruner told me, 'If you've got a good nose, you can smell if there's any mildew around' (Eric, 15 August 2012).

---

5   Biodynamics is a system of organic farming based on the esoteric philosophies of Rudolf Steiner, and it is popular among many growers in in McLaren Vale. It treats agriculture as a holistic integration of humans, plants, animals and 'cosmic and terrestrial forces', and contains spiritual and mystical elements that could be viewed as rather more magical or occult than strictly scientific (see, for example, Kirchmann 1994).

6   Here it must be pointed out that notions of 'quality' vary greatly between producers. There is often some degree of 'reverse-engineering' (Paxson 2010) to try to achieve a particular style, such as undertaking particular canopy management practices with an aim towards slower ripening and higher acid levels for a more savoury, 'French'-style wine. The quality of the grapes is in these cases judged in relation to the pre-formed image.

Since antiquity, vineyards have in Western cultural traditions been potent symbols of human civilisation and settlement, rootedness and belonging: a cultivation of the wild. Like wines, vines are themselves also often anthropomorphised, with different types of vine said to display different human characteristics. While, for example, Grenache and Mataro are said to be hardy, pessimistic misers who can survive in poor soils without much need for irrigation, an employee at one winery told me that 'Cabernet Sauvignon is the "princess" of the vines: it really spreads out its root system, and likes very luxurious soil — thick and rich — and it doesn't mind moisture' (Fiona, 5 February 2013). The passing of the years also gives older vines, rooted in place, a certain maturity. Young vines are often likened to unpredictable teenagers, while the old vines are depicted as wise elders, treasured and respected in McLaren Vale for the way they have borne witness to the ongoing passage of the seasons, longer-term oscillations in climate, and the ongoing march of human activity over their life spans. Very old vines of a century or more still bear upon their gnarled trunks the scars of generations of vine pruners, whose past decisions (to trellis in a certain way, to snip off new growth in a particular fashion, to lop off certain limbs, and so on) still influence the sensory qualities of the grapes that hang from each season's new canes. Old vines are said to possess a stability and depth of character that young vines lack, and, although the quantities of grapes they yield are often much smaller than the quantities that vigorous young vines yield, the quality of the wine is usually thought to be superior, with more intense, complex flavours and aromas. The vines themselves also hold an emotive power beyond their productive capacity. They are repositories for memories — of a long succession of vintages, of cold, wet and disease-ridden years and the hot, dusty years of drought — and are thus integral to both the physical and emotional fabric of the landscape.

Many growers placed great importance on ensuring that their grapes were as reflective as possible of their distinctive 'terroir'. Although definitions of the term are hotly contested, terroir is broadly understood as the unique sum of environmental factors and conditions of production (usually both 'natural' and 'cultural') in a particular place, influencing the flavour and other qualities of a wine and granting it a particular 'sense of place' (see, for example, Bohmrich 1996; Demossier 2011; Trubek 2008). Discussion of terroir usually focus on the way foods and wines 'of place' can become endowed with a unique and significant distinctiveness, whether physically 'real' or imagined: an essence of place. The tasks and processes of wine production, especially those undertaken by small-scale producers (planting, pruning, harvesting, crushing, pressing, and so on) may be said to facilitate, bring forth or unlock the wine's terroir, which may be tasted upon consumption. Such wine, then, acts as a conduit linking the drinker with the wine's place of origin, as well as with the lives of the people who are involved in its production.

For small-scale growers, vineyard work with an aim to the production of high-quality, unique or interesting wines often entails a very close and personal relationship with the vineyard and a 'communication' of sorts with the vines. This involves close and focused observation of the conditions and the 'signs that the vineyard is giving you', an awareness stemming from accumulated knowledge and familiarity. While growers usually describe this simply as 'good farming', such attention also engenders an emotional link between person and the place of the vineyard. The rhythm of familiar tasks and activities is comforting; the winegrower feels *at home* in the vineyard. The exposure to the ever-changing elements of the weather — the cold winter rain, hot summer sun, the gully winds of the morning and the sea breezes of the afternoon — is cherished by farmers, who contrast it to the *inauthenticity* of a working life spent indoors. Some vignerons in McLaren Vale have spent their entire lives tending the same land; for some, their land has been farmed by their family over five or six generations and they know it 'like the back of their hand'. Such winegrowers can, by smell and taste alone, immediately discern in which of their vineyard blocks a particular bunch of grapes was grown. To those so attuned, the very particular soil, geology and growing conditions of the site are rendered *sensible* in the fruit. Wisdom sits in places (Basso 1996), and the occupation of the small-scale farmer or winegrower is perhaps best thought of as a mutual sharing in this emplaced wisdom through the performance of their ordinary, everyday tasks.

The vineyard, as an anchoring point for emplaced memories and knowledge, may be embedded with deep feelings of belonging and loyalty, but may also act as a reminder of past tensions and hardships: years of drought, disease-ridden wet seasons, and economic downturns. As winegrowers plant, manage and maintain their vines with an eye to future cycles of weather, climate, culture and economy, the vineyard is also a locus for hopes and aspirations, and anxieties and uncertainty about the times to come.[7] The main sense expressed by small winegrowers, however — as people who have

---

7   For vignerons in McLaren Vale, there are several common anxieties. These include the vagaries of market, industry trends and government taxation regimes which may affect their future ability to sell their wines profitably. Many of the growers I spoke to were worried about the increasing buy-up of vineyard land by foreign investors, particularly Chinese companies looking for stakes in the South Australian wine industry. People also frequently shared concerns about the ongoing financial sustainability of agricultural land uses like winegrowing in a region under pressure from the sprawl of nearby suburban areas. Another often-expressed anxiety stemmed from the South Australian government's apparent relaxation of biosecurity regulations that have to date preserved the State as one of the few major wine-producing areas worldwide to have escaped the ravages of the Phylloxera vine root louse (Campbell 2004). With the pest having destroyed vineyards across Europe and many 'new world' regions including other Australian states, forcing replanting onto Phylloxera-resistant North American rootstocks, South Australia's untouched old vines and Phylloxera-free status are a source of great pride among vignerons.

chosen to spend a good proportion of their lives engaging in the often solitary tasks of the vineyard — was that it is primarily a place of positive emotions. The attentive observation and focus required when dealing with this world of plants, weather, insects and soils, and the repetitiveness of tasks like pruning, can bring about a meditative state of mind:

> You can clear your mind of anything else you really don't need to be thinking about, and concentrate on the task directly in front of you, because you're constantly thinking about the next cut you're going to make, the next plant in front of you. That just zones a lot of things out. (Mark, 25 June 2014)

Many of my informants told me that they often looked forward to the time of year when they could leave the majority of their winery tasks behind and get back into the vineyard, to 'reconnect with the land' in a way that is peaceful and contemplative yet — as it involves an interaction with the dynamic rhythms of the 'natural world' — quietly energising.

Fermenting emotions

Wineries, where the harvested grapes are crushed and fermented into wine which is then matured before bottling, may be marked with similarly deep contours and currents of emotion. Such places are the locations of a powerful melding of the focused energies of human labour (particularly during the heightened intensity of the harvest and 'vintage' period) and of those of the wine itself in the microbial processes of fermentation and maturation. For small winemakers, who can avoid many of the technological and chemical interventions that become necessary in large-scale wine production, their wineries are not mere 'factories' for beverage manufacture which seek a mastery of nature and replication of results. Instead, these wineries are better thought of as places of artisanship, wherein the skilled processing of the grapes and wine (hand-plunging a ferment, pressing new wine off skins, 'racking' wine between barrels, and so on) requires a deep perceptual engagement with the tasks. Here, winemakers take into account, and work with, the physical properties of their materials in response to dynamic environmental conditions.[8]

The engagement of winemakers with their work in the winery is genuinely multisensory. Response to visual cues is crucial, as the practitioner keeps an eye on the activity of the bubbling ferment and carefully observes changes in the brightness of colour of wine maturing in barrels. But other senses are just as important. 'Hands-on'

---

8   As Ingold notes, even processes that require a high degree of mechanisation (bottling being the most obvious example in the winery) require such skilled human attention, a 'conjunction of rhythmicity and concentration' (2011:61). The fleshly, living practitioner is not separated from these machines but 'is *among* them, working with machines that work with him' (62, italics in the original text).

winemaking techniques are just that: during primary fermentation, as yeasts convert the sugars in the grape must to alcohol and carbon dioxide, the vintner must ensure that the 'cap' of grape skins carried to the surface of the ferment by the gas does not dry out, as this risks bacterial infection and undesirable flavours. This may be done in various ways (for example, by using an electric pump), but many small producers prefer to manually push the cap down and stir the ferment using implements like rakes, paddles, or — if the fermentation vessel is small enough — bare arms and hands. The energy created by microbial action during fermentation gives off significant heat, and although thermometers are usually used to monitor temperature, winemakers will often also use their own hands to stir the ferment and feel the warmth of the must in different parts of the vessel. The tangible warmth of the must as it is transformed into wine is significant as yet another way in which the liquid may be thought of as a living entity, a vital, blood-like substance that carries the weight of human emotions. One of my informants told me that she likes to think of the winery as a 'nursery' where wines, like human babies, grow and mature before being turned out into the world: 'I don't really like thinking of myself as a winemaker. More of a babysitter, looking after the wine while it does its thing' (Margie, 5 April 2012).

To walk into a winery is to walk into a rich world of olfactory stimulation. The microbial and chemical world of winemaking is one of smells, ranging from the fresh, sweet, sticky smells of a new ferment to the dark, earthy, musty aromas of red wine maturing in oak barrels in the cellar. The sense of smell can have a very direct link to emotions and memories: it is a sense that may, bypassing conscious thought, immediately conjure up a suite of linked sensory experiences, evoking 'vivid, emotionally-charged memories of past events and scenes' (Tuan 1990:10). The recollection of past odours and the emotional transportation which the experience of winery smells can bring on is significant. For most of my interlocutors, the smells of the winery and the barrel room were generally seen as pleasant, comforting and familiar. Some, moreover, described very specific, emotion-laden smell-memories. For Dennis, smelling a particular barrel of maturing Cabernet Sauvignon while working as a cellarhand at the age of fifteen was a moment of epiphany — although he was not yet a wine drinker at that stage, the unearthly aroma that he encountered sparked an interest in wine which was to become a lifelong vocation:

> There was a puncheon of wine at the back of the barrel room, in the dark — it was Cabernet Sauvignon —[and] I took the bung out and the smell just hit me. I'll never forget it. I can still smell that wine right now, sitting here. And that set me on this course, on this journey. (Dennis, 15 August 2012)

More than simply experiencing the smells of the winery, the winemaker must pay close attention to them, as the particular aromas transmit important information about the state of the wine much more immediately — and accurately, in the opinion of some — than laboratory chemical analysis can provide. People sensually attuned to the material processes of winemaking may identify potentially unwelcome odours, such as those associated with certain chemical compounds (like hydrogen sulphide or ethyl acetate) or microbial organisms (like the brettanomyces yeast or various spoilage bacteria) at very low levels.

Taste, also, is critical for the winemaker, as it conveys important information about the state and qualities of the wine at different stages of production. Vintners will taste their wine frequently throughout the processes of fermentation and maturation: such practice brings about a deep familiarity with the wine, which both enables them to quickly identify any potential problems and shapes their ongoing methods. A familiarity with certain parcels of grapes from certain vineyards over numerous vintages furthermore enables producers to gradually develop their own 'styles'; for many, this evolution over time of a relationship between winemaker(s) and vineyard is a key element of terroir. The 'cellar palate' of artisanal winemakers attuned to the specific conditions of their own winery is not always regarded in a positive light, however, as winemakers' senses of smell and taste may become conditioned to the presence of particular yeasts or bacteria that produce flavours and odours which other tasters might regard as undesirable. Nevertheless, the diversity of winemaking styles among artisan producers (compared to the 'homogenising' tendencies of mass production) forms a large part of these wines' consumer appeal: handmade wines with 'individuality' and 'uniqueness' are often celebrated and valorised within the world of wine critics and consumers.

The sensations of smell and taste are fleeting and ephemeral, yet memories of them may be powerfully present and emotionally charged. For winegrowers, part of the pleasure of their work comes from chasing and attempting to recapture certain elusive sensorial experiences, like the Cabernet Sauvignon barrel in the cellar of Dennis's youth. As we can see, these people are simultaneously producers and consumers, continually reacting to, and reflecting upon, their interactions with the wine, modifying and adjusting their actions in order to bring their wine and themselves into closer alignment. This is truly working *with* the wine rather than acting *upon* it. West notes with respect to artisanal cheesemakers that '[w]orking with the curd, they learned from the curd itself' (2013:332); further, craft winemakers similarly learn from the actions of the wine 'as it move[s] through time and space, *doing* one thing or another' (332, italics in the original text). In some cases, this learning is completely accidental, as in the case of a barrel of Chardonnay that Mark neglected during his busy 2006 vintage:

> At the end of vintage I thought, 'Let's have a look at that stuff'. There was a lot of airspace in the barrel, and the wine had grown this flor [a layer of yeast cells on top of the wine] which was sort of protecting the wine from the air. It looked weird, but it wasn't totally oxidised and stuffed. It had an interest to it, a nutty character. It's very sherry-like, like a Fino. Now it's holding itself in this state: from '06 to 2014,

it hasn't changed much at all. It's got more complexity: there's a little bit more in the mouth, more flavour and character. (Mark, 25 June 2014)

A frequently heard maxim among artisanal winegrowers is to 'trust your senses'. For skilled practitioners, trusting and giving priority to the human senses and to *instincts* developed over years of attentive engagement with the processes of winemaking rids them of what they see as the artificial constraints of production 'by numbers' or 'to a recipe'. Some of the best wines, as several producers told me, come from happy accidents or creative experimentation. While many of these winegrowers have formal qualifications in oenology, agricultural science or other disciplines, they usually view large-scale winemaking as restrictively scientific — a form of manufacture further removed from the primacy of sense-experience than that undertaken by the artisan. For the artisanal producer, improvisation is not only accepted but also necessary in order for the processual relationship between human and liquid to run smoothly. The skill of practitioners, as Ingold puts it, lies not in their ability to impose onto matter a preconceived form, but rather 'in their ability to find the grain of the world's becoming and to follow its course while bending it to their evolving purpose' (2011:211). Through the senses, wine and person work together. By smelling, tasting and drinking wine, artisanal winegrowers bring its substance into themselves, literally embodying it. In such a process, there is a feeling that the wine also comes to embody the *person* of the winegrower who has poured some of his or her own 'heart and soul' or 'blood, sweat and tears' into the production of the wine. This is a relational view that fits well with theories of terroir, which claim that wine embodies an essence of *place*. To adopt Gray's (1999; 2014) terminology, such a view sees the wines, people and places of artisanal production as *consubstantial*.

The emotional topography of the winery itself is varied, as different spaces may become imbued with different flows of emotion. In most wineries, for example, the areas where grapes are crushed into large primary fermentation vessels are seen as places of energy and liveliness. This is where all the action takes place during the hectic vintage period. Winemakers must perform numerous tasks very quickly as various parcels of harvested grapes arrive for crushing; juice is pumped between storage vessels; fermentation times and temperatures are monitored and adjusted; and decisions are made as to when each batch will be pressed and skins removed. Vintage work is long, busy and tiring, but it is also an intensely social time of year, as people throughout the region pitch in together to help one another. The wine itself is highly vigorous during the initial ferment, and the melange of smells and sounds coming from the bubbling vats adds to the general ambience of activity and energy.

In contrast to the noise and activity of the fermentation room, informants Peter and Sophie see the barrel room of their family winery as a contemplative place: quiet, dark and cool, and filled with the close and heavy smell of maturing wine. There is a sense of silence and the stillness of deep repose: the wines are quietly alive, and indeed Peter tells me that he often listens to the subtle, almost inaudible crackling sounds of malolactic fermentation, as bacteria slowly convert malic acid into the smoother lactic acid. The cellar of a house, according to Bachelard, 'is first and foremost the *dark entity* of the house, the one that partakes of subterranean forces' (1964:18, italics in the original text). It is a place of deeply hidden dreams and memories. This description might also be applied to the cellars of a winery, where barrels of wine solemnly slumber for months or years, biding time before bottling begins. In older wineries, the cellar is literally an underground chamber: a cave or tunnel carved from the rock, where the wines may quietly mature in the dark, cool subterranean air. For most newer wineries in McLaren Vale, a devoted 'barrel room' is more likely to be simply a well-insulated shed or other storage space; or, alternatively, the maturing wines are stored in the same room in which primary fermentations take place. Nevertheless, there is a feeling that such places, where the wine 'rests' and matures, are connected to slower, deeper and more grounded rhythms than are the energetic places of primary fermentation.

Conclusion

In the skilled performance of their tasks, winegrowers in McLaren Vale engage intimately with the world around them at a sensorial level — including touching the soil and the vines, feeling the sun, wind and rain in the vineyard, smelling and feeling the warmth of the fermenting grapes, and tasting the wine at different stages of its production. It is this sort of deep and attentive engagement of people with their environmental surrounds over time which produces not only practical and intellectual 'knowledge' but also a rich topography of feelings and emotions of belonging, love, loss, nostalgia, tranquillity and struggle. The emotional depth fostered by the hands-on tasks and activities and direct sensorial experiences of small-scale wine production is, I believe, an important aspect of the ontological perspective shared by many of my interlocutors, which sees people, land, vines, and wines as fundamentally interrelated and codependent, partaking of and manifesting a sort of shared *essence*. The mutual engagement of people and 'nature' in this production means that a wine may be said to embody both the intent, love and care of the winegrowers, and the ineffable 'sense of place' of the particular vineyard from which it originated. Similarly, a vineyard or winery may be seen to be indivisible from the unique and specific wines it has produced and the people who farm it, especially in cases where several generations of the same family have worked the same land.

For winegrowers, the vineyards and wineries into which they pour so much of their time, labour and attention may lie at the very centre of their emotional lives, shaping their ongoing experiences of the world. They are places of activity and excitement, of peace and refuge; over time, they can become places of dwelling. This sort of intense emotional connection to places, forged through particular sensual experiences and interactions and embedded deep in the psyche, is by no means limited to winegrowers or farmers. However, these relationships are given material form by such people, whose products spring directly from their concerted physical, intellectual and emotional interactions with the soil, vines, grapes, presses, vats and barrels of their places of production. The wine itself is seen to be embedded not only with the physical traces of the geographic location — as a result of the particular geology, rainfall, aspect, micro-climate and so on of the vineyard — but also with the emotional rhythms and currents which give it its life and vitality, its unique value and depth of meaning.

Processes of production can serve to imbue material objects with a sort of agency, enmeshing them in relational networks with the people who produce and consume them (Appadurai 1988; Gell 1998). Their interactions with humans in the processes of production, circulation and consumption work in some cases to animate these items, granting them social meaning and thus de-objectifying them. However, these things are not just agents of action, but rather come to embody feelings, emotions and memories. In wine, as in art and elsewhere, the valorisation of the handmade, unique product of a skilled practitioner — more *special* and more valuable than the mechanically reproduced version identical in every other respect — demonstrates just such an animic, relational perspective. For wine, this perspective is made explicit by the commonly expressed belief in terroir, which emphasises not only the relational and substantial links between people and product but also, perhaps even more significantly, with *place*. Consumers are brought into this relational meshwork with the wine as participants themselves, linked to the world of production through the physical incorporation brought about by smelling, tasting and drinking the wine.

This processes of consubstantiation that lie at the heart of artisanal winegrowing in McLaren Vale involve the sharing of a physical essence: the specific tastes and smells of a vineyard and winery coaxed 'out of the land and into the bottle' (Sternsdorff-Cisterna 2013:53) by human efforts and action. But there is also a deep emotional resonance at play. The tasks and activities of dwelling in the world invest places and landscapes with currents of emotion and meaning, and it is through the committed and personal engagement of artisanal producers with their worlds that these emotions come to reverberate throughout the places and products with which they are intimately connected. Emotions are not disembodied: in McLaren Vale they may find a home in vineyards, fermenting vats and oak barrels, and in other, more portable and comestible places: the bottles of wine that flow from the wineries of the district to shelves and cellars all over the world.

References

Appadurai, A. 1988. *The Social Life of Things: Commodities in Cultural Perspective*. Cambridge: Cambridge University Press.

Bachelard, G. 1964. *The Poetics of Space*. Trans. M. Jolas. New York: Orion Press.

Basso, K.H. 1996. 'Wisdom sits in places: Notes on a Western Apache landscape'. In K. Basso and S. Feld (Eds.), *Senses of Place* (pp. 53-90). Santa Fe: School of American Research Press.

Bohmrich, R. 1996. 'Terroir: Competing perspectives on the roles of soil, climate and people', *Journal of Wine Research*, 7(1): 33-46.

Bourdieu, P. 2010. *Distinction: A Social Critique of the Judgement of Taste*. London: Routledge.

Campbell, C. 2004. *Phylloxera: How Wine Was Saved for the World*. London: HarperCollins.

Davidson, J. and C. Milligan. 2004. 'Embodying emotion sensing space: Introducing emotional geographies', *Social & Cultural Geography*, 5(4): 523-532.

Davidson, J., M. Smith and L. Bondi (Eds.). 2007. *Emotional Geographies*. Aldershot, UK: Ashgate.

Demossier, M. 2011. 'Beyond terroir: Territorial construction, hegemonic discourses, and French wine culture', *Journal of the Royal Anthropological Institute*, 17(4): 685-705.

Durand, G. 1999. *The Anthropological Structures of the Imaginary*. Trans. J.C. Hatten and M. Sankey. Brisbane: Boombana Publishing.

Gell, A. 1998. *Art and Agency: An Anthropological Theory*. Oxford: Clarendon Press.

Goode, J. and S. Harrop. 2011. *Authentic Wine: Toward Natural and Sustainable Winemaking*. Berkeley and London: University of California Press.

Gray, J. 1999. 'Open spaces and dwelling places: Being at home on hill farms in the Scottish borders', *American Ethnologist*, 6(2): 440-460.

Gray, J. 2014. 'Hefting onto place: Intersecting lives of humans and sheep on Scottish Hills landscape', *Anthrozooös*, 27(2): 219-234.

Heath, D. and A. Meneley. 2008. 'Techne, technoscience, and the circulation of comestible commodities: An introduction', *American Anthropologist*, 109(4): 593-602.

Ingold, T. 1993. 'The temporality of the landscape', *World Archaeology*, 25(2): 152-174.

Ingold, T. 2011. *Being Alive: Essays on Movement, Knowledge and Description*. New York: Routledge.

Jefford, A. 2012. *Wine and Astonishment*, Wine Communicators of Australia. Viewed 10 July 2014. <http://www.winecommunicators.com.au/site/files/ul/data_text14/3755588.pdf>.

Jones, O. 2007. 'An ecology of emotion, memory, self and landscape'. In J. Davidson, M. Smith and L. Bondi (Eds.), *Emotional Geographies* (pp. 205-218). Aldershot, UK: Ashgate.

Kirchmann, H. 1994. 'Biological dynamic farming—An occult form of alternative agriculture?', *Journal of Agricultural and Environmental Ethics*, 7(2): 173-187.

Paxson, H. 2010. 'Locating value in artisan cheese: Reverse engineering terroir for new-world landscapes', *American Anthropologist*, 112(3): 444-457.

Paxson, H. and S. Helmreich. 2014. 'The perils and promises of microbial abundance: Novel natures and model ecosystems, from artisanal cheese to alien seas', *Social Studies of Science* 44(2): 165-193.

Sternsdorff-Cisterna, N. 2013. 'Space and terroir in the Chilean wine industry'. In R.E. Black and R.C. Ulin (Eds.), *Wine and Culture: Vineyard to Glass* (pp. 50-66). London and New York: Bloomsbury Academic.

Suárez Toste, E. 2007. 'Metaphor inside the wine cellar: On the ubiquity of personification schemas in winespeak', *Metaphorik.de*, 12(1): 53-64.

Trubek, A.B. 2008. *The Taste of Place: A Cultural Journey into Terroir*, vol. 20. Berkeley, CA: University Presses of California, Columbia and Princeton.

Tuan, Y-F. 1990. *Topophilia : A Study of Environmental Perception, Attitudes, and Values*. New York: Columbia University Press.

West, H.G. 2013. 'Thinking like a cheese: Towards an ecological understanding of the reproduction of knowledge in contemporary artisan cheesemaking'. In R. Ellen, S.J.A. Lycett and S.E. Johns (Eds.), *Understanding Cultural Transmission in Anthropology: A Critical Synthesis* (pp. 320-345). New York and Oxford: Berghahn Books.

This book is available as a free fully-searchable ebook from
www.adelaide.edu.au/press

www.ingramcontent.com/pod-product-compliance
Lightning Source LLC
Chambersburg PA
CBHW081206020426
42333CB00020B/2630